A Life in Illustration

THE MOST FAMOUS ILLUSTRATORS
AND THEIR WORK

gestalten

Preface

The business of illustration now doubtlessly glitters in facets more varied and enigmatic than it has ever before. Holding this book in your hands, you are likely to share our fascination in one of life's most beautiful careers and the many mysteries that shroud it. How do illustrators work these days? For whom, what, and in which media format? How do art and commerce go together? What career paths are there, and which are particularly worthwhile to follow? Who are the ones that have made it, and what are the stories behind their success? What is illustration, today, anyway?

While the web is full of empty phrases, wishy-washy biographies, and statements à la "I have always loved drawing and turned my passion into a living," truly insightful information on the workings of the business is astoundingly rare. *A Life in Illustration* gathers extensive portraits looking into the lives and careers of 23 remarkable professionals. Sparkling stars in the increasingly nebulous and immense sky that is the contemporary creative industry, they provide intriguing personal accounts of their day-to-day practice and how it relates to, and occasionally clashes with, the many myths that distort the illustrator's job description. Some specialize—in visualizing information, in drawing logos and letters, in editorial or advertising, or in fashion or surface design for products. Most, however, work across business sectors and applications.

The numerous markets that currently exist for illustrators constitute a surprisingly deep pool of career opportunities. Too limited in scope to represent the field in its entirety, this selection leaves out many lesser-known, supplementary markets to focus on the most densely populated avenues for professional assignments. Structured around six areas that provide particularly fertile ground for the work of contemporary illustrators, it provides an overview of core fields that do not put artists into boxes. Obvious overlaps and decidedly ragged chapters reflect the very nature of the illustration business where clear-cut categorizations are largely untenable. The resourceful transgression of borders is in fact the mainspring of the many career paths portrayed here.

Martin Haake and Jonathan Burton appear in a chapter entitled "Commercial Illustration," but with numerous successful projects in the editorial field. The unmistakably voguish flow of Tina Berning's drawings belies the fact that her work is not only à la mode in fashion circles, but has earned her commissions by car companies, news journals, and cultural institutions alike. Alex Trochut and Jessica Hische mainly draw letters, but do so for brands, musicians, and magazines. The informative illustrations by *National Geographic*'s Juan Velasco, the *New York Times*' Jonathan Corum, and Francesco Franchi of the Italian newspaper *Il Sole 24 Ore* thrive on investigations at the crossroads between graphics, illustration, and journalism, and present themselves as exemplars of how the boundaries between various disciplines occasionally blur to an extent where they no longer exist. An expert in writing and creating children's picture books, Oliver Jeffers also produces editorial work and exhibits in galleries across the globe.

The tiresome argument that one can only be a commercial illustrator or a fine artist, as if there is no in-between, is rebutted repeatedly, most persuasively by artists like Andrea Ventura and Olaf Hajek, who not only illustrate, but also paint by commission for fine art collectors. Tina Berning and Christoph Niemann, among others, give striking proof of the symbiotic relationship between self-directed and commissioned work, highlighting the former as a particularly worthwhile investment in the latter. House Industry's Ken Barber is just one of many illustrators who refer to their teaching position as a highly informative counterbalance to professional practice.

Brimming with revelations that otherwise tend to be drowned by the hurdles of an ever more indeterminable creative industry, *My Life in Illustration* features illustrators who live the dream of thousands upon thousands of aspiring creatives. But what is it actually like at the top of the ladder? How thin does the air get up there? How does one climb all the way up in the first place? What is it like to juggle art and commerce, to run one's own business while being tied up in educational assignments? How have new technologies changed work processes and the way illustrators communicate with clients? Is it hard to hand over responsibilities to assistants and agents? What is efficient time management in the business of illustration? There are plenty of questions addressed in this book and many answers given. Above all, however, stands the richly substantiated fact that the field defies formulas and standards. Transitions are fluid, guidelines relative, values erratic, and rules extremely hard to pin down. All of this contributes to our fascination. Instead of explaining a stunning industry to death, this book explores and thrives on both its myths and realities, careful not to confuse one for the other.

Commercial Illustration

The illustrations in this section sell and promote products, services, and ideas. Commissioned by corporate clients, they adorn product packaging, brochures, and book jackets. They serve as key visuals for billboards, posters, and other forms of advertisement, be it as a cohesive set of corporate communications, or as one-off visuals. It is especially, but not exclusively, in the commercial field that clients recognize illustration's facility for abstraction. More generic than photography, illustration can liberate characters from age, race, gender, and other real-world contexts, creating brand messages for everyone. More malleable than photography, it can adapt precisely to the wants and needs of very specific target groups. Encompassing a broad range of applications and business sectors, commercial illustration occurs in manifold styles. Correspondingly diverse is the group of artists featured in this chapter. Featured here are Martin Haake's scribbly product packaging and dada-inspired book jackets and maps for corporate publications; Jonathan Burton's delicately drawn movie posters; and Olaf Hajek's

shop window backdrops. In addition to classic commercial commissions, collaborations with artists are becoming an increasingly important mode of commercial illustration work. With more and more businesses harnessing the emotional value of art, a growing number of clients waive extensive campaigns in favor of marketing projects. Approaching these illustrators as artists rather than service providers allows a creative approach to move beyond a clear-cut commercial brief and into an unexpected aesthetic venture.

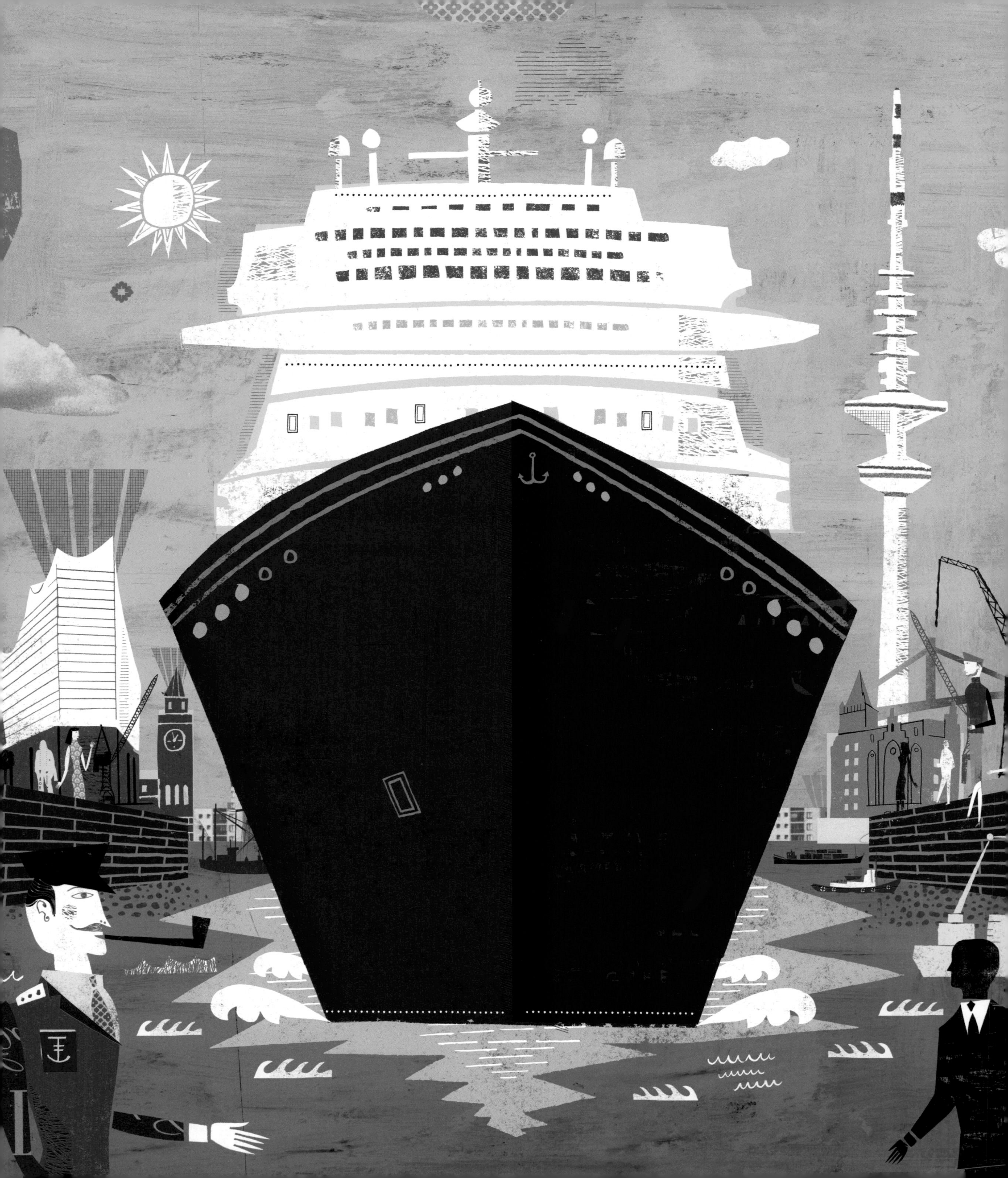

Martin Haake

PLACE AND DATE OF BIRTH
Oldenburg, Germany; 1970

COUNTRY OF RESIDENCE
Germany

FAMILY STATUS
Married, 2 children

EDUCATION / DEGREE
Communication Arts, Hochschule der Künste
(University of the Arts), Berlin

ACTIVE IN THE FIELD OF ILLUSTRATION SINCE
1995

BREAKTHROUGH PROJECT
Süddeutsche Zeitung Magazin

KEY CLIENTS
Penguin Books, Playboy, the New York Times,
Vanity Fair

MOST RENOWNED PROJECTS
Famous Germans made out of sausages for
Süddeutsche Zeitung Magazin;
illustrated maps for various illustration

COMMISSIONS PER YEAR
125

AVERAGE TURNAROUND TIME PER COMMISSION
1 week

WORKSPACE
Shared studio

EMPLOYEES
None

AGENTS
Germany: 2 Agents
U.K.: Central Illustration Agency CIA
U.S.: Lindgren & Smith

HOW MUCH COMMISSION DO YOUR AGENTS TAKE
25–30%

TEACHING POSITIONS
None

AWARDS (SELECTION)
D&AD British Art Directors Club, Yellow Pencil,
Silver Award (2004); ADC German Art Directors Club,
2 Silver awards (2002)

MEMBER ASSOCIATIONS
None

GALLERIES
Direktorenhaus Berlin

"CLIENT COMMUNICATION USED TO BE A LOT MORE PERSONAL WHEN I STARTED. YOU WOULD GO TO THE BRIEFING IN PERSON, BRING IN THE ORIGINAL ARTWORK FOR PRESENTATION. I DO MISS THE SENSE OF PROXIMITY AND DIRECT COLLABORATION."

There is a lot going enchantingly wrong in the illustrations of Martin Haake. Perspectives. Proportions. Curves and cuts. There is a lot going on, too: strange scenes set on motley textured backdrops, populated by misshapen figures that are cobbled together from mixed media snippets, garnished with doodles, letterings, and Haake's characteristic cursory, yet endeavored handwriting, evoking script on chalkboard. The merry mingling of such things is roughened by contrast and friction. Haake loves the coexistence of high and low, trash and treasure, pop and renaissance. What he does is sweet but scruffy, finished but flawed. Imperfection has always fascinated him. He draws inspiration from folk art, the collages of Dada, and the paintings of outsider artists. Neither illustrator by education, nor designer or visual artist in any other form, Haake is, in a way, an outsider too.

Originally from Oldenburg, a midsize city in northern Germany, Haake moved to Berlin in 1989 to study Social and Business Communications at the Berlin University of the Arts. Planning to go in the direction of advertising and work as a copywriter, he took quite a few classes in semiotics. Exploring the meaning of signs, he found that he was more drawn to image than text. Haake claims he was never particularly talented in drawing and painting, at least not naturally, but he was ambitious enough to turn his lack of expertise and formal training into opportunity and a characteristic style of his own. After graduation, when more or less everyone else from his course took on jobs at advertising agencies, Haake went to Hamburg to pursue a career as a freelance illustrator.

Emphasizing the amateurish style of his drawings, he tinkered around with different materials to create a portfolio that he carried around to the offices of Hamburg's leading magazine publishers. One of the first to show keen interest were the editors and art directors at Gruner+Jahr, who asked him to create an illustration for the women's magazine *Brigitte.* "When I first showed them my idea they didn't like it, so I created eight alternative proposals," Haake recalls. "I think they were impressed by the mere quantity." He had five different styles back then, in the mid-nineties, thinking that would be a great advantage. In any case, he got the job for *Brigitte,* and others soon followed. Almost a decade ago, Haake moved to Berlin, where he set up a shared studio with the illustrator Olaf

CRUISING DAYS
(PAGE 6)
Client: Cruising Days Hamburg, 2012
Art Direction: Kathrin Dyrssen

DANUBIA
(BIG LEFT)
Client: Picador, 2013
Art Direction: Stuart Wilson

WINTER TRAVEL
(TOP LEFT)
Client: Neue Zürcher Zeitung, 2012

EDWINA ERMITTELT (EDWINA IS INVESTIGATING)
(TOP RIGHT)
Client: Judith Homoki, 2013

THE MANDELBAUM GATE
(BOTTOM LEFT)
Little Brown Publishing, 2013
Art Direction: Ceara Elliot

THE TRIFLE BOWL
(BOTTOM RIGHT)
Random House Publishing, 2013
Art Direction: Lisa Horton

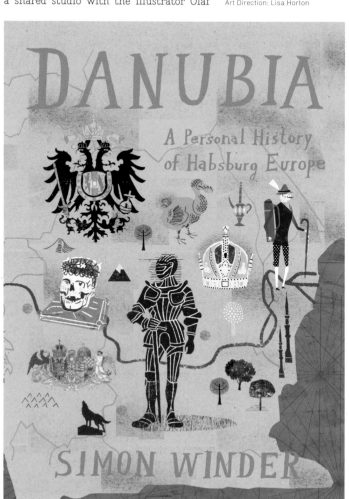

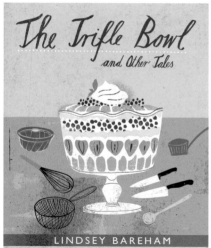

Hajek. The two have been working side-by-side ever since, not collaboratively, but in lively creative exchange.

Haake was, and still is, putting everything he likes into his work. His diverse styles have merged into one of great diversity. He likes to compare his technique to meat processing. Through his grinder go letterings, doodles, collage elements, drawings, and paintings, all raw and coarsely minced, to be concocted to taste without a recipe. The comparison of a meat grinder is suited to a project Haake realized for the *Süddeutsche Zeitung* back in 2001. It was the time of a big beef scandal, and he portrayed 10 famous Germans using meat and cold cuts: Michael Schumacher, with his red cap, and aspic, corned beef, blood sausage, and turkey breast and salami; Claudia Schiffer with her blonde mane, and curry turkey breast, Thuringian pate, and tongue sausage.

Getting his material from the meat counter is the exception rather than the rule. Usually, Haake draws, paints, or writes what he needs, and combines this with elements he finds in vintage magazines, catalogs, old schoolbooks, postcards that he buys at flea markets or on Ebay, or on discarded paper sheets from the streets of Berlin. His archive has grown considerably over the last decade or so, and part of it moved to the digital realm when he started to process things in that way.

Haake had frowned upon computers for a very long time. He would create a background using acrylic and scraps of paper, then glue all collage elements on top, and finally paint and draw on top of the collage. He turned to desktop publishing at some point out of necessity. "I found that many of my images, especially colors, came out poorly in print. Aware that Photoshop offered the possibility to do color corrections, I taught myself how to use it, peu à peu." When he found out how convenient it was as a tool to put things together, he began to use it regularly in place of glue.

In fact, Haake's analog collages are barely distinguishable from the ones put together in Photoshop because all the elements and structures are still analog. Digital filters or Google image searches are not part of his methodology. A dilettante at heart, Haake's desktop publishing skills never went beyond the basics of adjusting color and moving things around on layers. "I had an intern here for two weeks who showed me so many things and functions

I didn't know and would never have thought possible. I am a pro in nothing," he says. But this does not hamper amazing results. Haake still draws, paints, and scribbles, so all the patina and structures in his illustrations are genuine and created by hand. His motley multimedia backgrounds are thickened by materials such as acrylic paint or discarded paper sheets, cut-outs, and found photos or scribblings, giving them their distinctive textured surface.

BALLADA
(LEFT)
Client: Hanfgarn und Ufer Film Production, 2010

DAS LEBEN IST EINE NUDEL
(LIFE IS A NOODLE)
(RIGHT)
Client: Kindler, 2010

PHONE CARD
SHOP
AFRICA
BUSINESS
JOB OFFER
WEATHER FORECAST
JOB CENTER

Haake likes the fact that the technique is not immediately identifiable. He likes the sense of mystery. "When I did this cover for *3x3*, the illustration magazine, one of my first digital pieces actually, Charles Hively, Publisher & Design Director, called me up asking if he could have the original for his collection. He was quite surprised when I said that there is no original. He couldn't believe it. I still have some of this analog work on my website. But no client ever asked me to do an analog piece. Why should they, if the result looks the same anyway?"

Haake: "Analog pieces are often difficult in practice, and the fact that they cannot be altered is something many clients simply do not want to understand. The flexibility Photoshop offers is great, oftentimes necessary." He did a spread for the weekly newspaper *Stern* recently, where he had to move the elements out of the binding edge, for example. "Minor adjustments like these have to be made frequently. Major changes and requests for revision are getting rare. I guess projects just need to be finalized quicker these days, budgets are tighter." Haake mainly works in the editorial

feel of the final version. He emails them to his clients for agreement, as in-depth telephone conversations are not frequent anymore. "Client communication used to be a lot more personal when I started," Haake laments. "You would go to the briefing in person, bring in the original artwork for presentation. I do miss the sense of proximity and direct collaboration. After all, personal contact builds trust and gives the opportunity for open discussion. On the other hand, I certainly appreciate digital communication for making it possible to work with clients across the globe."

Although about half of his clients are German, Haake hardly works for clients who are based in Berlin. "As the world gets smaller, the number of my international clients increases. Currently, I am doing a job for a commissioner from India, for instance." As a large part of Haake's clients are from the U.K. and the U.S., he decided to work with the agents Lindgren & Smith in New York, and CIA in London. "A local contact makes life a whole lot easier, especially when it comes to complex copyright issues, rights of use, and things like that."

CAN YOU HEAR US NOW?
(LEFT PAGE)
Client: Heifer International, 2010
Art Direction: Donna Stokes

PEINLICH! PEINLICH?
(EMBARASSING!
EMBARASSING?)
(TOP)
Client: Dogs magazine, 2013

EVEL KNIEVEL DAYS
(LEFT)
Client: Zürcher Zeitung

KÖRUNG
(RIGHT)
Personal work

field, where time is short anyway. The advertising industry has changed a lot since the time that Haake wanted to become involved in it as a copywriter, not for the better, he finds. "I find a lack of courage on the creative side, too many people involved. More often than not, the client has the final say. Creatively, the editorial field is much more exciting." Its short deadlines become easier to handle as experience grows.

Haake used to do numerous sketches in the early days of his career, up to 12 at a time. "Nowadays, I know a bit better what idea works and what does not, so I usually sketch one or two, which allows more time for the final art." He does not do pencil sketches, but mixed media roughs to give a sense of the look and

Apart from organizational issues, Haake does not see major differences working for clients from other countries. He does agree that the British packaging industry is very open to playful illustrations like his, which may explain why his style is particularly popular among British clients. He did a multicolored collage design for Waitrose's recently, to be wrapped around the supermarket's range of "Food-of-the-World" sandwiches. When his packaging illustrations for the organic soup company Yes Please Food came out about five years ago in Germany, they truly stuck out from the supermarket shelves. Illustrated from top to bottom with funny faces for key visuals and handwritten typography, the design was received really well. However, it seems no coincidence that the responsible agency as

well as the owner of the small company are originally from the U.K.

"I guess my style appears to be a bit British," Haake says. During his early career in Hamburg, his wife was offered a job in London, so they moved there and stayed for four years. "A great time, and incredibly inspiring," Haake recalls. "Clients in the U.K. pay far less than those in Germany, or in the U.S., and I really don't know why."

Be that as it may, the British have always been valuable clients for the German illustrator. Only recently, his poster campaign for the Royal Mail was put up everywhere across the country.

"Money is usually not the most important motivation for me to do a job," Haake declares. Fees appear arbitrary to him. "You can do the same thing, and the funny thing is that, for the same amount

FRIEDRICH NIETZSCHE
(LEFT)
Client: Philosophie Magazin, 2012
Art Direction: Iris Ströbel

FRIEDRICH II
(RIGHT)
Client: Rotary Magazine, 2012
Art Direction: Matthias Scheil

of effort, one client may pay you 500 Euros, the next 10,000. Of course, it depends on the scale of the project, the rights of use and so on, but the range is unreasonably wide and hard to navigate. Olaf has much better negotiating skills than I have and I learned a thing or two from his example. Still, I am just not the biggest businessman."

He is not the most industrious networker, either. "I should do more Facebook, and stuff like that, I guess. But I think a good website is the most important thing. Mine is already six years old or so, but I still get a lot of positive feedback." The site generates quite a few direct job inquiries, too. Haake is represented by 2agenten in German-speaking countries, but still administers occasional jobs himself. Since he is getting better in his negotiation skills, he usually succeeds in getting fine deals.

MACHIAVELLI
(LEFT)
Client: Hohe Luft, 2012
Art Direction: Gabriele Dünwald

WAGNER AND BAYREUTH
(RIGHT)
Client: Rotary Magazine, 2013
Art Direction: Karsten Middeldorf

"Agents take 25–30% commission, plus expenses for promotion, which can easily go into the thousands a year. Of course one would prefer to avoid all these costs. I highly appreciate the work of my agents but enjoy handling commissions on my own, as long as the volume and scope are manageable."

Over the last few years, Haake has been flooded with commissions from all directions, and he manages to realize about 125 a year. "Freelancing has worked well for me straight from the beginning. But this really is the best time ever," he says. "I am in the studio every day, including weekends." Fixed working hours are impossible to maintain for the time being, but Haake likes to work on weekends, especially Sundays. "Everything is nice and quiet then—perfect working conditions." He regrets that free time for family life has become rare these days.

He often thinks that he needs to learn to reject some projects to free up time for personal projects.

"I would love to do my own book. Books embody such an enduring value." He envisions something that works as a picture book, but with no stringent story-line, rather, structured around information—an illustrated edition of the *Guinness Book of World Records*, for example. "Or unnecessary knowledge in pictures. Also, my two sons are twelve and nine years old now, and I always wanted to do a picture book for them. Unfortunately, that didn't happen yet. I just cannot commit to such a long-term project now that there are so many nice jobs coming in all the time."

The good order situation is further enhanced by the recent appreciation of maps. Haake has illustrated Africa, India, Berlin Mitte, London, St Tropez, and the

THE GENERAL
(LEFT)
Client: 3x3 magazine, 2009
Art Direction: Charles Hively

PROFESSIONALS AT SCHOOL
(RIGHT)
Client: Scholastic, 2013
Art Direction: Frank Tagariello

RIVIERA IN THE 1960S
(RIGHT PAGE)
Client: Lodenfrey, 2012
Art Direction: Dan Popa

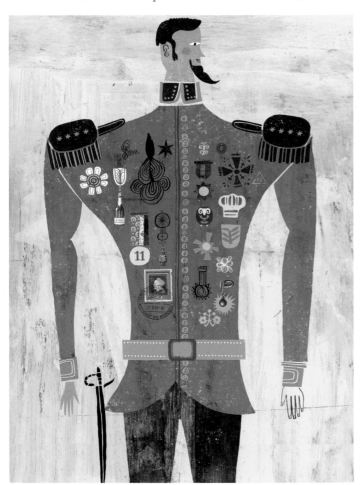

whole happy planet in one quirky chart. "Maps have become so en vogue these days. They are used for various applications—editorial, of course, but also corporate communications." Haake's maps merge information with a good deal of personal interpretation. They are not necessarily very accurate. Therefore, they are highly emotional. "Initially, I didn't care if they could actually be used or not. But when I did an extensive map of Berlin on the occasion of the Berlinale, and people actually got lost, I reconsidered my approach." Today, Haake consults reference material to create maps that can actually be used. Currently, he is working on one for a conference hosted by Switzerland Tourism. "That will be huge, to be displayed on a twenty-meter screen, with animated elements."

Notwithstanding Haake's effort to present cities and landscapes truly and fairly, subjectivity remains at the heart of his maps, and creative freedom is what he enjoys most about drawing them. "In maps, I can bring together everything that I love and combine it in manifold ways. Which elements, symbols, or land-

marks I choose to bring out and enlarge upon is almost entirely up to me, and also, the way in which I portray them." And so, the Berlin TV tower grows arms, or the Queen grows taller than Big Ben. Anything seems possible in these places that Haake illustrates. Laws and principles seem suspended in favor of idiosyncrasy and cartographic experiments.

"Experimentation is so important, it makes you reinvent yourself," Haake says. It is due to the lack of time for personal projects that he does his best to experiment in his commissioned work. Maps, he says, allow him to experiment as no other project, so he considers them to be his specialty. Though he has proven adept in his craft, he asserts that he is still "a pro in nothing," doing his best to start each new assignment as an amateur would. As he told Charles Hively of *3x3*, he'll use new tools, new mediums, new brushes, and change his source references so as to constantly create new challenges and ventures. "Sometimes, I'll say to myself, 'let's try to do this image as if Saul Bass, Bill Traylor, or Jean-Michel Basquiat would have done it.'"

PLACE AND DATE OF BIRTH

Rendsburg, Germany; 1965

COUNTRY OF RESIDENCE

Germany

FAMILY STATUS

Not married

EDUCATION / DEGREE

Diploma in Design

ACTIVE IN THE FIELD OF ILLUSTRATION SINCE

1993

BREAKTHROUGH PROJECT

Süddeutsche Zeitung Summer riddle cover and
3 following issues of illustrations

KEY CLIENTS

The New Yorker, the New York Times, Macy's, MontBlanc

MOST RENOWNED PROJECTS

Macy's, Hotel 25hours, Goldene Kamera,
Afinal, o que querem as Mulheres?

COMMISSIONS PER YEAR

100 plus exhibitions

AVERAGE TURNAROUND TIME PER COMMISSION

Depends on commission

WORKSPACE

Shared with Martin Haake

EMPLOYEES

None

AGENTS

7 worldwide

HOW MUCH COMMISSION DO YOUR AGENTS TAKE

25%

TEACHING POSITIONS

None

AWARDS (SELECTION)

Gold Award Association of Illustrators UK (2012);
Silver Award UK (2003); Art Directors Club Europe, Gold
Award (2003); Art Directors Club Germany, Silver Award
(2003), Leadaward Gold (2004); Leadaward Silver (2004)

PUBLICATIONS

1998–2011 American Illustration 18–31
2005 Illustration Now!,Taschen
2005–2011 Best Illustrators Worldwide,
Lürzers Archive Special
2007–2009 Freistil 12–14
2009 Monograph Flowerhead, Gestalten
2012 Monograph Black Antoinette, Gestalten

MEMBER ASSOCIATIONS

Association of Illustrators (AOI)

GALLERIES

AJL ARTS; Berlin
Whatiftheworld Gallery, Cape Town

Olaf Hajek

"THERE ARE NO RULES IN THE BUSINESS OF ILLUSTRATION, EVERY JOB IS A LITTLE UNIVERSE OF ITS OWN."

"One of the most daring challenges in the life of an illustrator is to seize the freedom you have and make the best of it," says Olaf Hajek with substantive conviction. He just returned from South Africa, where he spent three months cut off from his everyday life as an illustrator and all its routines, putting together his solo show "Strange Flowers" at Capetown's Whatiftheworld Gallery. "Brief, sketch, produce, deliver. I was longing for a project of greater scale, duration, and depth and realized that there would be no time off until I'd consciously take it."

Parallel to realizing around 100 illustration commissions annually, for clients as diverse as the *New Yorker,* Macy's, and Volkswagen, Hajek has built up a considerable artistic oeuvre over the past years, exhibiting in galleries across the globe, and painting on commission for enthusiastic collectors. When a friend introduced him to a South African artist who offered him studio space in Kapstadt for three months, he decided to take the time off from illustration and focus solely on his art. "Turning down lucrative illustration commissions was not easy. Financial strain is one thing, but I mostly feared not being able to sustain my mission, mentally." The internet connection in Kapstadt was quite bad, so that helped him disconnect. "I really never felt so productive as in these three months in Kapstadt this year," Hajek declares, noting the importance of the change of scenery.

Both Hajek's art and illustrations are imbued with carnevalesque narratives. Alive with detail, flowers, plants, patterns, and texture, they tell of the relativity of life. Enclosed in his syncretic pageants are figures that metamorphose into plants,

has arrived at the point of setting priorities. After returning to Berlin, Hajek found that many illustration clients hesitated to send him inquiries. "I guess they think I am concentrating on my art and gallery career now, which is my fault, of course, and to some extent true." In the long run, Hajek may see himself as a painter, rather than an illustrator. But while he has focused on his transition from illustration to fine art over the last years, his illustration work has undergone an exciting transition too.

While editorial work used to be the core of Hajek's early illustration career, it has long become one specialty among others. A new affinity for commissions that go beyond the daily illustration business has led him to create a shop window for Montblanc, wallpapers and paintings to adorn interiors, such as those for the restaurant Rigoletto in Stockholm and

birds that accumulate into lumps, and trees full of overripe fruit, dripping sap. Amazonian belles carry bouquets, bearing blooming, over-flowering, or withering blossoms. Blurred by a surreal dimension, Hajek's folkloric tales wed the beauty with the grotesque, the macabre with the innocent, the sacred with the profane, and realism with mise-en-scène.

Boundaries have always dissolved in Hajek's work, opposites have always blended. Craft and fine art appear to form the ideal symbiosis. What flourishes in Hajek's free projects is soon to sprout and grow in his commercial work too. "Existence is transition," writes Dr. Philipp Demand, head of Berlin's Old National Gallery, so aptly in his introduction to Hajek's second monograph. But however seamless the transition between Hajek's art and illustration may seem, he

AFRICAN BEAUTY
(LEFT PAGE)
Personal Work, 2011

HAND MADE
(TOP)
Catalog cover
Client: Burgbad, 2011

LOST PARADISE 2
(RIGHT)
Personal Work, 2011

ORANGES ARE NOT THE ONLY FRUIT
(PAGE 16)
Cover for a novel by Jeanette Winterson
Client: Groove/Atlantic, 2011

the Hotel25Hours. Recently, the Swedish fashion brand Minimarket commissioned Hajek to paint a flower pattern to be used for various items from their collection, from jackets or dresses to shoes. Currently, he is working on packaging for the cosmetics brand Cacharel. "I take great pleasure in the variety, seeing my work applied in different contexts and become part of every day life," Hajek says. Yet one does not find many pictures that show his work in application. Agents and clients may like to see illustrations in use, but to Hajek the image must, most importantly, be able to stand alone.

Hajek stands by his artistic position with poise, despite it not necessarily tying in with commercial interests. To him, the challenge of applied illustration lies not least in the endeavor to put an idea forward and win over the client. "I don't feel like a service provider. Luckily I am in a position where I can think twice before taking on a project that involves too many rules and limitations. In fact, my clients often approach me with rather vague ideas of what they'd like, oftentimes struggling to put it in words, and invite me to draw upon it as per my own style and creative vision. In an effort to reduce costs, more and more business clients, even large ones, are turning their backs to major campaigns, in favor of smaller marketing projects." Recognizing art and design as a tool, many collaborate with artists like Hajek to produce small merchandising editions in the stead of huge billboards. "Less money, more creative freedom: the latest trick," Hajek comments. He recently created a set of postcards for the organic cosmetics brand Weleda and one for Chevrolet, too.

As is usual in advertising, projects like these often begin with a pitch. "Mostly unpaid, for minimal remuneration, you are asked to propose your idea. Some seriously ask you to present a finished piece. Then, at worst, you have done it for nothing." Unacceptable, finds Hajek. His agents

MONTBLANC
Client: Montblanc Intl., 2012
Creative Director: Carlo Giordanetti

in New York once talked him into pitching a series of advertising illustrations to Coca-Cola. The project was not realized, but reasonably remunerated to make up for all the time and effort. Chevrolet accepted black-and-white sketches, which they paid for, but then deducted from the final fee. Hajek is fast in finding ideas and doing first sketches. Working on an editorial piece, for example, the idea usually comes to him while reading the text. "One might accuse me of not thinking enough," he says, "but I just really focus on the implementation, and like to have as much time as possible for that."

Hajek's work is intensely detailed, so his labor costs are high, regardless of the type of project. Fees differ considerably, and to Hajek, the assessment of value feels random at times. "There are no rules in the business of illustration, every job is a little universe of its own. In terms of money, that is, but also in regard to requirements and expectations. But within the editorial field, you may be asked to illustrate a personality test in a women's magazine, or a topical political article for a newspaper. Needless to say, the approach is entirely different. Then, the degree of creative leeway depends a lot on who acts as your counterpart. Are you talking to the creative director, the picture editor, are marketing people involved? How free is the commissioner? How many people

FLOWERS
Client: MiniMarket, 2011

are part of the discussion?" By and large, editorial clients are more prone to taking risks than the advertising industry, which acts under the permanent pressure of customer expectations and marketing departments.

"American advertising clients are most difficult," finds Hajek. "They have all these excessive business hierarchies." He rarely does large commercial jobs anymore, but recalls absurd situations with some he has done in the past. One time, for example, he was commissioned to illustrate an advertisement to promote an African style beverage. The scene was conceived to feature a black man, but marketing feared potential negative connotations

and suggested a white protagonist instead. The black man turned into a blonde girl in the end. "Much of the advertising industry ticks that way, like much of the world unfortunately does," Hajek says. "I prefer not to be a part of that." He carefully chooses what he considers aesthetic approaches in advertising—projects that value art as a form of emotional communication and thus like to let the art speak for itself.

Hajek is lucky enough to have that choice. He enjoys an ongoing flow of commissions. However, he never thinks of himself as truly safe. "The fate of the illustrator is to never know what happens next. To never be able to plan in advance.

You never now what jobs pop up. Two or three weeks is the maximum future timeframe that you may sometimes be able to oversee. No matter how successful you are, existential fears pop up every once in a while." This is the flipside of the great freedom you have, working freelance. And Hajek has never known anything different.

He moved to Amsterdam to become a freelance illustrator right after graduating from the Department of Design of the University of Düsseldorf. "While most of my fellow students on that quite advertising-oriented graphic design course worked to become big names of the advertising industry, I always knew that I wanted to

cites valuable basic skills in typography, design, and layout, thinking pragmatically, and coming to terms with the commercial art scene. Occasional side jobs in design studios during his studies eventually enabled Hajek to create the financial cushion he needed for his move to Amsterdam, and a year of precious preparation time. "I sat down to build up my illustration portfolio, worked on self-initiated drawings and paintings, combined them with some university assignments, and produced little booklets to show to potential clients."

He was hired for occasional editorial jobs, first in Holland, then in Germany. Around 1994 Markus Rasp, art director at the *Süddeutsche Zeitung* magazine for many years, took notice of Hajek's work,

my way, and question whether it was the right one or not."

After two years in Holland, Hajek moved to Berlin, where he shares a studio with the illustrator Martin Haake. He does not self-impose fixed working hours, but naturally maintains a rhythm that comes close to a nine to five structure. "I don't know the split between job and free time. My work is an essential and integral part of my life. But I can easily count the number of night shifts I did over the past 20 years on a single hand. Or wait, did I ever work late at night? I really don't even understand how one can get into that situation in the first place. And I never ever exceeded a deadline."

Despite his natural talent in handling deadlines and daily schedules with

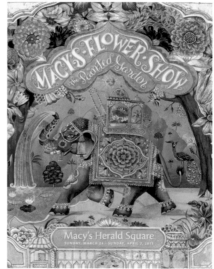

be an illustrator, however that may work out." The interest in painting had emerged early in Hajek's life. He recalls a workshop in oil painting he attended while still in high school: "This artist would let us paint with our fingers, and tell us things like 'If you don't like the image, just flip it around and continue painting.' Then I took a nude and portrait workshop at an adult education center, but that was fantastic, too. The teacher there told us things like 'If you can't draw a nose, leave it out, the main thing is to create a good image.'"

Ideas like these encouraged Hajek to think freely, and influenced his approach to scale and perspective, and color and painting as haptic experience. In fact, this education related more closely to his work than all that he learned at university. He

INTERNATIONAL FILM FESTIVAL
(LEFT)
Client: Ile de France, 2012
Agency: Rampazzo & Associés

MACY'S FLOWERSHOW
(MIDDLE)
Client: Macy's Inhouse Agency, 2013
Creative Director: Gregory di Bisceglie

LITTLE GURUS
(RIGHT)
Publisher: Bohem, Switzerland, 2012
Author: Olaf Hajek

causing Hajek's career to gather momentum. After two smaller commissions, Rapp entrusted Hajek with illustrating the big summer quiz—three issues in a row, with illustrations throughout the entire magazine. The project was well-received and made Hajek's work popular in no time. "I was lucky to be able to make a living out of illustration from the beginning. Extremely lucky, that is. In fact, I have never been forced to do anything else. I also never had to quarrel

ease, Hajek shuns specific appointments and long-term obligations beyond his own creative practice.

He lectured at the Universität der Künste Berlin for a while, but quit. "It was an interesting experience, but they ran out of money, and the payment had been very bad anyway." He has been invited to take on teaching positions by other universities, but always rejected the offers. "I don't see myself there at the moment. I could well imagine a professorship some day, but not for the time being. Such things take responsibility and a whole lot of time that I would rather spend on other things now." He enjoys the opportunity to do occasional lectures, has traveled to speak at the Minneapolis Institute of Arts, and has an upcoming speaking engagement offered in Los Angeles.

The global village of illustration knows no boundaries, and Hajek finds the immense scope of his profession both absurd and extremely fascinating. "Compared to many other creative industries, the platform for illustration is vast and diverse. As an illustrator, you don't have to be on site, like a photographer for a shoot, and you are not confronted with language barriers like the writer." Hajek travels a lot, and cherishes a network of

UNCENSORED
(LEFT)
Client: African Museum, 2012
Art Direction: Gijs Sluiters
Famous Agency NLm, Belgium

GLYNDEBOURNE FESTIVAL
(RIGHT)
Client: The Guardian, 2012
Art Direction: Marc Reddy
Agency: Bartle Bogle Hegarty,
London

clients from all over the world, working with agents in Berlin, London, Paris, Stockholm, Amsterdam, New York, Sydney, and São Paolo. He does not get a frequent flow of work from all of them, but they keep him present and connected on an international level.

"It is not easy to find a good agent," says Hajek, "but it is worth trying." He has recently broken up with his New York agent Bernstein and Adriulli after 10 years to join Art Department, and compares the experience to that of divorcing a partner. "It can be extremely hard but you have to figure out if you are good for each other." Hajek does his best to occasionally meet agents, and sometimes clients, so as to build up a sense of trust and longstanding work relationships. I met with Montblanc's creative director once, to discuss my first project for them, a calendar for their Arts Patronage Award. A few years after he commissioned me again, to design the Montblanc window, and bought one of my paintings. Now he works for Swatch, and called me up to do this artist edition watch." Hajek also notes a friendly long-term collaboration with Markus Rasp and the *Süddeutsche Zeitung*, which has yielded a whole string of commissions.

Just as important as personal communication is, for Hajek, the broad, global reach of his agents. "You really need someone on the spot. Agents usually don't work across countries, however bustling and networked they may be." That is also why he would strongly advise any illustrator against signing an exclusive contract with only one agency. "For one thing, you have to work globally these days, otherwise you would not get enough jobs. For another, being part of that global network, and dealing with commissioners from various fields and cultures, is one of the most enjoyable and valuable assets of being an illustrator these days."

An international spectrum as broad as Hajek's would have been unthinkable

back when he started his career in the pre-internet era. Desktop publishing was slowly starting to emerge, but never played a role in Hajek's practice. He scans his paintings to be reproduced as illustrations. Apart from that, his process is entirely analog. When starting a project, he makes it a point to state this to clients, so that they know upfront that he won't make adjustments or move things around. "I do a black-and-white sketch to agree upon the image buildup with the client." A clear agreement is key, as he then paints in full detail and characteristically vibrant tones. The latter is often problematic to reproduce in print, and respective disappointments are part of his day-to-day business. However, Hajek has never wrapped his head around color-management solutions. "The client is in charge of reproduction, so things like colors are impossible to control for me, even if I knew how to do it." He could do minor changes in Photoshop, but shuns digital tools.

"There is some fantastic digital illustration work out there, but also an incredible amount of illustrators who believe that the computer compensates for a lack of skill and talent," finds Hajek. Both technology and trends boost the interest in creative jobs, causing the field to grow somewhat inflationary. "There are so many illustrators, both good and bad, these days, they cannot even be sure to get an agent." Hajek remembers the wonderfully unhurried times of carrying his portfolio around to local art directors. "Today, you can't just call up a publisher, as they get thousands of portfolios emailed." The situation is aggravated by the media crisis that does not only affect traditional print media, but also various fields of advertising. Hajek poses questions about the

HOTEL 25HRS WIEN
(THIS PAGE)
Client: Hotel 25 hrs, 2011
Photo: Steve Herud, Berlin
© dreimeta – Armin Fischer

WINTER
(RIGHT PAGE)
Client: Saisonküche, 2010

state of his profession: "What is illustration today? In what forms is it successfully used, or will it be used in, in the future?" He says he really does not know, but is curious to see.

For Hajek's part, his direction seems set and certainly promising. Due to his growing popularity as a painter, he gets more and more inquiries for projects as an artist, rather than as an illustrator. Quite recently, he designed an anniversary edition of a classic Bauhaus teapot for Crate & Barrel, a Chicago-based company dedicated to making fine European home- and tableware. The minimarket collection was a great success. An Olaf Hajek

art watch by Swatch will be available soon. "That is in fact exactly the course I want to take in illustration," Hajek says. "Lending my art to a fine selection of beautiful projects."

Patrick Morgan

PLACE AND DATE OF BIRTH
London, United Kingdom; 1977

COUNTRY OF RESIDENCE
United Kingdom

FAMILY STATUS
Married

EDUCATION/DEGREE
BA (hons) in Graphics and Illustration,
Kingston University

ACTIVE IN THE FIELD OF ILLUSTRATION SINCE
1999

BREAKTHROUGH PROJECT
Selfridges 2003

KEY CLIENTS
Tom Ford, Coca-Cola, YSL, Telegraph, FT,
the Observer, Siemens, Carling

MOST RENOWNED PROJECTS
Selfridges 2003 Annual Report

COMMISSIONS PER YEAR
100

AVERAGE TURNAROUND TIME PER COMMISSION
1–4 weeks

WORKSPACE
Private studio

EMPLOYEES
3

AGENTS
Début Art, London, Paris, New York

HOW MUCH COMMISSION DO YOUR AGENTS TAKE
35%

TEACHING POSITIONS
Program leader, graphic design (BA),
Tutor, fashion design (MA)

AWARDS (SELECTION)
D&AD (2009/2010/2011) as a tutor

MEMBER ASSOCIATIONS
AOI, DESIGN AND ART DIRECTION (D&AD)

GALLERIES
Coningsby Gallery

"MANY PEOPLE IN THE FASHION INDUSTRY LOVE ART LIKE MYSELF AND HAVE A GREAT VISION OF DESIGN AND THE WORLD CULTURALLY."

Patrick Morgan is a hard worker with clear ideas on how to move forward. Now that his award-winning illustrations appear worldwide and his style has been endorsed by fashion brands such as Yves Saint Lauren, Celine, and Tom Ford, and by businesses such as Coca-Cola, Hewlett Packard, Selfridges, Virgin Mobile, and Waitrose, it is hard to imagine that the beginning of his career was rather hard and stony. One might not know that he built up his first illustration portfolio while working as a laborer on a building site. Looking at his career in retrospect, Morgan has often noted how times of struggle with few positive returns have pushed him to bigger heights, and ever closer to his aim of making his mark in the design industry.

Growing up in north London, Morgan began to seriously pursue his goals during a one-year foundation course at the local Middlesex University. He explored the school's workshops and his "love for screen printing and any other printing processes," and moved on to work his way through the BA program in Graphics and Illustration at Kingston University. Under the creative lead of RCA professor Brian Love, Morgan followed the path of printmaking through drawing and painting, with a growing focus on commercial illustration. Recalling his time at Kingston as a tough battle of the best, he learned to deal with criticism and the fact that, in the shark pool of commercial art, only the strongest survive. Time would soon show that Morgan was among this category.

The London-based illustration agency Début Art had become aware of Morgan at the Kingston degree show and took him on right after his graduation in 1998. Immediately convinced of the commercial value of his work, they pushed him to refine his art and prepare for the professional world that was still largely unknown to him.

One year would pass before his first paid commission. Illustrating the members of the band REM for *Q Magazine*, Morgan experienced what daily business demanded beyond raw talent, creative passion, and the ability to draw. "I was starting to use Photoshop in my work for coloring and didn't have a clue about resolution, size, anything. I think it all came out half pixelated. I had only had one lesson in Photoshop… They commissioned me again so maybe it wasn't too bad."

CHANEL PRODUCT
(PAGE 26)
Client: Stylist magazine

TOM FORD
(THIS PAGE)
Client: Stylist magazine

Surely not, for further commissions were not long in coming.

Early editorial jobs were followed by bigger commercial ones. In 2000, Morgan took on a position as art director for the

ITE Group, an organizer of international trade fairs and conferences. Continuing to work freelance, his commissions increased steadily. The one that Morgan highlights as a turning point in his career was *The Selfridges Annual Report 2003*, "a real money spinner and great creatively." As Morgan noted in conversation with fellow illustrator Halil Yildirim, "I had total artistic control and tried to push them to put as much cash into the cover artwork using Fluro inks and special blacks—anything to really make me feel totally in control, not being a control freak. Attracting clients is one thing; getting them to feel comfortable and happy to allow you to work your wonders is another thing."

Flying all over England illustrating for the various Selfridges stores was a good way of self-promotion, which Morgan has taken very seriously since the early days of his career.

He gave Yildirim an example of his investments over a year: 1,500 GBP for a double-page advertisement in the print edition of *Workbook*, a creative resource for photography and illustration portfolios, 1,700 GBP for a double-page advertisement in their U.S. edition, 980 GBP for a single-page advertisement in *The Art Book*, Phaidon's A-to-Z guide to the "greatest" artists, 300 GBP for an online portfolio on the Association of Illustrators website,

a quick update." Looking at all the big names that have accumulated in Morgan's client list over the years, his strategy has certainly paid off.

Working for big money, Morgan is very aware of not selling his soul. Pushing through his ideals wherever he can, he rejects too much compromise. "It will

for YSL and Jack Purcell for Converse and they both just said do what you do best and make ART. This made me push hard trying new techniques and it makes you feel that the industry does have some people with an open mind commissioning you to be the best at what you know best (...) However, when the budget is big,

350 GBP for promotional images, and 120 GBP for an online portfolio on the creative platform The Black Book. "Promoting yourself is not cheap. But if you don't do it then keeping in the art world is very hard. Your own website will generate a lot of student viewings but that's it really. I have had a few big jobs from my site, but people really go to your site to have

**TOP 10 PRODUCTS
BY UK TOP ILLUSTRATOR**
Client: Stylist magazine

destroy your creative heart." In the same breath, he declares that he never really had issues with large corporate clients asking for directions he would not take. "In fact, it is the big clients who tend to give you lots of freedom. Often smaller, more independent clients are less open, as they think they are the artist too, and it's a real clash of minds. I worked with Loreal

and something is going wrong, you have to just keep going until one party crashes. Usually the client breaks. Illustrators are used to a hard life. Fighters."

Arming himself to become the tough fighter he is today, Morgan went through various jobs and working conditions. Apart from the aforementioned position as art director at the ITE Group, which he

Yves Saint Laurent
PARIS

held from 2000 to 2005, he was an illustrator in-house for the Telegraph from 2010 to 2012. "I think if I had gone straight into establishing my own business (Morgan Creative, which he launched as PMA Associates after having left the ITE Group), I may not have lived the test of time," he states with the wisdom of hindsight. "Working as an art director taught me professionalism and the *Telegraph* showed me how to deal with tight deadlines."

Morgan still works in the editorial field, cherishing it for its immediacy and the compact process. "Spontaneous art, you can't beat it." As a matter of principle, and in regard to commissions of all kinds, Morgan has found that simple, clear-cut approaches are the ones that sell best. "If the idea is too clever the client just won't accept it. Whenever you try to be too smart they change it." Of course, simple ideas are not always easy and quickly made. And so Morgan spends a great deal of his time on preliminary research such as finding suitable images to support his compositions or taking photos to be used for reference. 60% research, 30% working, 10% experimenting is how he breaks down his process.

Having worked as a commercial illustrator for quite awhile now, Morgan has seen the field grow more complex, and expand into new markets and territories. The greatest challenge for him today is to carve out a unique path and move along on it. "The industry is saturated with artists and lots of people are doing the same thing, so there is no point in trying to be a fish in a big pond. I always wanted to specialize but now seeing that the other illustrators are doing many styles—being a one trick pony is not a way to survive. I like to constantly change and play, never staying the same. I'm really starting to move away from standard mediums and trying to do really complex computer work collaborating with 3D artists. I think collaboration is the only way forward for the best arts, as illustration alone is lowly and hard."

Most of Morgan's work uses a combination of traditional drawing and printing

YVES GLASSES
(LEFT PAGE)
Client: Yves Saint Laurent

COCO CHANEL
(TOP)
Client: Chanel

PARIS HOME
(RIGHT)
Client: Casa abaitaire, Italy

techniques. "My style has changed from pen to pencil to printmaking but it's all about mark making," he explains. "I just draw and experiment all the time. EVERYDAY. Pen, pencil, silk screen, rollers, block printing, relief printing. You name it, I'm trying it." Digital finishing techniques like coloring and occasional renderings facilitate updates and speed up the production process. Lately, however, Morgan is trying to be "as artistic as possible, as so many students are using Photoshop and computers in their work so you have to be one step ahead." He mentions making art with terracotta now, and implies that he will give away a bit more on that later.

Spurred by creative ambitions, which do not always go hand-in-hand with commercial projects, Morgan soon learned to balance bread-and-butter commissions with self-initiated experiments, and how the former benefits from the latter. Aware of what the industry and his clients want "now," he always tries to work ahead, thinking of what will work in the time to come. "I experimented with pen and ink about three years ago and it is starting to come in vogue now. A real planned process."

Trends are always changing, especially in the field of fashion, which Morgan works in a lot. "I work in many areas, but as time goes on you need to find your areas of love. I have always loved fashion. For example, I am a real fan of Paul Smith, as he's always young-minded and very contemporary, and Karl Lagerfeld, whom I have grown to admire. Workwise I think fashion is quite iconic, so creating works for the likes of Tom Ford or Yves Saint Laurent has been rewarding."

Apart from enjoying fashion and its products as a theme, Morgan appreciates the industry's quirky individuals. "Many people in the industry love art like myself and always have a great vision of design and the world culturally." As a course director in drawing and print design at Istituto Marangoni, a prestigious Italian fashion academy, Morgan works at

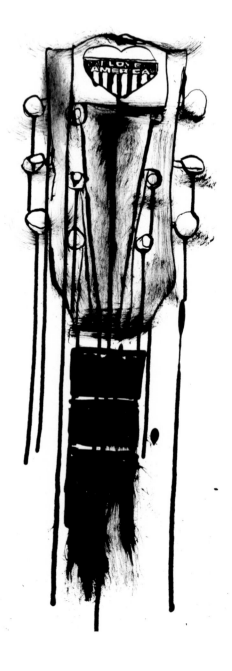

Besides teaching and running his own business, Morgan has extended his work relationship with Hewlett Packard over the years to become their creative consultant. Sharing the position with Tony Chambers, *Wallpaper** magazine's editor-in-chief, he is entrusted to experiment

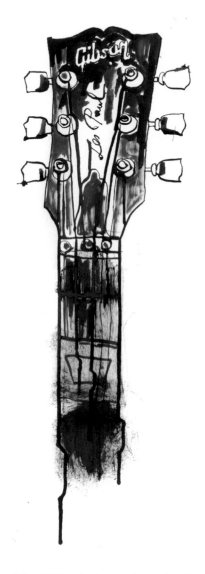

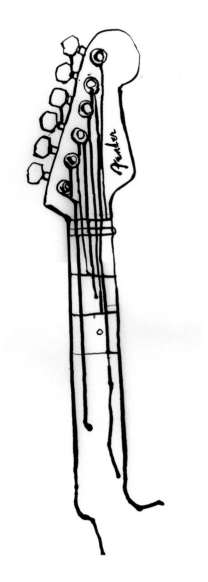

created videos, and did global advertising campaigns—a great work in progress."

The insights Morgan gained as an essential part of HP's marketing campaign have sharpened his already early marked sense for self-promotion. "Although my agents do most of my marketing and

the crossroads of fashion, styling, and the graphics industry. Holding the teaching position since the academy launched its London location back in 2003, he has been passing on his skills in design, advertising, and image-making to generations of fashion illustration graduates.

GUITARS
(THIS PAGE)
Client: Live Nation

CRY BABY
(RIGHT PAGE)
Client: St. Malo Avenue Clothing

with all HP printing products that have come out over the last 10 years, the HP 130 Large Format in particular. "Big printers and funky papers," as Morgan sums up. What emerges from the experiments is used for Hewlett Packard's PR and marketing. "They sponsored exhibitions,

promotion by now, I am starting to think more about having to branch out and market myself. I am starting to work with my wife on a fashion label, St Malo Avenue, and we have just created prints for clothing for a band, Citizens!, managed by Kitsune.

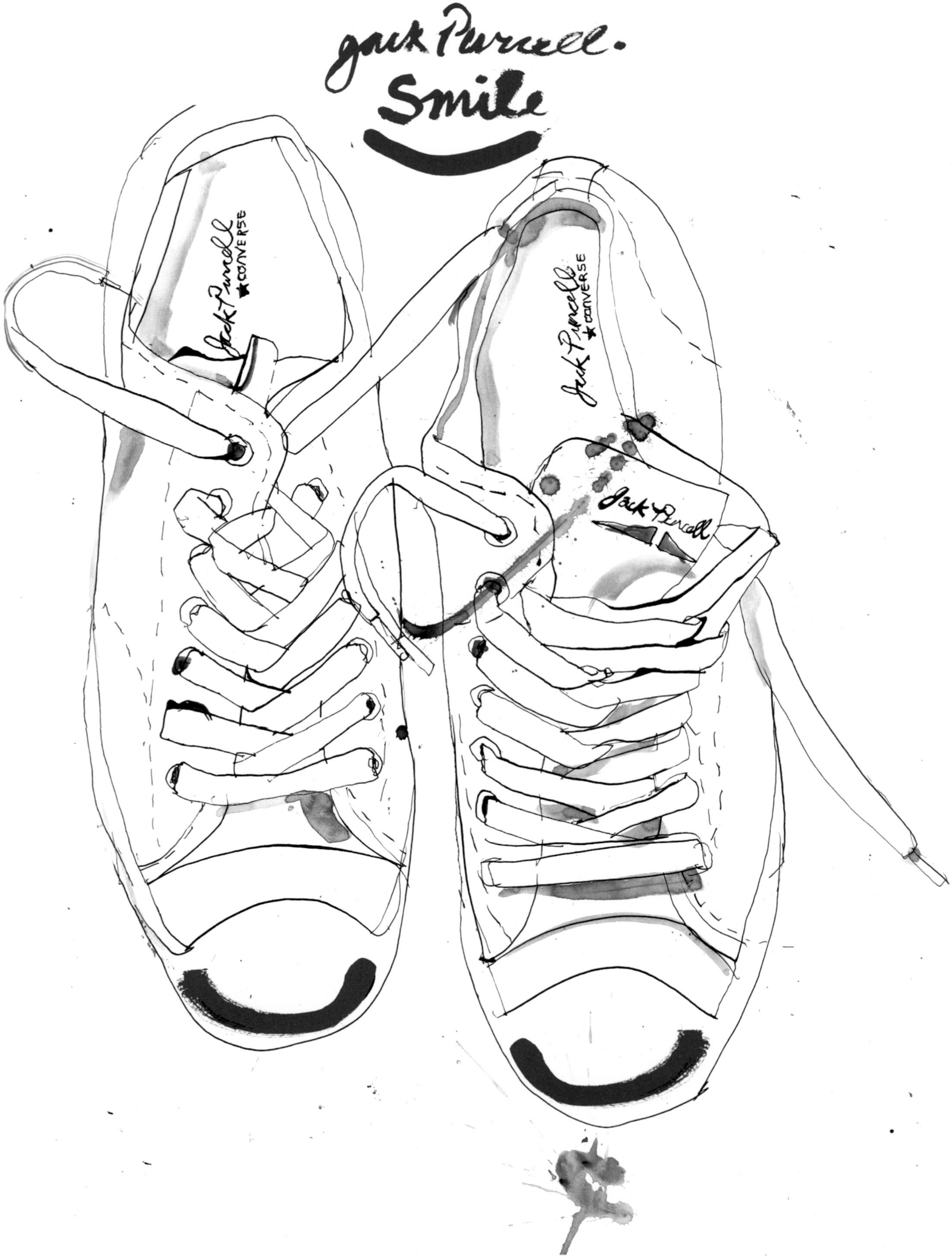
Jack Purcell.
Smile
Jack Purcell
CONVERSE

Is there still time for doing illustrations at all? At PMA Associates, which has recently been renamed Morgan Creative because many people thought it was a consultancy, Morgan works with a collective of illustrators who support him as colorists and assistants. He has three employees at the moment, but the team varies in size, depending on commissions, and includes a screen printer, a fabric printer, and Morgan's brother Mark as an intern. Morgan also works on commissions with his students at Istituto Marangoni, most recently for POD, a healthy fast-food chain with restaurants throughout the U.K. Altogether, he realizes around 100 commissions per year, but is trying to slow things down a bit, and reduce work to an even finer selection of clients and briefs. He still does pitches, but not the kind that call for unpaid proposals.

About 70% of Morgan Creative's commissions come in through agents, the rest through direct contact. "The commissioning process is very direct, so you get the money side out of the way fast to get on with the real part, THE ART." Morgan still works with his agents at Début Art, who mainly operate from London and New York, where geographically the bulk of his clients now are. Whether they are in London or the U.S., Morgan prefers to communicate with his commissioners by email. "Some clients like to bring you in, but this can really take too much time depending on budget. Britain is expensive so time is money and you really need to work time and budget. Otherwise you are overworking the piece, and better off just doing it for free."

Morgan's time and work management reflects his keen business acumen. The commercial side, however, is only one facet of his successful creative ventures. "Teaching varies throughout the year, but life is full with at least one exhibition a year now. I have one in London supporting a charity, The House of St Barnabas for the Homeless, or I donate work to charities, like recently to The English National Ballet to support dancers. I am also working on a print collection with MCG Italian fashion

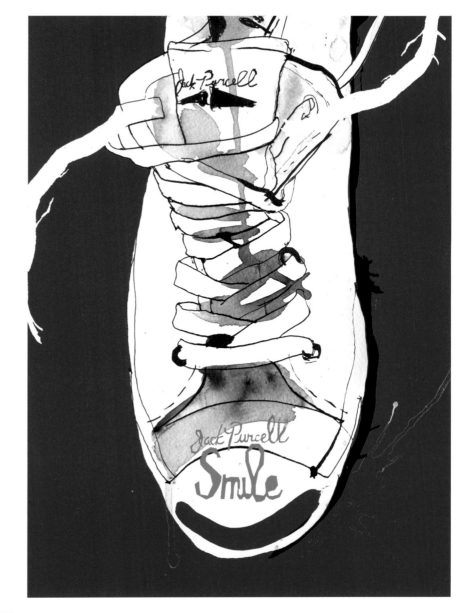

JACK PURCELL ADS
(BOTH PAGES)
Client: Converse

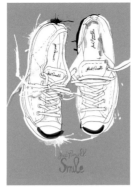

designer Massimo Casagrande on his next menswear shirt collection, creating prints, and finally a personal collection of terracotta reliefs on work I did with Tom Ford for the national ballet, "The Fire Bird." A few years ago, Morgan announced a future plan to open an illustration and design school, helping people push forward in the industry, so as not to lose themselves to the corporate machine, instead getting back to creating real original art.

Is there still time for a life, beyond professional practice? "I work all the time and only have time out to pick my kids up from nursery or school, and then wash the kids at night to help my wife—the real world things that bring you back into reality. Three years ago I went on holiday before I had my third daughter Raffaella, but since then I have been working and stay at home, as most jobs always come when you are packing and ready to leave." Recently, Morgan has been speaking to Apple, a dream client for many. "I think they are pushing design to the highest level, so let's see." One may either be overwhelmed by or infected with Morgan's untiring willingness to work and thrive. "No rest for the Wicked," he announces. The capital W is well-deserved.

Jonathan Burton

PLACE AND DATE OF BIRTH
Nottingham, United Kingdom; 1972
COUNTRY OF RESIDENCE
France
FAMILY STATUS
Married, 2 children
EDUCATION / DEGREE
Diploma in Art & Design, North Linsdey College, Scunthorpe; Higher Diploma in Art & Design, Blackpool & Fylde College Degree in Art & Design, Bradford College; MA in Illustration, Kingston University, London
ACTIVE IN THE FIELD OF ILLUSTRATION SINCE
2000
BREAKTHROUGH PROJECT
The Folio Society book, Cover Her Face by PD James
KEY CLIENTS
Folio Society, Penguin Books, Asset International, the New York Times
MOST RENOWNED PROJECTS
The Folio Society books, Folio Playing Cards, BAFTA posters, tickets, and brochures, Penguin Modern Classics series of Kingsley Amis books
COMMISSIONS PER YEAR
50
AVERAGE TURNAROUND TIME PER COMMISSION
Editorial a few days, books a few months
WORKSPACE
Home studio
EMPLOYEES
None
AGENTS
U.K.: Handsome Frank, U.S.: Riley Illustration
HOW MUCH COMMISSION DO YOUR AGENTS TAKE
25% editorial; 33% advertising
TEACHING POSITIONS
None
AWARDS (SELECTION)
Silver and Bronze awards from the Association of Illustrators for Advertising, Editorial, and Book Illustration; Society of Illustrators, Silver medals for 3D Illustration and Sequential Illustration; Recognized by Communication Arts 53/54, and American Illustration 29/32
MEMBER ASSOCIATIONS
AOI, The Society of Illustrators
GALLERIES
None

"THE BEST ILLUSTRATION HAS THE RIGHT BALANCE OF IMAGINATION AND CONTEXT. I REMEMBER MY OLD TUTOR SAYING 'DON'T ILLUSTRATE—ILLUMINATE.'"

Photo: Sophie Pawlak

"It's always fascinating to watch artists at work. It's almost like a magical process is taking place," says Jonathan Burton. A bubble of perfectly creative harmony flies before the mind's eye, going 'bang' as he continues with unwavering professionalism. "The reality behind that illusion is that the artist had to develop over a long period in order to get to that level. The ability to draw is well-respected with those around me, who have always been impressed by what they tell me is my 'natural' talent. I've heard that since I was very young. This now starts to bug me slightly, as I don't think the ability to draw is at all natural, it's more to do with patience, interest in observation, and continual hard work."

Burton grew up in Lincolnshire in the U.K. and studied art and design in Scunthorpe and Blackpool. He then received a degree in Bradford before deciding to head to London to fine-tune his skills in illustration with a master's program at Kingston University. "I was more drawn to illustration than any of the other disciplines because of the storytelling aspect. I always loved Edward Hopper's work, for example, where we the viewer are invited to create a narrative about the characters. His paintings look like illustrations for a story or a still from a film. So illustration gave me the chance to create a believable world in which to tell a story."

Burton's drawings possess a strong narrative dimension suggestive of storytelling, and a sense of theatricality that translates into a style evocative of a bygone era. Illustrating for *Time*, the *New York Times*, *New Scientist*, the *Wall Street Journal*, and Penguin Books, the stories vary in nature, providing a starting point for Burton's work. "For books, there are certain scenes that fly out of the page that I think need to be illustrated. For editorial I always try to break the text down to a phrase or theme that will spark an idea. I think it best to work from a point where I am open to any possibility, and to do that I need a simple starting point that will let me 'go off on one.' An Illustrator risks being too much of a slave to the text, the work becoming just about the content. The best illustration has the

LUCKY JIM
(PAGE 36)
Cover for the Modern Classics series
of Kingsley Amis novels
Penguin Books
Art Direction: Jim Stoddart

CRIME SCENE
(BOTTOM)
Illustrations for Cover Her
Face by PD James
Client: The Folio Society
Art Direction: Sheri Gee

GOD'S SHACK
(RIGHT)
Illustrations for The Hitchhiker's Guide
to the Galaxy/The Restaurant at the
End of the Universe by Douglas Adams
Client: The Folio Society
Art Direction: Sheri Gee

right balance of imagination and context. I remember my old tutor saying 'don't illustrate—illuminate.'"

Aside from editorial and book cover illustrations, Burton's portfolio includes a fine selection of diverse corporate commissions. Recent standout projects

ARGO
(RIGHT PAGE)
Alternative film poster imagery
for the annual awards evening of
BAFTA (The British Academy of
Film and Television Arts)
Client: BAFTA Awards 2013
Art Direction: Guy Marshall/
Studio Small

include a poster campaign for the 2012 season of the cultural institute Centre François Mauriac, and a deck of playing cards for The Folio Society, which won a silver medal at the Society of Illustrators. Burton also cites his series of illustrations for the BAFTA Film Awards 2013 as a breakthrough project, albeit a belated one. With his images adorning the cover of the award night's printed programs and serving as the key visuals for ticket and booklet designs, the project certainly earned him broad media attention.

"I'm happy that my work over the last few years has been so varied in its usage. Working on editorial commissions keeps me on my toes with the short deadlines,

continual variation, and sometimes difficult subjects. Part of the business of working for advertising clients is that the briefs are much more restrained. It's more of a challenge to keep the energy up with all of the criteria to consider, but it's inevitable, as big budgets mean more risk. This means the client having more of a say and it's my job to adapt to that and still be as imaginatively creative as possible."

Book cover commissions especially allow for relatively broad approaches and lengthy creative processes. While editorial projects usually need to be finished within a few days, books allow Burton to immerse himself in a topic for several months—a situation he highly

appreciates. "I enjoy looking at old prints and trying to recreate the look to make it convincingly antique. The process has unleashed nothing but positive influences and has loosened up my figure drawing, made me use more unusual colors and think about printing techniques. For the

BAFTA AWARDS 2013
(LEFT PAGE)
Alternative film poster imagery for the annual awards evening of BAFTA (The British Academy of Film and Television Arts)
Client: BAFTA
Art Direction: Guy Marshall/ Studio Small

illustrated for The Folio Society in 2009, noting that the story was so descriptive in its characterizations and settings that in order to get the details right, he felt the need to make note of everything—the characters' ages, clothes, hairstyles, what was where in each room, and even where

As the editors of the "It's Nice That" blog once put it, Burton's drawings "blend realism and imagination with studied care." It is editorial and publishing work in particular that allow him to bring in idiosyncratic visions. "Usually when the text is very dry and business-oriented,

book work I really enjoy getting into the characters, researching the time period and putting them together in a 'narrative moment.' With the long deadlines in book illustration, I have time to jump into the world of the story and rummage around. I suppose the research I put in to get the details right is my 'specialty,' and I feel most at home when I have an interesting subject to sink my teeth into."

In this context, Burton refers to the PD James novel *Cover Her Face,* which he

LES MISERABLES
(LEFT)
Illustrations for Cover Her Face
by PD James
Client: The Folio Society
Art Direction: Sheri Gee

WHODUNIT MOUSE ATTACK
(RIGHT)
Illustrations for The Hitchhiker's Guide to the Galaxy/The Restaurant at the End of the Universe
by Douglas Adams
Client: The Folio Society
Art Direction: Sheri Gee

the light was coming from in each scene. This was particularly important for the overhead crime scene, which became the most complex illustration. He documented the extensive process on his blog "The Unreachable Itch." "I got a little obsessive and enjoyed putting every item and person in their correct place. All of that research into detail becomes incidental, though only serves to make the settings more authentic. The most important thing to get across was the sense of drama."

it's more interesting to think about what it is I like to draw and create an image that feels personal and exciting to me. If I approach something with that sense of fun and freedom then that comes across in the work and hopefully invites the reader to see the text in a different way. I've been lucky to work with art directors that respect the ability of their illustrators to interpret the given text in a visually exiting way. There has to be trust in the relationship and it's great to get to know art directors that come back and have confidence in me."

Burton speaks from experience. "For art directors to gain confidence in you as an illustrator, you need to first of all show you can work to brief and deadline." Looking back on the early days of his career, he recalls how having the first real piece of printed work in his portfolio really got things rolling. "My first commission after university was for *Reader's Digest* and I'm thankful to their design director Martin Colyer for taking a risk on using a 'newbie.' I met him in person which helped—maybe he saw the need in my eyes."

Burton worked in 3D and collage at the start of his career. "It was a pretty original style at the time and it earned

GIRL, 20
(BOTTOM)
Cover for the Modern Classics series
of Kingsley Amis novels
Penguin Books
Art Direction: Jim Stoddart

BAFTA TICKET
(RIGHT)
Alternative film poster imagery for
the annual awards evening of BAFTA
(The British Academy of Film and
Television Arts)
Client: BAFTA
Art Direction: Guy Marshall/
Studio Small

LA GRACE
(RIGHT PAGE)
Poster campaign for the Cultural
Season of 2012
Client: Centre François Mauriac
Art Direction: Julie Chabrie

me several regular spots for *Q Magazine*, the *Observer*, and Classic FM, which meant I could survive on illustration alone. Afterward, I did my first Billboard ad campaign for Mini/BMW called "Look At My Mini." Eventually I phased out that style and concentrated on good old-fashioned drawing." Today he mainly works in pencil and then scans his drawings to color them in Photoshop. "Occasionally I will use watercolor, ink, and colored pencil to color the line work if I feel it will work

better for the subject, and also to enjoy the 'real' materials."

Working for The Folio Society on the illustrations for PD James's above-mentioned book was an important step for Burton in developing his work. The prolific work relationship with The Folio Society continued with a richly illustrated edition of Douglas Adams's *The Hitchhiker's Guide to the Galaxy* and considerably raised the profile of his drawings. How commissions are gained, however, remains a bit

of a mystery to Burton. Certainly many of Burton's clients approach him directly after they've come across his work in sourcebooks and on his personal website, while others find him through his agents. Represented by Handsome Frank in the U.K. and Riley Illustration in the U.S., Burton is one of a fine and relatively small association of artists. "Working with an agency, it's important for me to feel like an important part of it and not just one name on a huge list."

On top of the inquiries he receives directly and through his agents, Burton does a few direct mailings on his own, making sure they are personal, well-tailored, and sent to the art director with whom he wishes to work. "I try to be selective

SELECTING FROM OPTIONS
(TOP)
Work for Plansponsor/Planadvisor
On several themes ranging from "Selecting Options," "Building Something Better," and "Picking the Best," Asset International publishes investment magazines
Client: Asset International
Art Direction: SooJin Buzelli

THE PERILS OF ARCHIBALD
(BOTTOM)
Handmade book using ideas from participants on Burton's blog
Personal Work

PLAYING CARDS
(RIGHT PAGE)
A specially designed deck of playing cards to be given to Folio Society members. The work has gone on to win a silver medal at the Society of Illustration in New York
Client: The Folio Society
Art Direction: Sheri Gee

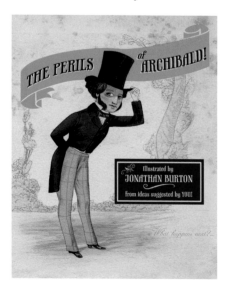

and that works more than anything else." However selective he is in picking projects, the free time between specific jobs keeps dwindling. Burton regrets having less and less time to work on self-generated projects, knowing that doing so would be advantageous for him. Creative workflow gathers momentum through experimentation, and not at the push of a button. Burton adds that he must be in a particular state of mind to do his best work. "Sometimes after hours of drawing I start to feel like something is working."

Burton works best early in the morning, so if he has a busy day ahead he will get to his desk by 6:15 am to enjoying drawing in uninterrupted solitude. He has created his workspace in a separate and spacious room within his house. "I like the idea of working in a shared studio, but when I've tried I've found that I can't concentrate properly. I envy other illustrators' studios such as Oliver Jeffers's studio in New York and Quentin Blake's in London. They are hives of huge activity, chaotic and full of life. Unfortunately, I need to be alone to be productive and I think a lot of illustrators are the same." Working productively in peace and quiet, Burton usually finishes work around 4 or 5 pm. He doesn't do evening shifts anymore, as he is too busy with his kids. "I have two young girls, so hectic work periods can be tricky to reconcile with family life. Fortunately my wife is very forgiving. Children teach

you that work isn't everything and that you have to have time off. They grow up too quickly to ignore this. I take breaks when the school holidays come and a longer break during summer, so sometimes I have to juggle projects around and I work hard to make time."

Burton is due to start an illustrated picture book with Milan Jeunesse this year, and he has written and illustrated a book that he is hoping to get published soon. Working with BAFTA has given him a taste for film posters, he says, leading him to interpret some of his favorite films into limited-edition prints for sale. He welcomes the idea of working with a film company on a new release, too. In the end, however, he has arrived at a phase in his life in which priorities are clear. "In the end, I would rather turn work down than sacrifice a family holiday. Everyone needs a holiday after all!"

Editorial Illustration

In editorial offices across the globe, art directors and picture editors are on the lookout for images to accompany the written content of publications in both newsprint and pixels. The artists they commission are usually facing tight deadlines and demanding subjects, especially when assigned to illustrate topical news. In return, they enjoy considerable freedom of subjective artistic interpretation, as well as the opportunity to work alongside aesthetically trained professionals. While all of the illustrators in this chapter agree that editorial work environments—with their fast pace and substantial art direction—prove challenging but also worthwhile in shaping their own professional development, their creative approaches could not be more different. Conceptual illustrators such as Christoph Niemann focus on ideas of satiric wit to translate the essence of the editorial story. A painterly representative, Andrea Ventura bank on moods, atmospheric representations, and artistic renditions. While few are limited to facts, aiming to contribute to the reader's comprehension, many enrich the text with additional layers of meaning, and some do so by establishing a tension between the visual and verbal. By and large, editorial illustrators investigate rather than decorate, which makes the field fertile and rich with creative ambition. Today, as thousands of trade magazines and independent publications become potential clients and springboards for aspiring illustrators, the editorial sector offers a rich breeding ground for the industry of illustration. As the ongoing digitization of media changes the editorial landscape, some of the illustrators featured here venture into new territories and expand their work into the digital and interactive realm.

Christoph Niemann

"TIED UP IN DEADLINES, YOU DON'T TAKE RISKS. IT IS JUST TOO EASY TO SAY 'NO TIME, THANKS, NEXT.' I THOUGHT I HAD TO LEARN TO MAKE MISTAKES AGAIN."

PLACE AND DATE OF BIRTH
Waiblingen, Germany; 1970

COUNTRY OF RESIDENCE
Germany

FAMILY STATUS
Married, 3 children

EDUCATION / DEGREE
MA in Fine Arts, Academy of Fine Arts, Stuttgart

ACTIVE IN THE FIELD OF ILLUSTRATION SINCE
1995

BREAKTHROUGH PROJECT
N/A

KEY CLIENTS
The New York Times, the New Yorker

MOST RENOWNED PROJECTS
Abstract Sunday Column for the New York Times, Covers for the New Yorker, Petting Zoo App

COMMISSIONS PER YEAR
N/A

AVERAGE TURNAROUND TIME PER COMMISSION
Between 45 minutes and 18 months

WORKSPACE
Studio

EMPLOYEES
1 assistant

AGENTS
None

TEACHING POSITIONS
2000–2002: School of Visual Arts, New York

AWARDS (SELECTION)
Hall of Fame, Art Directors Club New York 2010

MEMBER ASSOCIATIONS
Alliance Graphique Internationale

GALLERIES
None

In truly living life, one can't be afraid to take risks or gloriously fail. Christoph Niemann's Petting Zoo, an interactive picture book app, represents just one of the risky ventures the illustrator takes with pleasure and keen creative ambition. For the App, Niemann spent considerable time learning Divs, Javascript, and CSS in the risky, yet ultimately successful process of its creation. "As an artist you have to try new things," Niemann says. "You have to experiment, and not care about whether the new things actually make sense. You can sketch and plan all you want. But, to discover new territory, you have to get your hands dirty and benefit from the flaws and accidents. Eventually, however, you may arrive at a point where even well-meaning minds won't be able to get your idea, let alone realize that there even is an idea to be gotten in the first place."

Niemann's work thrives on great ideas, and more often than not, he succeeds in turning the complexities of life into cheerful visual nuggets. With a signature style that is less defined by form than by striking pictoral humor, a stroke of irony, and a refreshingly casual tone, Niemann masters conceptual illustration like few of his contemporaries.

Niemann studied at the Academy of Fine Arts in Stuttgart, close to his hometown of Ludwigsburg. Illustration would have been his first choice, but it only existed as an extension of graphic design, so he enrolled for that. Out of this necessity and the broad basis the course offered emerged the virtues of his approach. "My access to illustration was a design-oriented one from the beginning, meaning that I didn't concentrate on individual style so much, like 'this is the way I draw, and that style is what I will impose upon the world.'" Much like a designer would do, he appropriated the different fonts he had to choose from. Niemann works out his idea first, and then decides what style or technique feels most suitable to convey it. That may be reductionism or realism; drawings or photographs; numbers or M&Ms. The possibilities are virtually endless.

The illustration path Niemann took during his fifth semester of studies combined drawing with advertising under the creative lead of Heinz Edelmann. Niemann's own focus on editorial illustrations came naturally through his interest in politics, economy, and everyday themes. He was also inspired by the editorial illustrations he found in magazines like the *New Yorker*, the *New York Times*, or *Rolling Stone*. "U.K. design was very present at the time, with all the then-ground-breaking 1990s typography and graphic design put forth by people like Neville Brody. But I felt that was all about form, and experimenting with all the possibilities that desktop publishing newly and excitingly offered. In New York, it seemed to be about 'the big idea.' American magazine design was just another league."

Niemann considered a semester abroad, but repelled by all the administrative stuff that went along with that he figured that an internship during the university vacations would be more worthwhile. He mailed applications to New York, work samples and little booklets, tailor-made and directly addressed to the designers he wanted to work with, and got his first internship at Paul Davis's studio, where he spent a semester break fixing computers and doing some of his first real design work. Pentagram then took him on as an intern during his next summer break. All of a sudden, he found himself working alongside Paula Sher, having lunch with Michael Beirut and Woody Pirtle, or sitting next to Brad Holland having a beer. "Interestingly, they all worked together somehow," he recalls, "passing me around. Paula Sher called up Steven Heller, saying 'I have someone here, you may want to

CRIME COLUMN
(THIS PAGE & PAGE 48)
Client: New York Times Book Review, 2009–2013

meet him.' The people at the *Times* were friends with those at the *New Yorker*." And all warmly welcomed Niemann and his fresh approach.

Niemann's first freelance project in New York came about because Paul Davis had recommended his former intern to Fred Woodward, the art director at *Rolling Stone*. "It was a full page for a review of a record by Alice in Chains. I had to fly back to Germany two days after they gave me the brief, and didn't dare to tell them. I listened to the music, and liked it but didn't know how to get started. There was nothing palpable to it, it was just rock. Yeah, baby yeah. I was really freaked out that I might propose something that would not work out in the end—that the sketch might be better than the final. So I started to draw finals, and turn them into a sketch to hand in. When I didn't hear back from them immediately, I reckoned they had long commissioned someone else. I called them up, weak-kneed, on the way to the airport to go back to Germany, as summer break was over." Friendly but nonchalant, they informed Niemann that they'd be printing it. "A great experience, but absolutely nerve-wracking," he recalls.

The good thing about routine—apart from the fact that one actually gets better—is the healthy degree of emotional distance it entails, finds Niemann, noting that it took him about five years to develop a sense of confidence: "To learn to go to sleep today without worrying about what's on my table tomorrow. That I'd be able to get things done without making a fool of myself. That things would be fine, even if not the greatest artworks. That, once I had an idea, I would be able to realize it

one way or the other." Having done a few posters at Pentagram, and the full-page illustration for *Rolling Stone*, Niemann was asked to do some illustrations for the *New York Times Book Review*, and other commissions followed. Nevertheless, he returned to Stuttgart after every summer break to finish the course, which he felt to be an important and still enjoyable

LET IT DOUGH!
Abstract Sunday Column
Client: the New York Times, 2010

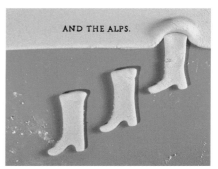

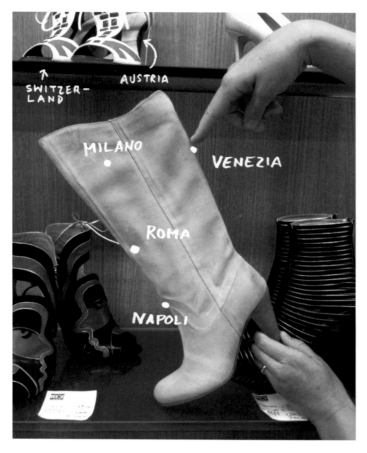

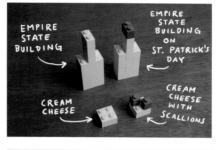

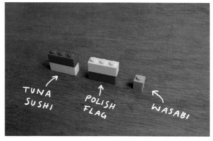

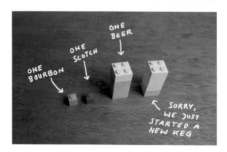

commitment. Careful not to be lured by opportunity and get drawn into the market at a stage he considered too early, he rejected commissions in favor of working on his portfolio. Three weeks after graduation he moved to New York.

Working for the daily press, like the *New York Times* op-ed page, Niemann found himself challenged with extremely tight deadlines. "It was not exceptional for the editors to come up with a rough idea of what they wanted to write at 3 pm when at 6 pm the whole thing needed to be finished. I had half a day or a day if I was lucky, two if I was really, really lucky." But he soon learned to appreciate the pace of news media. "The pieces were printed, consumed, and discarded, for me to start fresh. I really enjoyed that rhythm and being able to keep up with it." Niemann's drawings are relatively quick and straightforward, hence their characteristic, dynamic lines. It may take him a while to figure out his approach and get into the flow, establishing

72 HOURS IN VENICE
(LEFT)
Abstract Sunday Column
Client: the New York Times, 2011

I LEGO N.Y.
(RIGHT)
Abstract City Column
Client: the New York Times, 2008

a consistency to hold individual drawings together. But more time does not mean more depth and quality to him.

"Time allows for angst, doubt, and too many opinions, like in advertising, where there's always another week for revisions, always someone knowing it better. All this open brainstorming is complete and total nonsense to me. Also, all the prattle about details that doesn't have anything to do with quality, most of the time. In the end, advertising illustrations are no better, no more detailed or elaborate than editorial ones." The professional editorial work ethic Niemann praises so highly thrives on clear decisions based on substance. "There are some art directors without whom I don't think I would have been capable of doing the stuff I do. You need someone to bounce things off, come in with a suggestion, or someone with a larger view of how your design will actually function in context." The *New York Times* op-ed page was art directed by

Nicholas Blechman, who remains one of Niemann's closest friends. "We always discussed political issues and the day-to-day news a lot, which helped me to develop a greater confidence in dealing with politics as a theme of my work. The actual drawing is only one part of the job, and part of your own creative vision that you contribute to the publication."

Niemann sees his illustrations as the visual equivalent of a headline. "It should function as a teaser, give you a first idea about what an article is about. It can be funny and witty in itself. Ideally, it contains a second layer, some kind of meta info, or metaphorical reference, that you only get once you have familiarized yourself with the content." Niemann masters a visual language that is unexpected and somewhat off-the-wall, and yet befits expertly researched content, like James Surowiecki's economy column in the *New Yorker*. "How much liberty can I take? How absurd can

I be?" These questions are explored with every new assignment.

"The key benefit of illustration, as opposed to photography, is its ability to be abstract," Niemann says. "I can draw a character that is ageless, even one that is genderless. A stickman is everything: man, child, Chinese, Indian... It gives me the opportunity to play, stretch the concept of a human being to become incredibly broad, and then reduce it to become really precise." This scaling of realities fascinates Niemann, but he is careful in bringing in his own opinions and interpretations. "I rather try to contribute to the author's stance, even though I might not always entirely share it. If an article goes against my ideas, I do not commit to illustrating it in the first place."

With his work frequently appearing on the *New York Times* op-ed page, the *Book Review* and the *New York Times Magazine*, Niemann never has to worry about the quality of content. Plus, he has earned enormous popularity, the trust of many clients, and a continuous flow of commissions. However, having pursued his career in New York for about a decade, he started to miss the sense of challenge. "As I got better and more experienced, I realized that I had become a bit too comfortable. Routine is a good thing, as it helps you deal with yourself and with clients. But at the same time, it tempts you to safely navigate around obstacles and potential pitfalls." For Niemann, professionalism had turned into breathlessness, security into assumed dependencies.

"Tied up in deadlines, you don't take risks. It is just too easy to say 'no time, thanks, next,' and keep within your comfort zone. You know how to evaluate yourself and timeframes, choose the techniques that feel most reasonable to work with in view of a given amount of time. You don't experiment but avoid disasters and play safe. One thing is economic pressure, another the environment: If everyone around you is very straightforward, professional, following schedules, you are easily carried along by that. I hope that I still did halfway

innovative stuff, but I felt that in the long run, I would be using up my creative reserves. Even though I had all the jobs I had always wanted, I felt there might be something beyond that that I wanted, too, but just didn't know then. I thought I had to learn to make mistakes again."

Certain that to start fresh, he would need an overall change of scene, Niemann relocated to Berlin. "Moving home yields so much energy. Being forced to reorient yourself takes effort, of course, but on the other hand it enables you to see things again. After such a long time in New York, I felt like traveling my daily routes had blinded me. Home, subway, studio, lunch at always the same places, subway, pick up kids, playground, subway, home. I was hoping that the move to Germany would be just as reinvigorating as my move to

New York had been eleven years before." Workwise, it is above all the column for the *New York Times* blog that represents Niemann's fresh departure.

Conceived as a format that would allow the *Times* editors to publish alternative content relatively irrespective of readership counts and beyond the physical limitations of print media, the *New York Times* blog soon gained popularity as a site for ambitious editorial experimentation. Niemann had been part of the project since its inception. "Do whatever you want," the editors said to him at the outset, "but make it personal!" They had asked him to generate content himself, so he proposed a few topics and they slowly carved out the direction. The blog was launched under the title "Abstract City" in 2008, coinciding with Niemann's move

STATE OF THE ART
Abstract Sunday Column
Client: the New York Times, 2012

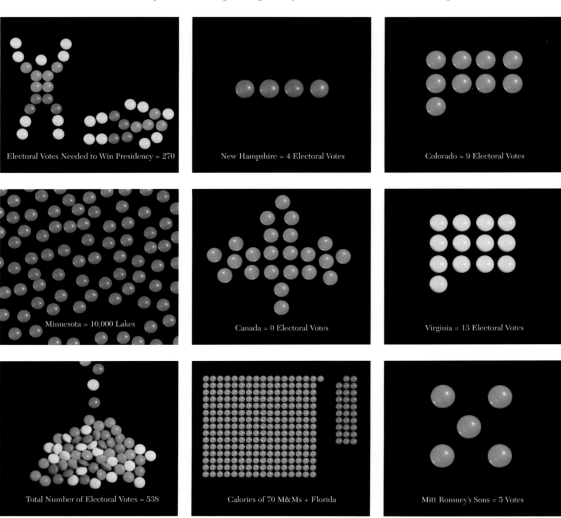

Electoral Votes Needed to Win Presidency = 270

New Hampshire = 4 Electoral Votes

Colorado = 9 Electoral Votes

Minnesota = 10,000 Lakes

Canada = 0 Electoral Votes

Virginia = 13 Electoral Votes

Total Number of Electoral Votes = 538

Calories of 70 M&Ms + Florida

Mitt Romney's Sons = 5 Votes

Wireless Gingko

Swiss Army
Tree

Tree-Shirt

Kansas
Tree

Regular Tree

Alder Ego

California
Tree

Cloud Tree

Cloud-That-Actually-
Resembles-a-Car Tree

Laurel

Hardy

Hawaii
Tree

1957-Ford-Thunderbird Tree

Willow

Pillow

to Germany. "All of a sudden, I lacked everything that had made me so comfortable over the past years: rigid deadlines, experience, confidence, and editorial content to relate to. Writing was the most daunting challenge. I did not need to write

long texts, but struggled with things like sentence structure, or superfluous adjectives. It gave me hard times, but certainly set things free, creatively."

Niemann soon arrived at a point where his words and images formed ensembles. Most of his quirky sketches, snapshots, or bricollages make big words obsolete, in favor of brief notes. "My theory is that image and text need to add up to 100%. If they are at 90, it's no good. But if they are at 110 it's no good either. If the text part feels complete in itself, you do not need an image, and the other way around. So if you want to have a meaningful interplay of both, you need to either reduce the text to a point

where it needs the image, or make the image more abstract to not reveal too much. It took me a while to develop the feeling for it, and realize that usually I'd say too much. Today's readers are incredibly smart. We tend to underestimate them."

Indeed, the visual comprehension of the average reader has improved considerably over the past years. Niemann points to infographics as an example. "Twenty years ago, pie charts were for bankers and scientists. Today, you can establish intelligent narrative structures with them, and they are integral to the broader public's visual vocabulary." Niemann does not do infographics, but plays with its vocabulary. He notes how the internet

BIODIVERSITY
(LEFT PAGE)
Visual Essay for Abstract City Blog
Client: the New York Times, 2011

**COVERS FOR
THE NEW YORKER**
(THIS PAGE)
Client: the New Yorker, 2001–2013

has trained the contemporary readership's grasp of visual abstraction and its irony, allowing for visual language to use less literal expressions. Niemann's blog column challenges and delights millions with visual wit and tongue-in-cheek simplification. Obviously, it is not easy to come up with continually new ideas.

There is no formula, no reliable technique that Niemann employs. Therefore, a lot of trial and error goes into his work, and explorations into various techniques and forms of visualization. During his stay at the 2011 Venice Biennale, Niemann conducted live drawing sessions as a roving and illustrating reporter, documenting the event non-stop with quirky sketches

that he scanned and blogged—one every third hour—from his hotel room. At the 2011 New York Marathon, he drew live while running, equipped with a piece of cardboard as a table. He completed about 40 drawings, which he live-tweeted throughout the six hour–race and put up on the *New York Times* blog the day after. Sketches included his hunger pangs during the race, a self-portrait showing himself as a discharged battery around mile 3.2, and scribbles drawn with broken paintbrushes to communicate the exhaustion he felt during his final steps of the race. As *Time* magazine reported, "Niemann provided a better view of the action across the five boroughs than even the best news camera." Indeed, he brought perspective to the event that most other journalist missed or failed to convey.

Although the bulk of Niemann's work appears in editorial context, his characteristic cheerful and refreshingly unpretentious nature and somewhat casual tone is valued by commercial clients, too. Quite recently, he designed a series of classic tourism advertisements for the Swiss winter sports hotspot St. Moritz, as well as a customer magazine, a tote bag, and an exclusive silk scarf for the high-end department store Bräuninger in Stuttgart. He has also illustrated a series of visual guidebooks on language and the internet for his frequent client Google, which he praises for their remarkable sense of close collaboration.

Niemann rarely meets his clients in person, but he appreciates amicable, longstanding relationships. He still works for many of his old New York clients, enjoying that having moved to Germany, time is on

FIRST PERSON
Client: Print magazine, 2005

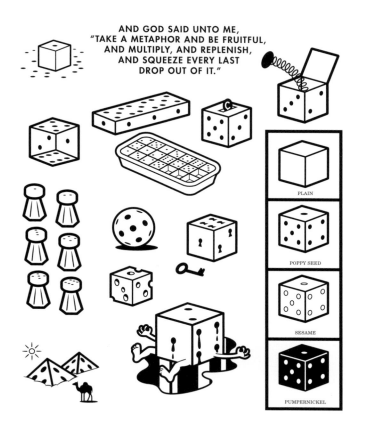

his side. "You have six extra hours, before they start, to get everything done. And when they come to the office, I can offer them a range of fresh ideas. The other way around, working for German clients from New York, was horrible. When you wake up in the morning, they have had all their meetings, so you are constantly trying to catch up."

Except for a very brief and "very unfortunate" testing phase, Niemann has never worked with an agent. He considers the concept problematic. "As agents get money for every job you do, their fundamental interest is you accepting as many jobs as you can. That is not much of a help, to me. I would need an agent to tell me which jobs to turn down. I did start to

work with someone with a background in marketing, who assists me with contracts and maintaining existing client contacts. But this person works for me as a service provider, not as an agent. So she doesn't have an interest in getting me as many commissions as possible, as an agent would. It would be great to have someone to negotiate fees and stuff like that, but then I find these things impossible to outsource. The bitter truth is that you are the only one able to evaluate your work. The question of whether a job is worthwhile or not very much depends on the time, effort, emotional, and creative energy you put into it." In that sense, projects like his blog column or the Petting Zoo app are "actually priceless," as Niemann puts it.

Niemann cites a rule from the employee management model his frequent clients at Google had once shared with him: "Take 20% of your time to work on free projects. It sounds crazy, but is in fact incredibly smart." With the app, Niemann exceeded Google's 20% rule significantly. "I think I reached 50% last year, with the app as a self-initiated, essentially free, project." Having leaped into the deep end that animation and programming were to him, Niemann was overwhelmed with things to learn. "I didn't even react to emails or invoices for a while." Niemann's other

PETTING ZOO APP
Client: Abstract City Media, 2013

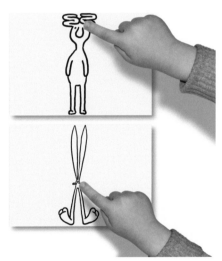

In view of the latter, with all the time (about a year) and effort (immense) Niemann invested in it, he just managed to break even, he notes. The full amount of revenues from the app store still remains to be seen, but they will certainly stay well below what he could have earned with commissions in the same time instead. The value of experimentation, however, cannot be measured in terms of money. Neither can the gain in reputation.

The first of its kind, the Petting Zoo app attracted great media attention. Magazines like *Wired*, *USA Today*, and

CNET featured it, as did Apple Japan on their homepage, introducing Niemann to audiences that had not necessarily been familiar with his work before, an effect that he considers priceless. "It was important for me to not have to bear the costs of the project. Much more important than the revenue from the App store, however, was to break new ground and open new doors."

big experiment, the work on the blog, which has now moved to the *New York Times Magazine* under the title "Abstract Sunday," has become less frequent, too.

In order to create sustainable headspace to continue his work on self-initiated projects, Niemann started to work with his assistant Mathilde Walter in late 2011. "Accepting help meant going through a very painful process of admitting to my

MY LIFE WITH EDITORS

HOW AN EDITOR THINKS:

Too retro! Can't she have a stun gun or something?

Why are these shorter? We don't want to imply that they are less important!

Why stars? Can't we rather have the outlines of the states? That would be so much clearer.

Uh-oh...a woman and a scale! Our readers will think this is about a diet.

DID YOU KNOW that there is actually no friggin' $ sign on a dollar bill?

How can she see the scale when she's blindfolded? Duh!

Can you try a vertical?

ILL-O-MAT

BTW, WHAT'S WITH THAT APPLE? How did a kid's giving an apple to a teacher end up being the visual essence of education?

THIS IS BRIBERY!!!

What's next? Jimmy Hoffa as the metaphor for the legislative process?

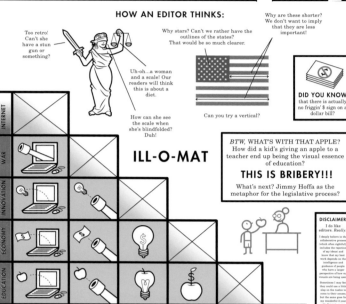

DISCLAIMER
I do like editors. *Really.*

I deeply believe in the collaborative process which often rightfully includes the rejection of my ideas and know that my best work depends on the intelligence and guidance of people who have a larger perspective of how my visuals are being used.

Sometimes I may feel they could use a little slap on the tushie to come to their senses, but the same goes for my wonderful 3-year-old. Yet just as my little son is afraid of vacuum cleaners, some editors seem to be strangely afraid of illustration.

I hear of great unease about the ambiguity of drawings and concern about readers misunderstanding a particular metaphor. Then again, nobody seems to worry about readers wondering why a stupid pork barrel costs billions or why the Army is just putting boots on the ground instead of whole soldiers.

Instructions: Find the two most important elements of the story (example: "Article on insufficient funding of No Child Left Behind Act"...pick economy and education. Combine metaphors according to chart and you will have a 90 percent success rate of getting the sketch approved. (Also: the chart covers about 90 percent of all possible topics of illustrated articles.)

ART, SHMART

A lot of illustrators seem obsessed about being recognized as fine artists.
NOT ME!
I don't have to be a fine artist, because as art history proves, they are actually just like me.

1913: Malevich makes first pixel illustration.

1961: Somebody teaches Warhol how to ⌘-C and ⌘-V.

1944: Art director asks Morandi to take another stab at it.

1885: Cézanne sells out.

1958: Yves Klein sends in four sketches.

1949: Minutes before deadline, Pollock has an accident.

1958: Fontana gets portfolio back from client.

1928: Editor LOVES Magritte's concept, points out little mistake in headline. *Ceci n'est pas une pipe.*

1889: For $79, Van Gogh sells self-portrait and grants irrevocable rights to edit, crop, or otherwise manipulate the art, and to republish in print, Web, CD-ROM, DVD and any other medium existing or yet to be invented.

PERIODIC TABLE OF METAPHORS

(I) THE CLASSICS
Steadfast and reliable: they are an illustrator's best companion.

`010010010` `100111101` `101000101` `100111101` `101000101` `100111101` `011000101`

(II) THE TRICKIES
Beware of this team, it's like butter. They look so promising, but as soon as I try to twist them, they fall apart.

(IV) THE ZOMBIES
They should be long dead, but they keep crawling out of their graves and there is nothing I can do.

(V) THE TOXICS
Use at your own peril.

(III) THE EDITORS' FAVES
I have empirical proof that editors just LOVE these, though I have not the slightest idea why.

(VI) THE NO WAYS
Don't even think about it now!

I WANT YOU

HOW TO MAKE A CONCEPTUAL ILLUSTRATION

A lot of conceptual illustrations are simply a graphic combination of two metaphors.
For example, let's take the following assignment:
Make an illustration for an article with the headline,
"SEARCHING FOR AN EXIT STRATEGY."

Step I:
Consult the Table of Metaphors and find appropriate symbols for A: "Searching" and B: "Exit."

Step II:
Mix Metaphors.

Step III:
TA-DAH!

DEPT. OF TIPS AND TRICKS

FUN WITH LABELS

Using labels in drawings is a cheap trick we mostly encounter in cartoons. Putting a random word on an object always makes some strange sense, which is why labels are usually used to hide weak ideas.

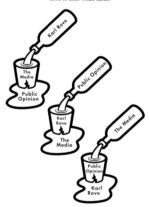

(labels: Karl Rove / The Media / Public Opinion)

THE DICTIONARY
The guide to Art Director/Illustrator-Speak
What they say = What they mean

ART DIRECTOR:

"Well...I got your sketch..."
=
"It's killed."

"This is interesting."
=
"What the hell is this?"

"We don't get it."
=
"I don't get it."

"We're wondering if you can give it another try?"
=
"This is $%&# embarrassing and an insult to Western culture!!! Do you remember we are paying you MONEY to do this? So you'd better sit down and try for a little longer than two minutes, will you?"

ILLUSTRATOR:

"You didn't receive it?"
=
"I am sending it NOW."

"I thought this was funny."
=
"I had a hangover."

"I really think it works the way it is."
=
"I am meeting Nicholas and Paul in a bar in 10 minutes."

"I understand."
=
"This is a $%&# joke!!!
I told you from the beginning that this ridiculous idea of yours doesn't work, and now you want ME to clean up your mess."

THE ABSTRACT-O-METER

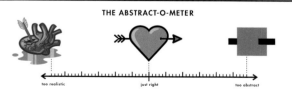

too realistic — just right — too abstract

own shortcomings and the accumulated backlog that they had caused over time." In working by himself all the time, Niemann also feared that the organizational system he had built up over the years would be incomprehensible to anyone else but him. "With the benefit of hindsight, however, the decision to get help was exactly right and somewhat overdue."

Creative exchange is a widespread catchphrase these days. "It is always great to have someone around, to discuss ideas, and toy around with them. For a series of screen prints I just did, I sat down with Mathilde to figure out what to do and how to do it. In the end, we decided to just start printing, and raffled a few. Then we did a few more." The prints are for sale on Niemann's webshop, which Walter manages and maintains. Only recently, they received a call from the secretariat of Germany's Federal President Joachim Gauck, who deemed one of Niemann's prints—featuring a drawing of the Brooklyn Bridge originally published on the *New York Times* blog—a suitable present for Barack Obama's 2013 visit to Berlin. "It was really short notice, and nervous as I was, a stupid typo crept into the inscription before the print was picked up to be chauffeured to the Bellevue palace." Conscious of the honor, Niemann notes that, with projects like his screen prints, the financial aspect is secondary. "They are essentially a fun project. One of those that I would not have done alone, especially not back in America, where I was slightly obsessed with the idea that everything needed to be 'fit-for-purpose.'"

Back in America, creative exchange that did not directly relate to commercial projects came up short. Having given up his lectureship at the School of Visual Arts in New York to have more time for his three kids, Niemann now tries to attend and hold talks at design events every once in a while. To him, this is even fresher and more inspiring than teaching. Thinking of such events as platforms for personal exchange, rather than professional networking, Niemann takes pleasure in meeting

people, or having a chat over dinner. "It is not only about the work itself, but also learning about how other people reconcile it with life." How do they balance between free and commercial projects? Do they follow Google's 20% rule? Do they feel drained if they don't? How do they go about heavy workloads? For a commercial artist as acclaimed as Niemann, these questions are more daunting than those about the next commission.

As for his own part, Niemann does his best to maintain regular working hours. "Nightshifts can only end in disaster because there comes a point where you just don't get things right anymore. If I am sufficiently rested and creatively fit, four productive work hours a day, four days a week, is perfect. Just these golden hours, plus some for repro and administration. If I'd sit there 14 hours a day, the work would not be any better. Rather worse." Niemann is strict with his daily schedule, but has loosened that up a bit to go running during the day, even if there are deadlines. "Sometimes it is just good to take a break and clear your head. It took me quite some time and effort to put that theory into practice. And it's rather tricky to find the right balance. In the end, brooding over ideas at my desk has proven no more productive than getting up all the time, to draw some inspiration from books, the cinema, etc. I force myself to not work when I'm at home, which is not always easy. And during holidays with my family." Those are rarely longer than two weeks, Niemann notes. "I would like to do longer trips in the future, but then again, right now, I couldn't imagine not working for a month." That is surely because he cannot stop thinking about new challenges and how to develop his own creative practice.

"While classic editorial jobs used to be 95% of my work, they make up only about 5% now." Niemann's background in classic editorial extended naturally into the visual and verbal intermingling in the *New York Times* blog columns. Then came an evolution from the applied

editorial to the free editorial and self-generated content. This is showcased in a recent interview with the American cartoonist and musician Robert Crumb, for which the German *Zeitmagazin* asked him to come up with both image and words. And the experimentation for the Petting Zoo app led him to look into the latest trends in game design, finding that there are interesting things happening in that field. "Digital games are not all these elaborately rendered hyper-realities anymore, but also feature some more reduced, flat graphics. To me, that's exciting: narrative as hybrid, potentially intermedial, experience. There are great possibilities these days and the editorial field can certainly learn from that. I strongly believe that the separation between visual and verbal journalism is not reasonable in the long run."

**FIRST PERSON
72 HOURS IN VENICE**
(LEFT PAGE)
Client: Print magazine, 2005

Satoshi Hashimoto

"THE KEY TO GOOD ILLUSTRATION IS TO UNDERSTAND THE MESSAGE YOUR CLIENT WANTS TO COMMUNICATE AND THEN TO FIGURE OUT THE BEST WAY TO CONVEY IT. I AIM TO DRAW IN A WAY THAT IS ENJOYABLE AND EASY TO UNDERSTAND."

PLACE AND DATE OF BIRTH
Yokohama, Japan; 1971

COUNTRY OF RESIDENCE
Japan

FAMILY STATUS
Married, 1 dog

EDUCATION / DEGREE
Graphic Design and Photography,
Kuwasawa Design School

ACTIVE IN THE FIELD OF ILLUSTRATION SINCE
1996

BREAKTHROUGH PROJECT
N/A

KEY CLIENTS
Monocle, the Asahi Shimbun

MOST RENOWNED PROJECTS
N/A

COMMISSIONS PER YEAR
N/A

AVERAGE TURNAROUND TIME PER COMMISSION
Sometimes 1 week, sometimes 2–3 months

WORKSPACE
Private studio

EMPLOYEES
None

AGENTS
None

TEACHING POSITIONS
None

AWARDS
None

MEMBER ASSOCIATIONS
None

GALLERIES
None

A humble servant of clear-cut communication, Yokohama-based illustrator Satoshi Hashimoto likes to keep things simple. "I do not think about anything complicated when I'm drawing," he declares. "The key to good illustration is to understand the message your client wants to communicate and then to figure out the best way to convey it. I aim to draw in a way that is enjoyable and easy to understand. However beautiful, illustration is of no value if it is misunderstood." Hashimoto's practical approach to illustration was shaped by his first commissioned work, an illustrated English dictionary. "I prefer explaining a specific thing or event as simply as possible. The most fundamental task of illustration is to picture a thing in a very simple but accurate way."

Service-oriented, resilient, hard-working, well-educated, and dearly modest, one could say that Hashimoto fulfills certain Japanese clichés. On the outside his work does not reveal the origin of its maker, but combines stylistic elements of classic continental cartoons and American advertising illustrations from the mid-past century. One could be tempted to refer to another stereotype at this point, that of the Japanese person's great interest in Western things, but a note on the intercontinental appeal of Hashimoto's style is more appropriate. He illustrates for the likes of Tyler Brûlé's cross-media global affairs platform, *Monocle*, and the *Asahi Shimbun*, one of Japan's oldest and largest national daily newspapers.

Considering Hashimoto's pursuit of the greatest accuracy possible, one may be surprised not to find data visualizations in his portfolio, but documents of cartoonist ingenuity—vivid scenes of minstrels,

chambermaids, laborers, and flâneurs, wearing folk costumes, work-wear, or leisurewear; tourists parading down picturesque avenues or resting in sidewalk cafes; restaurant- and shop-goers; sporting, working, and cocktail-slurping fellows; playing children; artists, musicians, and wannabes, hanging out in studios, rooftop gardens, or musing over desks, laptops, or turntables. These mid-century styled but contemporarily-themed stories hold full-on narrative power. Representation is key, much more than imagination, says Hashimoto, who illustrates with a good portion of the latter, and with no fear of subjectivity and stylization.

JAPAN TRAVEL GUIDE
(PAGE 60)
Client: Monocle magazine, 2012

IN MY ATELIER
(TOP LEFT)
Personal Work, 2012

ENGINE
(BOTTOM LEFT)
In Engine magazine, Japan
Client: Shinchosha, 2009

SPAIN TRAVEL GUIDE
(TOP RIGHT)
Client: Monocle magazine, 2012

FARMING
(BOTTOM RIGHT)
Client: Monocle magazine, 2009

"I have one complaint, Mr. Hashimoto," wrote a travel blogger in regard to the limited-edition world map the illustrator drew for *Monocle* magazine. "Why did you put the Acropolis from Athens and nothing from Istanbul?" Hashimoto's admittedly free-spirited representation of the world highlights selected architectural landmarks and cultural icons. A claim of accuracy would be out of place here. Illustration may be there to communicate specific messages to specific audiences, as Hashimoto is so keen to underline, but luckily it can do so in a decorative, realistic, descriptive, conceptual, informational, technical, or narrative way.

Born in 1971 and raised in eastern Japan, Hashimoto received his higher education from the graphic design and photography department of the prestigious Kuwasawa Design School in Tokyo. He attributes the Western flavor of his illustrations to influences he took up in Jinbōchō, Tokyo's epicenter of used bookstores and publishing houses. "About 20 years ago, I found this American picture dictionary from the 1960s and was so impressed." He tells of how Jinbōchō's vintage

Besides reductionist approaches such as Braun's in product design or Paul Rand's and Saul Bass's in graphics, the visual language of the 1950s and 1960s propagated a keen sense of somewhat questionable optimism. Everything was deemed bigger and better, and the stars and moon were finally within reach. Smoking was portrayed as harmless, women were glad to do the dishes in pearls and heels, and to have a brand-new TV set was the greatest fortune on earth. The admen of

travel guide in the May and June issues in 2012. Hashimoto, who has contributed a fine selection of Thai-inspired illustrations, extensively worked on many subsequent editions. Both inside and on the covers, his drawings richly illustrate various international travel destinations. "I love traveling and I do travel sometimes, but there are tons of cities that I draw that I have never visited. When I have to draw these cities, I do research before. Sometimes I draw completely different things

publications got him acquainted with the visual language of the 1950s and 1960s, which has a visible influence on his work. Hashimoto's illustrations evoke a sense of nostalgia and an atmosphere of old cartoons, but without striving to do so, as the artist emphasizes. "I am barely conscious of the retro appeal of my work. I like nostalgic images, but it is not my purpose to mimic their style. I may draw like a cartoonist, but I am not trying to express anything like irony or caricature." He believes that the main reason that his style is reminiscent of cartoonists from the past is because both share a thrifty handling of color and a simplicity in their lines.

GALLERY BATON
(LEFT)
Illustration for gallery website
Client: Gallery Baton, Seoul, 2011

UNTITLED
(RIGHT)
Client: Monocle magazine, 2011

the bygone era packaged all of this quite nicely, and staged scenic stories drawing on characteristic illustrative cues such as figures with thick linear side profiles, soft watercolor-like tones, and contrasts with a limited range of bold splashes of color. While all of these have found refuge in Hashimoto's work, TV sets are superseded by laptops, cheerful domesticity by cosmopolitan savoir vivre, and honeyed hypocrisy by jaunty ingenuousness.

For *Monocle*'s travel guides, Hashimoto illustrates places across the globe, most of which he has never been to himself. The series of pullout travel supplements began with a Thailand survey and a Thai

from what I have researched, and develop ideas by brainstorming." Hashimoto usually spends two or three days brainstorming and researching, at which point he starts drawing with acrylic paints on flat paper. "Very basic," he comments.

Hashimoto's fruitful work relationship with *Monocle* goes back to 2008. "Chief editor Tyler Brûlé and his team think and work really globally," explains Hashimoto, "so they happened to find my artwork, and a Japanese staff member contacted me. Over time, I have established a very strong relationship with them." *Monocle*'s pages chronicle that relationship comprehensively. Popping up

GREAT BRITAIN

Portree
Inverness
Mallaig
Fort William
St. Andrews
Edinburgh
Glasgow
Carlisle
Newcastle-Upon-Tyne
Belfast
Isle of Man
Whitby
Scarborough
Harrogate
York
Douglas
Lancaster
Liverpool
Leeds
IRELAND
Chester
Hereford
Cambridge
Newport
Bath
London
Canterbury
Brighton
St. Ives
Penzance

throughout various issues, Hashimoto's drawings have frequently coincided with Brûlé's issue-ending "Observation" editorial. The visual atmosphere of the *Monocle* online shop bears his unmistakable signature too. Limited-edition prints by Hashimoto are part of the retail offerings, among them the "Map of the World," the "Happiness Index Poster," an overview of the 50 things *Monocle* staff considers most fundamental for a contented life, and the "Perfectly Serviced Hotel," printed on the occasion of *Monocle*'s first lobby shop opening in the Hyatt Regency London—The Churchill.

Although clearly concentrating on the editorial field, Hashimoto's portfolio also includes illustrated books and advertising and corporate illustrations. Working freelance since 1996, he never found it particularly challenging to set up his business and gain a foothold in the sector. "As the internet wasn't very common when I started, I had to make photocopies of my artwork and send them to various publishers and design companies. I used to go and meet them in person when I got good feedback. Right now, I use the internet to show my artwork." He does, but aside from his homepage, there's a surprising lack of information about Hashimoto out there on the web. Whether deliberate or mainly due to the different sign systems imping-ing upon search results, Hashimoto's on-line presence is certainly minimal. While many of his contemporaries thwart the idea of the illustrator as a service provid-er, aspiring to become mini-CEOs, poster-makers, puppet designers, or T-shirt war-riors, Hashimoto keeps a low profile. He is not a big networker, does no teaching or lecturing, and no self-directed work. "I only do commissioned work. That's how I spend all of my working time," he says, giving no indication as to whether he re-grets that or not. Regardless, he appears to be service-oriented, resilient, and cer-tainly hard-working.

"I usually work alone from 9:30 to 9:30 in my private studio that is just about a 10 minute walk from where I

GREAT BRITAIN
(LEFT PAGE)
A guide map for a traveling DVD
Client: Vap, 2006

PERFECT COMMUNITY
(TOP)
Client: Monocle magazine, 2008

SWITZERLAND
(BOTTOM)
A guide map for a traveling DVD
Client: Vap, 2006

live." Working alone is perfect for him, as he could not imagine giving up his inde-pendence. "It's a bit hard not having beer while I'm working," he adds with a smile. Not a big fan of irregularity, Hashimoto does his best to maintain his daily sched-ule. But every so often, when deadlines accumulate by the end of the month, extra hours and night shifts become necessary. "I sometimes reject job offers

when there are just too many," he says. It seems that more often than not, he ac-cepts heavy workloads with his ingrained industriousness. "It is not possible to take a day off every weekend. But my wife is also an illustrator, so she understands the situation very well." His wife works from home, focusing on magazine and ad-vertising just like Hashimoto. "We enjoy drinking beer in the evenings together, and spending time with our dog who also accompanies us while we work."

Business is going well and office matters like invoice preparation only take Hashimoto a couple of minutes per day. He works with agents on occa-sion, Visiontrack from Tokyo and Dutch Uncle from London, but he is not under contract with either. He usually receives client requests directly, and enjoys work-ing closely with art directors and editors. Much of his correspondence is by email, but believing that personal contact leads to better results, he meets his clients whenever he can. While 70% of them are based in Japan, the rest are spread across the globe. The internet has caused the world to shrink and global markets to expand, a development he considers to be of the utmost importance in the business of illustration over the past decades.

However much Hashimoto appreciates the international scope of his trade, he notes that language barriers remain. "While I don't notice major differences among countries in regard to creative strategies and requirements of clients, I do have a really hard time communicating in different languages. It is a huge problem for me right now. When I get an offer through an agent, I ask him to translate everything for me. If I get an offer directly, I try with very simple words in email communication. If that doesn't work, sometimes a client looks for a translator

CLASSIC CONCERT
(RIGHT)
Flyer for a children's concert
Client: Sony Music

STORAGE
(BOTTOM)
Title page illustration for
Croissant magazine. Client:
Magazine house, 2007

**THE PERFECTLY
SERVICED HOTEL**
(RIGHT PAGE)
Client: Monocle magazine, 2010

for me." He is fortunate with *Monocle* in that respect, perhaps one reason why the collaboration works so well. "They have brilliant Japanese staff there, so there is no stress working with them at all."

As opposed to words, Hashimoto's illustrations transcend linguistic and cultural differences with ease. That, he believes, is one of the big advantages of his

trade. Keenly interested in cultural and social anthropology and intercultural exchange, Hashimoto highly appreciates the opportunity to work on *Monocle*'s travel supplements and conventional travel guides. He could imagine to continuing in that vein, researching and drawing everyday habits of people from around the world in greater detail one day. "Just like

customs and traditions, the lives people live vary a lot from one area to the other, and can thus be very surprising. I love that kind of surprise."

Jan Van Der Veken

"IF YOU ARE ABLE TO SPEAK YOUR OWN VISUAL LANGUAGE, YOU CAN DRAW EVERYTHING, BECAUSE IT GIVES YOU THE FREEDOM TO DRAW IT YOUR OWN WAY."

PLACE AND DATE OF BIRTH
Ghent, Belgium; 1975

COUNTRY OF RESIDENCE
Belgium

FAMILY STATUS
In a relationship

EDUCATION / DEGREE
MA in Fine Arts

ACTIVE IN THE FIELD OF ILLUSTRATION SINCE
1999

BREAKTHROUGH PROJECT
The New Yorker

KEY CLIENTS
The New York Times, Wired, the New Yorker, Virgin Pacific, Vrij Nederland, Standaard Boekhandel

MOST RENOWNED PROJECTS
Two covers for the New Yorker

COMMISSIONS PER YEAR
90–120

AVERAGE TURNAROUND TIME PER COMMISSION
3–4 days

WORKSPACE
Home studio/atelier

EMPLOYEES
None

AGENTS
Comic House

HOW MUCH COMMISSION DO YOUR AGENTS TAKE
15%

TEACHING POSITIONS
Typography and digital design within the illustration field

AWARDS
None

MEMBER ASSOCIATIONS
None

GALLERIES
Petits Papiers Paris

"My images have a nice gentle atmosphere," says the Belgian illustrator Jan Van Der Veken in his equally gentle and kind manner. "If I am asked to draw a bunch of garbage, it may still be a bunch of garbage as I draw it, but garbage that is nice to look at." The joy of traditional Flemish cartoons reverberates in Van Der Veken's illustrations. To many, they recall the witty ventures of Tintin. To Van Der Veken they more importantly recall those of Blake and Mortimer, cartoon characters by Hergé's less famous collaborator Edgar P. Jacobs. Fond childhood memories, these cartoons have influenced his work unconsciously yet decisively.

Having attended an artistically oriented school in his mid-teens, Van Der Veken learned about printing and creative production, and then went on to study graphic design and typography at the St Lucas Art Institute in his hometown of Ghent. Driven by his growing interest in image-making, he took occasional extracurricular illustration classes with renowned Belgian illustrator and comic-strip artist Ever Meulen, creator of distinctive cartoons such as Balthasar the Green Stone Eater. "I never officially enrolled in that course, but found great pleasure in attending it," Van Der Veken recalls. Meulen, impressed by the ambitious entrant, encouraged him to continue drawing. He did, integrating illustrative elements into his graphic design projects. "While everyone else in the course was using photographs for their designs, I was using illustrations."

Van Der Veken notes that his illustrations were rather clumsy back then, essentially "normal drawings with curved lines." In an effort to add more structure to his creations, he experimented with contrast between architectural clarity and organic forms, surface and line. As his style began to take shape, influences from Hergé and Co. became more apparent. Characterized by the ligne claire technique, arguably the most distinctive feature of the works of the Belgian cartoon masters, Van Der Veken's illustrations evoke their limited and somewhat nostalgic color palette. The visual sense of "then," however, is contrasted with quite a bit of "now," as themes of modern-day culture and daily pressures involving new technologies, branding, health complaints, terrorism concerns, and material, legal, and intellectual property issues add up to what Van Der Veken explains as "retro-futurism." "I try to take the best things of long bygone

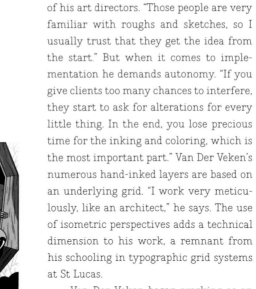

drawings, he depends on the schooled eyes of his art directors. "Those people are very familiar with roughs and sketches, so I usually trust that they get the idea from the start." But when it comes to implementation he demands autonomy. "If you give clients too many chances to interfere, they start to ask for alterations for every little thing. In the end, you lose precious time for the inking and coloring, which is the most important part." Van Der Veken's numerous hand-inked layers are based on an underlying grid. "I work very meticulously, like an architect," he says. The use of isometric perspectives adds a technical dimension to his work, a remnant from his schooling in typographic grid systems at St Lucas.

Van Der Veken began working as an independent illustrator right after his

financial worry, Van Der Veken got some of his first jobs through contacts who had picked him out of the crowd at his degree show. Soon he began to work with Comic House, a Dutch agency focusing on cartoonists, illustrators, animation, and 2D and 3D character design, and he also got his first extensive commission from the independent comic publisher Drawn and Quarterly. "I sent them a few illustrations and they got back to me immediately. Next thing I knew I was in charge of designing promotional work as well as a complete redesign of their website! The site is still in use today, though our relationship is not as strong anymore, mainly because I'm an illustrator pur sang, and not a comic artist. But the project was an important step that I am still proud of." Early on in Van Der Veken's career, he also

HISTORY NIGHT
(PAGE 68)
Client: Davidsfonds, 2012

DIVERSE
(BOTH PAGES)
Client: Standaard Boekhandel, 2011

times and combine them with the spirit of our present age."

Then and now also collide in Van Der Veken's work process, where a compass and ruler are as essential to him as Photoshop. Using a hand-drawn sketch as the basis for initial agreements with the client, Van Der Veken refines the illustrations with Chinese pen and ink, eventually adding color on the computer. Hoping to avoid adjustments to the original black-and-white

1999 graduation. "I thought at first that I'd present myself to graphical bureaus in order to have a steady flow of income, but they all turned me down because they sensed my determination and ambition within illustration. Eventually, someone told me to just try it as an independent illustrator, and to return to his bureau if it didn't work out—the best advice I ever got!"

Having moved back to his parents' house to set up his business free of

found clients by pouring through the yellow pages, searching for good design studios and cold calling them.

Today, Van Der Veken has built an impressive career for himself and an international client base which includes the *Belgian Post*, the *New York Times*, *Wired*, the *New Yorker*, and Virgin Pacific. Gestalten recently published his first monograph, which he calls "a brilliant tool to gain visibility." Van Der Veken, who kept an incredibly low profile for years, is now warming up to the idea of self-promotion. "Today, I made two A2-size posters with an overview of my best work so far. They fold into an A5 and are thus compact, so I send them to potential clients either digitally or by classic mail." He also maintains a Tumblr page that documents the daily routine of his company, Fabrica Grafica, from early sketch to final illustration.

Fabrica Grafica may sound like a large-scale enterprise but is in fact only Van Der Veken, with occasional assistance from his girlfriend. "I like the idea of people thinking it's a big company. It's funny, I keep getting applications from freelancers who would like to work for me." Located on the converted upper floor of the young couple's home, the "Fabrica" produces editorial and book cover illustrations, poster

designs, and related commercial art projects. Most jobs emerge from direct contact with clients, and the international network steadily expands by word of mouth. Recently, Van Der Veken's collaboration with the London-based illustration platform Nobrow yielded commissions for *Wired* and Virgin Pacific. This stemmed from the limited-edition screen print "City Lights," a picturesque urban scene featuring a man gazing at the evening sky

from his balcony, which gained popularity when it rapidly spread through the blogosphere.

Over the years, and as Fabrica Grafica's professional profile has grown, Van Der Veken has gotten into the habit of maintaining regular working hours. "I get up at nine, start working at ten to ten thirty, and

my main working period lasts until four in the afternoon. After that I do some coloring and inking but no design work anymore, rather technical follow-ups of nearly finished illustrations. I try to avoid night work or weekend work. Illustrating is the work of monks in fact—you have to do it in solitude. So at night I need to get out to a pub or do something with friends, and forget about my illustration work and the deadlines that come along with it."

"Editorial work especially is really tightly timed, so on average I work two or three days on one illustration." Other jobs may take up to two weeks, he says, adding that he usually works on four to five projects at a time. "Being an independent illustrator, I just do my best to work as much as I can. There is always the sense of 'if I turn this job down now, they might not return to me for the next one.'" He estimates the number of commissions per year to be somewhere between 90 and 120. Break times are rare. "If I get away for holidays, it's mainly for short trips that are close to home." The days of extensive travel to create travel books full of sketches are over, and Van Der Veken laments it. "I really wish I had more time for self-initiated work and experimentation. But you can't have it all I suppose."

"It gets to the point where clients approach you because they really want your style. On the one hand, that's great. On the other, it gets slightly repetitive and you sometimes think 'oh, no, I'm so done with this, I'm ready to move on.'" Despite the daily grind or narrow scope in stylistic development, Van Der Veken has learned to turn limitations into opportunity. Spurred by the aspiration to "create his own worlds," he approaches each job

as personal, and does his best to incorporate his own interests and ideas wherever possible. "To work in function of an article, for example, means to work within restrictions. But within these restrictions, there is always room for interpretation. Bringing these elements in allows me to evolve with every commission. And sometimes, the confines of a commercial brief are in fact a lot more inspiring than just starting from scratch."

Van de Veken's enjoyably accessible visual language, like his soft and muted tones, belies the depth of content. Nestled within the nicely diffuse light of old adventure stories are oftentimes themes of political and social relevance. "While I don't consciously impose a certain mood on my drawings, opinions enter in quite naturally," notes Van Der Veken. "I certainly aim to make drawings that are enjoyable, but not 'haha' funny." In the introduction to his monograph, he refers to the French filmmaker and comic actor Jaques Tati as one of his main influences, and a master in framing things. "I like that way of presenting life, with a quiet humor."

STEPPING STONE
(LEFT PAGE)
Client: Vacature magazine, 2007

HATE MAIL
(TOP)
Client: Humo magazine, 2012

TOO LITTLE TOO LATE
(RIGHT)
Client: Humo magazine, 2012

HOUSING CRISIS
(BOTTOM)
Client: De Standaard, 2008

ENERGY MANAGEMENT
(NEXT DOUBLE PAGE)
Client: Wired magazine, 2011

Tackling controversial topics with wit and disarming optimism, Van Der Veken's slightly naïve visual language thrives on a healthy dash of satire without ever being offensive.

Be that as it may, we are living in a time where Hergé and Co.'s often questionably stereotypical representations are edited meticulously, and even gentle forms of satire run the risk of being choked by anxiety and political correctness. Van Der Veken tells of a sketch he proposed to the *New Yorker* for an issue that focused on the Newtown, Connecticut school shooting in December 2012. It showed a scene of people in the streets, all appearing nice and friendly, but by means of x-ray vision, one could see that each person was carrying a handgun in their pocket. The art director loved it, and even encouraged him to add some children with guns in their pockets. That second sketch went to the editors-in-chief and was rejected. "I guess they considered it anti-American. I knew it would be a sensitive topic and that my approach was rather European and a bit sarcastic. But I thought it was worth trying, to see what they would say."

Van Der Veken has made it to the *New Yorker* cover twice, and, as is the case

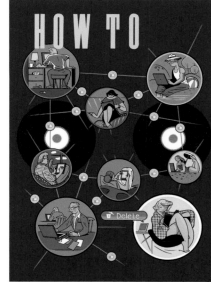

for many illustrators, the well-respected publication initiated his global break-through. Working with the *New Yorker* is special, even in terms of the commissioning procedure, he explains. "After I made my first solicitation to do a cover, they emailed back a list of topics for the upcoming issues. They ask you to do a black-and-white sketch for one of them, and send it over with a brief description of your idea. Phase two starts when they get back to you and ask you to continue working on it, refining the sketch, perhaps with some color. From all phase two sketches they pick a few to be finalized—phase three—and then they choose one to be on the cover. They pay you for phase two and phase three, but you only get

WINTER CHEERS
(LEFT)
Client: the New Yorker, 2009

NOBROW – LOGO DESIGN SCETCH
(TOP)
Client: NoBrow, 2011

TOP OF THE WORLD
(MIDDLE LEFT)
Client: the New Yorker, 2008

DELETE YOUR FACEBOOK ACCOUNT
(MIDDLE RIGHT)
Client: Wired magazine, 2012

ICELAND
(BOTTOM)
Client: Het Oog, 2004

VAKMO
(RIGHT PAGE)
Client: Vakmo, 2003

the full fee if you make it to the cover of course. Phase one is done for no money at all. I have done quite a few proposals that were rejected, but decided to just finalize them and add them to my portfolio any-way. They are nice drawings, so what the heck." Published or not, Van Der Veken's work has certainly made a strong impres-sion on Françoise Mouly, the *New Yorker*'s art editor and former publisher and co-editor of the comics anthology *Raw*. To quote her words on the Belgian illustra-tor, "Van Der Veken's line is so sharp that his world is beautifully streamlined. He transports us back to a time when the modern was exciting, everything was aerodynamic, people knew how to dress, and artists knew how to draw."

Himself living in a time of limitless possibilities, Van Der Veken knows how to combine multiple creative skills and use them to his advantage. All the letterings in his work are custom-made to match the style of his drawings. Endorsing inter-disciplinary approaches beyond categori-zation and the democratization of knowl-edge across various fields of creative practice, he believes that it is primarily due to his own combination of skills in graphic design and illustration that the Academy of Fine Arts in his hometown of Ghent recently offered him a teaching position—typography and digital design in the context of illustration. He was reluc-tant to accept the position at first, worry-ing that it would absorb too much of the time he would otherwise invest in com-missions, but eventually he agreed to do it. As it turned out, teaching for half a day per week does not interfere with his work too much, but greatly benefits it.

"Well, I do not consider myself a teacher in the school sense, as I don't place myself higher than my students. I have somewhat more experience, but they have their unlimited crazy ideas that I already have lost because of being in the business. That is, once you have a certain way of presenting yourself to the outside world, people only want that part of you, so you forget about your other artistic sides in a way. School is a laboratory that enables students to stretch out and do all sort of things to discover themselves. I am in-spired by the work of my students and see things in another perspective—very rewarding I must say!"

He, in turn, passes on to his students what he has learned through the business world. "Drawing is just half of the job. You have to reach out to and engage with a broad clientele, and seize the opportuni-ties the internet offers. Many Belgian il-lustrators concentrate greatly on the lo-cal market, which is a pity because that market is really small. I encourage my stu-dents to go through the world with open eyes and seek jobs internationally." Having worked on the global level for a couple of

THE CLEAR LINE OF
THE UNION
(LEFT PAGE)
Client: Convergences Paris, 2012

GLASS HOUSE
(TOP)
Client: Vara magazine, 2005

ALLERGIC REACTIONS
EXPLAINED
(RIGHT)
Client: Kwardrant Studio, 2008

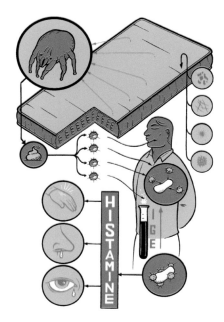

years now, Van Der Veken has acquired much experience, which he is proud to impart. "More than just individual proj-ects, I am certainly really proud of my personal development, the progress that I made over the years," he declares. "To be able to survive as an illustrator, the most fundamental thing is to develop a style of your own. If you are able to speak your own visual language, you can draw every-thing, because it gives you the freedom to draw it your own way. That process of development is ongoing, and you have to keep exploring and pushing yourself. It is crucial to understand that you'll never be finished, certainly not after a few years at the academy. School may be a great labo-ratory, but that is only the beginning."

PLACE AND DATE OF BIRTH
Milan, Italy; 1968

COUNTRY OF RESIDENCE
Germany

FAMILY STATUS
Married, 1 child

EDUCATION / DEGREE
High school degree

ACTIVE IN THE FIELD OF ILLUSTRATION SINCE
1992

BREAKTHROUGH PROJECT
His first assignment: 3 drawings for
the New Yorker

KEY CLIENTS
The New Yorker, the New York Times, Rolling Stone,
Time, Die Zeit, the Wall Street Journal, AD,
Boston Globe, Newsweek, the Progressive,
Frankfurter Allgemeine Zeitung,
Farrar Strauss & Giroux, Rizzoli

MOST RENOWNED PROJECTS
Covers for Newsweek, Time, Die Zeit,
the New York Times Book Review

COMMISSIONS PER YEAR
About 40

AVERAGE TURNAROUND TIME PER COMMISSION
About 5 days

WORKSPACE
Private studio

EMPLOYEES
None

AGENTS
Germany: 2agenten.com

HOW MUCH COMMISSION DO YOUR AGENTS TAKE
25%

TEACHING POSITIONS
None

AWARDS (SELECTION)
Society of Illustrators in New York (one Gold, two
Silver medals); Lead Award in Hamburg (Gold medal).
His work has been regularly featured in: American
Illustration, The Society of Illustrators Annuals,
Print Magazine, and Communication Arts.

MEMBER ASSOCIATIONS
None

GALLERIES
Baton Gallery, Seoul (Korea)

Andrea Ventura

**"AS AN ILLUSTRATOR, NO ONE REALLY
WANTS YOUR OPINION. THEY WANT YOU TO FILL
A CERTAIN SPACE IN THE ARTICLE."**

"Unlike an author of an article, I am not responsible for facts," says Andrea Ventura. "As an illustrator, I am free of all that. In a way, I am even free to lie." Ventura's illustrations don't lie, but their truth is wonderfully subjective. Approaching reality by intuition, Ventura shuns rigid concepts. There is no hidden agenda in his work, therefore only stunning immediacy. "I was never very interested nor strong in conceptualizing work," he says, which is why he always loved doing portraits. "It was easier for me. I was free of expectations, to come up with ideas and all that. I only had to worry about the likeness."

The term "likeness" belies the characteristic exaggerations and distortions that are so characteristic of Ventura's work. Albeit he claims to consider illustration "essentially servile," one senses a certain autarky in his gripping expressionist, largely gloomy style. Clients frequently ask him to paint brighter and reduce contrast, he says. Portraits of famous people especially are expected to soften and idealize, rather than to exaggerate and carve out potentially unflattering particularities. Ventura, however, neither paints to please, nor to get his work accepted. Initial hurdles and rejections have long been overcome.

Born in Milan, Italy in 1968, Ventura visited a local, art-oriented high school, firmly set on proceeding with his education at the affiliate fine art university located in the same building. But he failed the entrance examination twice, and put off by the fact that he would need to wait another year to redo the test while most of his high school friends had already been accepted, he abandoned his plan of

"Maybe it's some kind of personal inclination. The way I paint, instinctively, is just very dirty, heavy, and dark—too dark to appeal to business clients or advertising agencies, I guess."

Editorial commissioners and book publishers may try to reach the widest possible audiences, too, but many gladly avail themselves of Ventura's illustrations. Somberly absorbing atmospheres suit plenty of their themes. "Book covers are particularly adorable projects," Ventura says. "There is something so beautifully severe about them. Then book commissions allow for a longer and more substantial process, more thought." On the other hand, time allows for more doubt and revisions. Having worked in the editorial field for many years, Ventura has come to appreciate its fast pace. He has arrived at a point where he enjoys the compact and intense process of editorial projects, that they "don't drag on forever," but force him to solve a problem in

a traditional academic art education, and enrolled for history instead. A step motivated by only a casual interest and the desire to please his parents, Ventura meanwhile pursued his fascination with art, painting portraits. "I had the feeling that there was no alternative, really. I wasn't good at anything else." A friend would soon introduce him to the field of illustration, which he hadn't been fully aware of until then. Illustration was a good way to earn money with painting, the friend would say, and Ventura worked hard until the paychecks came.

The breakthrough came shortly after the move from Milan to New York in 1991, with three pieces appearing in the *New Yorker*. Commissions by other renowned publications like *Rolling Stone*, the *New York Times*, their *Book Review*, and *Newsweek* followed. Ventura's focus on editorial work came naturally. "My technique is painterly, painterly is editorial," he states. He also points to what he's heard clients refer to as dark and dirty moods, and what he refers to as his heavy hand.

HOTEL MEINA
(BOTH PAGES)
Client: the New York Times, 2012
Art Director: Honor Jones

INTERIOR OF BRYAN ADAMS APT IN PARIS
(PAGE 80)
Client: AD Magazine
Art Director: Ralph Stieglitz

a very limited amount of time. He compares tight briefs to exercise, the industry to a gym. "I never had enough time when I started, I was always unsure about the result. But I gained muscles and a sense of professionalism. I also learned to not worry too much, and let go. To just use the time I have and make the best of it."

Where other editorial illustrators work out narratives, conceptual symbolism, or political statements, Ventura focuses on aura. He does not attempt to imitate or replicate nature, but responds to what speaks to him, moods and impressions, often as captured in photographs. He tells of an image archive he used a lot during his early years in New York, a private collection of portraits of all sorts of famous personalities, located in a private apartment. He would first use it for a portrait of Lenin, commissioned by the *New York Times Book Review*. As more short notice inquiries for the fast-paced press landed on his desk, Ventura developed the habit of collecting pictures himself, focusing on personalities present in

major topical events. Around the time of the World Trade Center attacks, he had gathered a number of pictures of Osama Bin Laden, which he made use of when *Newsweek* approached him with the pertinent request. It is due to the gloominess

of his paintings that Ventura is often commissioned to draw "bad guys," or critically acclaimed personalities. He prefers to portray people he likes, or to whom he has at least some personal connection. Generally, he prefers artists or writers to politicians, because those types tend to be more open to accepting distortions; or men, rather than women, except for ones with very compact hair and heavy makeup, because he needs clearly defined shapes.

Ventura paints using acrylics, guache, charcoal, crayons, and pastels, and the occasional use of fragmented backgrounds may bring about edges and a sense of displacement. He prefers soft pencils—4B not 2H—whether it's Putin, Clinton, or Godard who he is portraying, as they are dark and of high, often unfathomable contrast. "As an illustrator, no one really wants your opinion," he declares. "They want you to

fill a certain space in the article." Aware that, in a way, all representation is interpretation, he claims to manipulate form, not content. "If I draw a face, I abstract myself from the personality, but concentrate on technical aspects like lighting, certain facial features, or physiognomy. Thereby I lose the sense of who it is I am portraying. I tend to be so busy with the detail that I forget the bigger picture—the who, the what, the why."

According to Ventura, it is publishers and magazine art directors, or the readers, who try to make sense of certain ways of representation, much more than he does. When he painted a portrait of Obama for the cover of Columbia University's alumni magazine shortly after the 2008 elections, the editors asked him to reduce contrast to avoid what could be taken as a negative aura. When he portrayed Clinton once, for *Newsweek*, with his face structured by pieced-together paper squares, it gave rise to public stir involving all kinds of farfetched interpretations. In fact, Ventura's reason to collage the image was merely technical: the face had been too wide, so he cut it in pieces and rearranged the proportions.

Portraits still make up about 90% of Ventura's work. Occasional nudes, landscapes, and interiors are as dark as the skin tones of the faces he paints. Berlin's winters are gray, too—perfect weather to work, finds Ventura, who has set up his workspace in one of Kreuzberg's nondescript rear buildings. He left New York about two years ago because he got married, and soon settled into his new environment, a shared studio where he works alongside fashion designers and other creatives. He is the only one who has an additional private space of his own. It is small and sparingly furnished—a desk scattered with pencils, charcoal, crayons, pastels, and a computer.

Ventura's work derives much of its energy from its painterly strokes, and it awakens a certain longing for the analog original. But technology has, however inconspicuously, altered the way he works.

Back in his earlier career, many editorial jobs ended in a last-minute back and forth of paintings, feedback, and revisions, carried through the nighttime streets of New York by express courier. Today, he reworks and revises his work digitally. "I cut and paste elements, and move them around in Photoshop. And I do color adjustments. Clients frequently ask me to lighten things up a bit, to compensate for the overall gloominess of my paintings with vivid color backgrounds," a compromise he has long past accepted.

"Being commissioned as an illustrator demands canalizing your own creative expression to suit a certain frame. You have to learn to work with the freedom you have inside that frame," Ventura notes. "However, personally, I like projects that have comparatively few constraints." What he struggles with most are predefined formats. "As an illustrator, it is naturally very important to be aware of the final size of a piece. I tend to disregard that. Sometimes I find myself in the end thinking 'oh my god, this is not the right format.' Defaults and conceptual formulations have always bothered me. When I did drawings in high school as a kid, I used to throw them all away at the end of the year, for the mere reason that they were created in adherence to predefined guidelines."

Confronted with the guidelines of commercial briefs, Ventura enters initial agreements on the basis of a quick sketch.

STAIRCASE IN MILANO
(LEFT PAGE)
Personal Work, 2003

CAPUTH
(TOP)
Personal Work, 2011

INTERIOR OF BRYAN ADAMS APT IN PARIS
(BOTTOM)
Client: AD Magazine
Art Director: Ralph Stieglitz

THE BAUHAUS SCHOOL
(NEXT DOUBLE PAGE)
Client: Richard Solomon, 2002

Then, he likes to go straight to the final version. "I do not show interim stages, unless I explicitly have to. It interrupts my workflow and indicates a lack of trust on the client's side. Doubt can be very draining. I don't like it when I feel too controlled or art directed, I need to feel a sense of trust." He recalls his early days working for the *New Yorker*, in the early nineties. The magazine had just undergone a major redesign, and Tina Brown had just started as its new editor. Ventura remembers how he was sent out to research by watching movie premiers, or theater plays, and that they did not even ask for sketches from him, but instead invited him to just do his thing and bring in a final painting. Such an amount of freedom is rare these days, and Ventura seems rather touched looking back. "The *New Yorker* feels like an album of my life," he says. "There are so many back issues that reflect various stages of my career." While this should dictate pride, Ventura cannot help but consider his old work with

harsh self-criticism. "It always feels to me that I have missed the point." Thanks to his critical mind, he finds himself in a constant process of progress and further development.

While Ventura continues to work for many of his long-standing clients from New York, he now has his bearings in the German-speaking arena too. In Berlin, he has started to work with the agency 2agenten, who got him commissions for many renowned magazines like the *Frankfurter Allgemeine Zeitung* and the *Zeitmagazin*. For the *Handelsblatt*, one of Germany's leading business and financial newspapers, Ventura portrayed a whole series of daily changing guest commentators. "Agents can be of great help, introducing you to a certain context, a foreign country, or culture," Ventura says. "They know the market, and bridge language barriers. It works really well for me with 2agenten." He used to work with an agent in the U.S., too, but finds it more convenient to take on commissions directly

from his clients now, and thus go around contractual obligations. "My old agent in the U.S. took 30%, plus I paid another 20% in taxes, so there already half of my income was gone." Asked about his overall experiences with agents, Ventura cites a fellow illustrator and friend of his: "An agent doesn't push you. It is you doing the work—for them it's just numbers. So for them, it's better to secure jobs for less than to command higher prices and try to get the most out of it. That is something only you can do, because you know the effort you put into the work." Ventura thinks he has a point there. "On the other hand, many illustrators are lousy business people. So an agent is good, as an accountant, your better business side, if you will." They can work as a promoter, too. "Of course, having quit working with him, I need to dedicate more time to maintain a presence in the market," Ventura admits. He is wrapping his head around a new, content-management website at the moment.

Ventura is not the kind of person who enjoys presenting himself and his work, but the ongoing digitalization and the physical distance that now separates him from a bulk of his clients make things a whole lot easier for him. "I always feel a bit vulnerable with my paintings, so meeting commissioners in person, to review and submit work, is always a bit of an examination to me. They look at your illustration, then they look at you. You see their faces. I prefer the detachment emails create. It's more comfortable for me." Client meetings are rare these days, anyway. In the editorial field especially, with its quick turnaround, meeting clients would be anything but economical. "It is often after two or three days that you need to hand things in," Ventura explains. "For me, it's a bit like having to find a new job every time, constantly having to make sure that you're hired again. I find that exhausting. It is the flipside to the otherwise great freedom I have. The freedom to do what I love to do. The freedom to live wherever I want,

FOREST ROMANCE
(LEFT PAGE)
Personal Work, 2009

PABLO NERUDA
(THIS PAGE, 3 IMAGES)
Client: Farrar, Straus and Giroux, 2002

and work for clients across the globe. The freedom to organize my life and my time myself." "Those who surrender freedom for security will not have, nor do they deserve, either one," said Benjamin Franklin. Freelancing, at times, means struggle and stress but it is certainly a price worth paying, says Ventura. "In the end, I am always amazed by the regularity with which inquiries come in."

With an average of forty commissions per year and a turnaround time of about five days for each, Ventura frees quite a bit of time in between for self-initiated projects and to experiment with other techniques. Over the last few years, he has developed a deep appreciation for pen and ink. "I like the fact that it's so clean, flexible, light. You need less space, less materials. Mixed media paintings have texture, dimensions—the process is very complex, and dirty. I sometimes like to draw at home, at the kitchen table, and pen and ink drawings allow me to do so, very spontaneously, and to put all the materials quickly away in a drawer once I finish. Also, there's something nicely immediate about the ink line. It feels so pure to me, so essential, direct. A bit like writing." Ventura's keen interest in writing and storytelling led him to author

"My Grandmother's War Stories," a short and very personal episode the *New York Times* published in 2010. "I never thought that I would be able to do it, but somehow writing and painting seem to come from the same place. It is just different techniques, and it was amazing to see how, together, they open up more possibilities." "My Grandmother's War Stories" became the starting point and first chapter of a graphic novel he finished only recently.

Ventura also sells and exhibits paintings. Estranged from the commercial art world as a whole, he works with a few select galleries, "friends," like the Galleria Rubin in Milan. "Selling a painting is just a great feeling," he says, "not only because

BOOKS
(THIS PAGE)
Rizzoli Publisher, Italy
Art Director: Matteo Bologna/
Mucca Design, NY

PINOCHET
(RIGHT PAGE)
Client: Time magazine, 1998
Art Director: Edel Rodriguez

Sigmund Freud
L'AVVENIRE
DI UN'ILLUSIONE
e altri scritti sulla religione
a cura di Alberto Luchetti

BUR
rizzoli

CLASSICI DEL PENSIERO

Arthur Schopenhauer
IL MONDO
COME VOLONTÀ
E RAPPRESENTAZIONE
VOLUME PRIMO
a cura di Sossio Giametta

BUR
rizzoli

CLASSICI DEL PENSIERO

Arthur Schopenhauer
SULLA VOLONTÀ
NELLA NATURA
a cura di Sossio Giametta

BUR
rizzoli

CLASSICI DEL PENSIERO

Immanuel Kant
FONDAZIONE DELLA
METAFISICA DEI
COSTUMI
a cura di Anna Maria Marietti
Introduzione di Amalia De Maria
TESTO TEDESCO A FRONTE

BUR
rizzoli

CLASSICI DEL PENSIERO

David Hume
DIALOGHI SULLA
RELIGIONE NATURALE
a cura di Gianni Paganini

BUR
rizzoli

CLASSICI DEL PENSIERO

of the money." In general, Ventura has always felt more comfortable working on free projects, with less limitations and more leeway. "That is not to say that commissioned illustration projects are of lesser value for me. There are certain briefs that give me the same pleasure as something I do for myself." In short, Ventura would not want to miss the opportunity of combining both free art and illustration. "It's a bit like having two rooms,

where you can go from one to the other. That is a very nice feeling. Ideally, there would be a couple of other rooms. One to compose music, another to make a movie; yet another to write a book, maybe one with no pictures at all."

PINOCHET

As the general becomes a senator, all the old passions erupt over his legacy

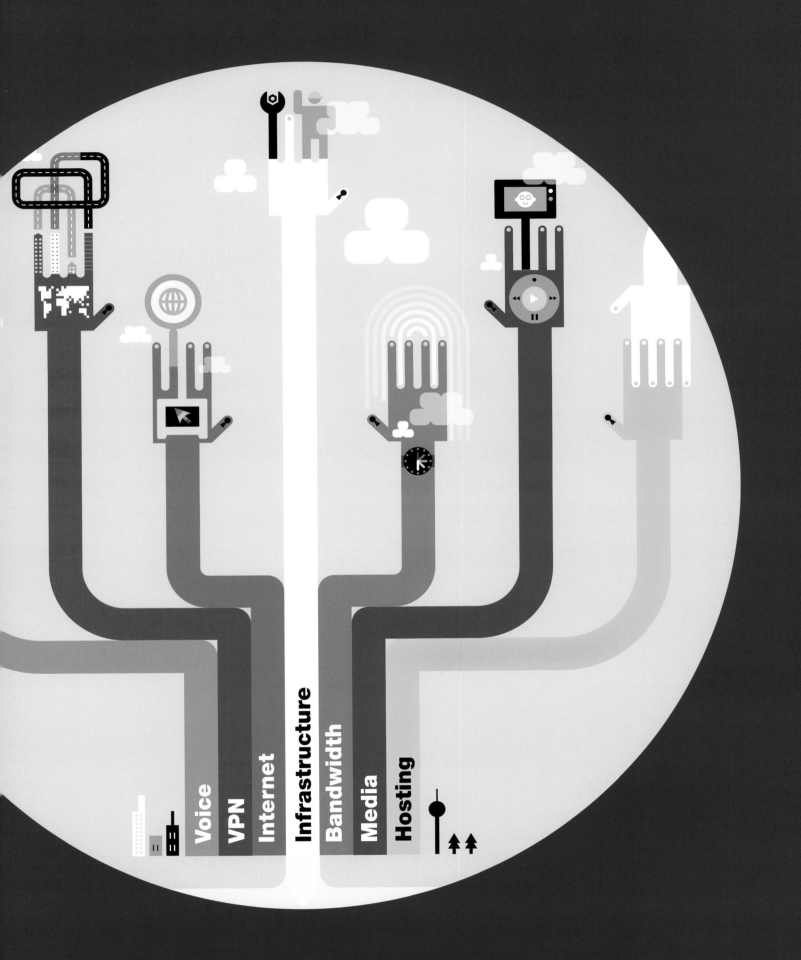

Informative Illustration

Historians credit illustrated maps and related forms of knowledge representation as the oldest form of art. With a history that is said to predate the written word, informative illustration is experiencing a boom these days. Its relevance grows continually, in line with the information age's torrents of data. Responding to the increasingly urgent demand for concise knowledge representation, the production of informative illustration has evolved significantly over past decades. Spurred by the fundamental human need to make sense of the world, artists explore new styles and techniques for diagrams, maps, charts, and other modes of data visualization. Expertly uniting graphic design, illustration, and journalistic skills, information designers like Francesco Franchi, Jonathan Corum, or Jan Schwochow team up with editors, journalists, and experts in international newsrooms. Digging deep into various specialist subjects, they cross limits and boundaries to render information in elegant, accessible, and, most importantly, highly informative ways. Astoundingly multilayered illustrations that stem from sophisticated journalistic approaches are contrasted with Peter Grundy's lighthearted and surprisingly subjective representations. In this chapter, technical illustration meets visual infotainment, politics pop culture, and drawings digital icons and elaborate technical renderings. Factoring out highly specialized sub-categories such as medical drawings or courtroom presentation art, the present selection concentrates on the communication of knowledge in popular media across printed, digital, and interactive formats.

PLACE AND DATE OF BIRTH
Milan, Italy; 1982

COUNTRY OF RESIDENCE
Italy

FAMILY STATUS
Not married

EDUCATION / DEGREE
BA and MA in Industrial Design,
Politecnico di Milano Graphic Design,
London Metropolitan University
Cum laude at Politecnico di Milano

ACTIVE IN THE FIELD OF ILLUSTRATION SINCE
2002

BREAKTHROUGH PROJECT
Editorial design for IL Magazine/Il Sole 24 Ore

KEY CLIENTS
Employed at Il Sole 24 Ore

MOST RENOWNED PROJECTS
IL Magazine/Il Sole 24 Ore

COMMISSIONS PER YEAR
Art director at IL

AVERAGE TURNAROUND TIME PER COMMISSION
1–2 weeks

WORKSPACE
Newsroom of Il Sole 24 Ore

EMPLOYEES
Working with a team of 10 at graphic department
of IL/Il Sole 24 Ore newspaper

AGENTS
None

TEACHING POSITIONS
Professor at IED Milan Master in Brand Design;
Visiting lecturer at Polytechnic University in Milan,
Catholic University of Milan, IULM Universtity Milan,
SISSA International School for Advanced Studies,
Il Sole 24 Ore Business School

AWARDS (SELECTION)
European Design Award (2009/2013); D&AD
(2009/2011/2012); SPD 48th, 47th & 45th Annual Print
Awards; XXII Premio Compasso d'Oro ADI Award; ADI
Design Index (2009); Selection for the XXII Premio Compasso d'Oro ADI Award; SND Malofiej Infographic Awards
(2009/2011/2013); 11th European Newspaper Award;
23rd International Biennial of Graphic Design Brno (2008)

MEMBER ASSOCIATIONS
Ordine Nazionale dei Giornalist; AIAP Associazione
Italiana design della comunicazione visiva; Society of
Publication Designers New York

GALLERIES / MUSEUM / EXHIBITIONS
Memory Palace Exhibition, V&A Museum London;
International Poster and Graphic Design Festival (2013),
Chaumont, France; Small Stories Bigger Pictures,
MOTI – Museum of the Image, Breda, Netherlands;
TDM5 Grafica Italiana, Triennale Design Museum,
Milano, Italy; The Best of Contemporary Italian Social
and Cultural Graphic Design, Rome, Italy; Unicità
d'Italia, Made in Italy e identità nazionale, Rome, Italy;
Spaghetti Grafica 2, Triennale di Milano, Milan, Italy

Francesco Franchi

"I SEE VISUAL LANGUAGE AS A SPECTRUM: ON ONE SIDE YOU HAVE THE ILLUSTRATION; ON THE OTHER SIDE YOU HAVE INFORMATION. I THINK THAT WORKS THAT ARE TOO CLOSE TO EITHER END OF THE SPECTRUM ARE RARELY INTERESTING."

"The need for stories is as old as mankind—it is through stories that we understand and make sense of the world," declares the designer Francesco Franchi. As the world rapidly changes, contemporary storytelling, be it verbal or visual, must be innovative and remain relevant. A new breed of visual journalists and graphic editors has taken on the challenge of reinventing news on paper through new forms of journalistic expression. At the vanguard, the 30-year-old Milanese designer has made it his mission to promote new editorial strategies where texts, headlines, photographs, and infographics are closely intertwined elements of visual stories, as opposed to stand-alone elements. In the name of processing and digesting knowledge, he encourages an interdisciplinary approach in which designers, journalists, and editors work together to develop a verbal and visual narrative language where content coexists.

Art directing *Intelligence in Lifestyle (IL)*, a supplement to Il Sole 24 Ore, Italy's leading economic and financial newspaper, Franchi works with Editor-in-Chief Christian Rocca to push the envelope of editorial design with a skilled team of illustrators, designers, and journalists in search of new ways to render the swelling torrent of information in our modern world. Decades after Godard famously declared that the beginning, middle, and end of a story should not necessarily appear in that order, Franchi's visual news stories take the dissolution of continuity and directional reading to the next level. "Well-considered and expertly rendered infographics can potentially fit the content of a 10,000-word (or more) article

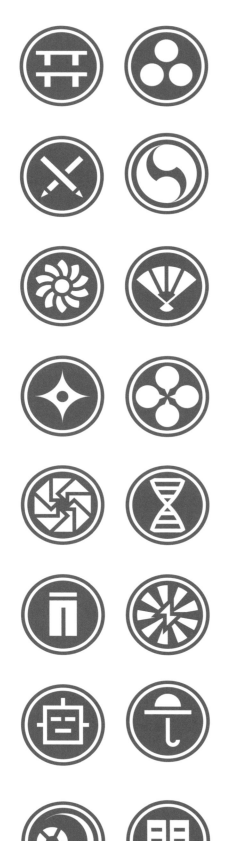

UNTITLED
(THIS PAGE)
For Intelligence in Lifestyle (IL)
Illustrator: Francesco Muzzi

UNTITLED
(PAGE 94)
For Intelligence in Lifestyle (IL)
Illustrator: Raymond Biesinger

into just one spread," he says. Visual language thwarts linearity with ease, and that is just one of its numerous virtues.

Packed with overlapping activities and manifold achievements, the story of Franchi's career appears non-linear, too, but it has a distinct beginning. Born close to Milan in 1982, he attributes his deep-seated interest in data visualization to his father, who created technical drawings and construction plans as a car designer at Alfa Romeo. The early acquaintance with the visual language of industry and engineering influenced his way of making sense of the world. "I always preferred to make a scheme rather than write something. Graphs, charts, maps, and schemes, and the manner in which they communicate concisely and unambiguously on the basis of a set of commonly understood conventions has always intrigued me." Over the years that fascination would develop into what he refers to as an infographic way of thinking.

In 2004 Franchi received a Bachelor's degree in Industrial Design from Italy's largest technical university, Politecnico di Milano, and then went to the U.K. for an Erasmus exchange to take specialized classes in graphic design at the London Metropolitan University. Back in Italy, he graduated cum laude at Politecnico

At Leftloft, Franchi worked alongside and under the creative supervision of the studio's partners, Andrea Braccaloni, Francesco Cavalli, Bruno Genovese, and David Pasquali. Following a first way-finding project for a park in Milan that combined illustration with information design and mapping, he worked on a range of commissions from corporate design and brand identity over advertising to information graphics for environments, digital, and print media. The growing number of projects for Leftloft's key clients in the editorial field, such as the *Corriere della Sera*, one of the oldest and most reputable Italian newspapers, would significantly form

element, integral to the creation of journalistic content. "I wanted to underline the importance of designers' modus operandi and their integration into the decision-making process and implementation of a successful editorial project, where innovation beyond distribution, form, and content is optimized in the production workflow; and where planning, creativity, and teamwork are at the heart of packaging the news. Designers can have a significant role in the process using their multidisciplinary, empathic, and creative skills, which are critical for the success of a good project or good redesign, understood not as re-styling, but as re-thinking in wider contexts."

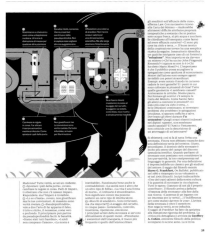

di Milano in 2007 with a Master's in Industrial Design and a thesis focusing on graphics. Bringing to the paper the practical experience he gained alongside his studies at the Milan-based studio Leftloft, Franchi proposed a new paradigm for forward-looking approaches in editorial design of news media.

TORO
For Intelligence in Lifestyle (IL)
Illustrator: Francesco Muzzi
Editor: Antonio Sgobba

Franchi's professional career. "I have learned a lot working at the studio—practical things and also how to deal with clients and with the other people involved in the design process. Thanks to numerous editorial projects I was able to learn the workflow inside large newsrooms in Italy." He gained a lot in an environment of intelligent and well-informed people, and also from observing that design was almost an afterthought in their processes, with not enough time or weight being given to it.

It was in response to his observations in Italy's newsrooms that Franchi's dissertation at the Polytechnic University in Milan suggested design as a functional

The dissertation, which Franchi developed under the guidance of Leftloft's Andrea Braccaloni as a thesis coordinator and Bruno Genovese and Alessandro Busseni as thesis advisors, earned him the attention of the editors and art directors at the Italian national daily business newspaper *Il Sole 24 Ore*. Walter Mariotti, at that time the publication's Editor-in-Chief, hired Franchi to give form to his new brainchild, the supplement *Intelligence in Lifestyle*, in May 2008, and appointed him its art director shortly after. The opportunity enabled him to put his theory into practice, building up the newsroom in completely new ways. "A design studio and a newsroom are two

RANE

| Anno | **II** | · **Qui non si canta al modo delle** · | Numero | **14** |

THE FICTION ISSUE

A cura di **FRANCESCO PACIFICO** | Illustrazioni di **RAYMOND BIESINGER**

Musica • Kaija Saariaho – *Du crystal* (1994), *Orion* (2002), *Notes on light* (2007)

very different professional environments, with very different dynamics, politics, and processes. At *IL Magazine* we tried to embrace a philosophy closer to the one I found in a studio like Leftloft than to the one I experienced in other newsrooms before. We adopted a more functional hierarchy where everybody recognizes the value of the expertise of the other practitioners involved, and where designers and illustrators are working hand-in-hand with the editors and are involved directly throughout the process." That process is complex, as Franchi explains. Data needs to be filtered, relationships established, patterns discerned, and information contextualized in a way that is aesthetically pleasing and informative at the same time. "I see visual language as a spectrum: on one side you have the illustration; on the other side you have information. I think that works that are too close to either end of the spectrum (too arty or too utilitarian) are rarely interesting. Design does not refer just to an aesthetic solution but has to aspire to becoming a primary aspect of a journalistic product, an intelligent representation that encourages critical thought."

In Franchi's theory of infographic thinking, design does not necessarily mean something sleek and beautiful. "We need to go back to the etymological meaning of the word design: the object, in becoming an industrial product, was destined to reach massive fruition and gain unprecedented dignity. Beauty is evoked, with harmony coming from the particular function and usefulness of the object. The composition criteria have to be founded in the intrinsic logic of the objects, in their function, and in their contribution to everyday life. This principle applies to every visual culture." To Franchi, the key challenge in designing information today lies in the designer's ability to access increasingly larger design databases that lure him into a "creative nirvana." "New software offers a dazzling amount of information and tools that give shape and meaning to massive amounts of data. In many cases the tool may become the message, and in other cases serendipity

RANE
(LEFT PAGE)
For Intelligence in Lifestyle (IL)
Illustrator: Raymond Biesinger

UNTITLED
(TOP)
For Intelligence in Lifestyle (IL)
Art Director: Francesco Franchi.
Illustrator: Maria Corte

MADRID
(RIGHT)
For Intelligence in Lifestyle (IL)
Illustrator: Elena Giavaldi
Designer: Davide Di Gennaro

BEERS
(NEXT DOUBLE PAGE)
For Intelligence in Lifestyle (IL)
Graphics: Francesco Franchi.
Illustrator: Laura Cattaneo
Editor: Alessandro Giberti

can point the way to new ideas and new ways of thinking."

"Editorial design, because it is a journalistic expression, acts as a vivid cultural snapshot of the era in which it is produced. Magazines printed in the 1960s, for example, not only evoke the visual vibrancy of their decade, but they also capture the spirit of an age that celebrated experimentation, innovation, and new directions." While his own visual language employs occasional nostalgia, Franchi generally propagates forward-looking concepts. "In order to become better at what we do I think it's good to start from the most simple and common display patterns for visual statistics and then try new things, experiment without being afraid of failing or being misunderstood." According to Franchi, the relationship between simplicity and complexity is complementary and while the right balance obviously depends on the context and target audience, one must be careful not to impair the complexity of matters for the sake of simplicity. "Sophisticated audiences will appreciate the designer's effort to present complex contents with subtly devised illustrations. I think underestimating the reader and therefore avoiding complexity is a bad idea."

Firmly anchored in the here and now, Franchi's graphs, charts, maps, and schemes are packed with concise information, his pages dense yet accessible due to their graphic rationale. He refers to the Swiss Style as a point of reference. "I'm used to working with type and grid, as well as a limited color palette, to create distinctive layouts and to signal a certain association to the reader, all while applying the publication's identity, appeal, aesthetics, emotional, and contextual considerations." In creating different layers of reading, Franchi's approach is that of a design author, calling for an active reader. "The main visual impact of the page is important. But we have to encourage the reader to explore the page in depth, and discover curious details and signals." In order to do so, Franchi thoroughly explores

SCHIUMA, PROFUMO, CREMA: SCEGLIETE IL BICCHIERE GIUSTO

La vulgata associa le "bionde" al boccale o al calice a tulipano e le "scure" alle coppe. È vero, ma non basta. Oltre alla forma si deve considerare tipo di vetro e spessore.

Calice a tulipano
330 ml
La bocca svasata impedisce un'eccessiva schiumatura e favorisce l'olfatto. Adatto alle birre belghe d'abbazia.
A

Boccale
400 ml
Il "classico". Quello in vetro tedesco, il "Mass", è perfetto per le "Märzen" per le "Pale ale" ci vuole il vetro britannico.
B

Colonna conica
330 ml
Vetro di spessore medio, a imboccatura larga per controllare la schiuma. È l'ideale per le vivaci e profumate birre danesi.
C

Altglass
425 ml
Cilindrico, per non esaltare né mortificare la schiuma. Il vetro, molto sottile, lo rende adatto alle ambrate "Alt".
D

La babele delle birre

CHI TANTO, CHI POCO. IL BORSINO DEI BEVITORI

I cechi bevono come spugne; irlandesi, tedeschi e australiani non scherzano; mentre in Gran Bretagna esagerare con "Lager" e "Stout" potrebbe ridurvi rapidamente sul lastrico. Consumi, costi, tasse e proibizioni: radiografia del mercato della birra nei cinque continenti.

- nazione di provenienza
- prezzo per 500 ml (in $)
- come si scrive "birra" nella lingua nazionale
- IVA sull'alcol

consumo pro capite

BIRRA — 0,00 — 0%

LUOGHI PUBBLICI E ALCOL

 OSPEDALI

 SCUOLE E UNIVERSITÀ

EDIFICI GOVERNATIVI

TRASPORTI PUBBLICI

PARCHI E STRADE

EVENTI SPORTIVI

CONCERTI

LUOGHI DI LAVORO

AAA ALCOLICO. TEMPI DURI PER PUBBLICIZZARE UNA MEDIA

Dai "Niet" assoluti – e assolutistici – iraniani, egiziani e algerini, al "tutto è lecito" per la pubblicità in Brasile, Cina e Sudafrica.

- illegale
- legale
- discrezionale

	TV	RADIO	STAMPA	MANIFESTI	EVENTI SPORTIVI	EVENTI DAL VIVO
ALGERIA	●	●	●	●	●	●
IRAN	●	●	●	●	●	●
GIORDANIA	●	●	●	●	●	●
EGITTO	●	●	●	●	●	●
VENEZUELA	●	●	●	●	●	●
DANIMARCA	●	●	●	●	●	●
FRANCIA	●	●	●	●	●	●
SVEZIA	●	●	●	●	●	●
ITALIA	●	●	●	●	●	●
INDIA	●	●	●	●	●	●
CANADA	●	●	●	●	●	●
BRASILE	●	●	●	●	●	●
CINA	●	●	●	●	●	●
CROAZIA	●	●	●	●	●	●
SUDAFRICA	●	●	●	●	●	●

Stati Uniti — 0,74 — CONSUMO PRO CAPITE 81,6 litri — Beer — 8,0% — ❶

Canada — 0,89 — 68,3 — BEER — 19% — ❷

Venezuela — 0,38 — 58,6 — CERVEZA — 14,5% — ❸

Messico — 0,81 — 51,8 — Cerveza — LA CERVEZA MAS FINA — 15% — ❹

Brasile — 0,35 — 47,6 — CERVEJA — 25% — ❺

Sudafrica — 0,38 — 59,2 — BIER — 14% — ⓫

Gabon — 0,56 — 55,8 — Bière — 18% — ⓬

Malawi — 0,32 — MOWA — 20% — 8,0 — ⓭

Algeria — 1,91 — بيرة — 17% — 3,8 — ⓮

Australia — 1,29 — BEER BEER — 10% — 109,9 — ⓯

IL

Glass types (top row)

Weizenbecker
500 ml
Capacità di mezzo litro. La svasatura serve a controllare l'abbondante schiuma delle birre di grano, le "Weissbier".
E

Calice a chiudere
330 ml
La sua forma rastremata alza la schiuma, impedendole di traboccare. Il suo vetro sottile valorizza le "Lager".
F

Coppa
250 ml
Forma emisferica, ideale per abbassare progressivamente la schiuma ed esaltare il profumo.
G

Colonna biconica
425 ml
Forma allargata al centro, bocca a chiudere. Per "Pils" belghe e per chi vuole la schiuma decapitata dalla spatola.
H

Pinta
473 ml
La forma a cono rovesciato neutralizza la schiuma delle "Bitter ale" e valorizza la *Cream* delle Stout.
I

Conosciuta già ai tempi dei Sumeri, la birra ha dissetato l'uomo per 5mila anni prima di consacrarsi, nel mondo contemporaneo, come bevanda universale

— *di* **Francesco Franchi** *e* **Alessandro Giberti** | *illustrazioni di* **Laura Cattaneo**

QUANTA COCA-COLA PER UNA BIRRA

Rapporto tra il prezzo di una birra e di una Coca-Cola: in Australia al costo di una birra media si compra poco più della metà di una Coca da 500 ml. In Iran una "bionda" costa 22 volte di più.

#	Paese	#	Paese
1	AUSTRALIA *0,61*	100	IRAN *22*
2	MONGOLIA *0,66*	99	ALGERIA *10,13*
3	MALESIA *0,67*	98	GUATEMALA *5,25*
4	ROMANIA *0,67*	97	BOLIVIA *5,07*
5	UNGHERIA *0,67*	96	PERÙ *4,22*
6	PARAGUAY *0,7*	95	ITALIA *3,88*
7	BIELORUSSIA *0,78*	94	LITUANIA *3,75*
8	COSTA RICA *0,8*	93	SEYCHELLES *3,68*
9	CROAZIA *0,8*	92	NORVEGIA *3,47*
10	PORTOGALLO *0,87*	91	ARGENTINA *3,29*
11	VENEZUELA *0,87*	90	CANADA *3,02*
12	GUINEA *0,88*	89	UCRAINA *3*
13	DANIMARCA *0,89*	88	KAZAKHSTAN *3*
14	BULGARIA *0,91*	87	GUYANA *3*
15	REP. CECA *0,93*	86	COREA DEL SUD *3*
16	MALAWI *0,94*	85	AZERBAIJAN *3*
17	STATI UNITI *1*	84	COLOMBIA *2,82*
18	POLONIA *1*	83	THAILANDIA *2,78*
19	SLOVACCHIA *1*	82	ISRAELE *2,78*
20	REP. CENTRAFRICANA *1,02*	81	NICARAGUA *2,7*

Bottles (first row)

156,9 — Repubblica Ceca — *0,22* — Pivo — 5%
131,1 — Irlanda — *2,07* — BEOIR — 21%
115,8 — Germania — *0,79* — Bier — 16%
99,0 — Gran Bretagna — *2,61* — BEER Outstanding — 17,5%
29,4 — Italia — *1,64* — BIRRA — 20%

Bottles (second row)

51,3 — Giappone — *2,02* — ビール — 5%
38,5 — Corea del Sud — *1,5* — 맥주 — 10%
22,1 — Cina — *0,6* — 啤酒 — 17%
20,0 — Malesia — *1,31* — Bir — 20%
1,5 — Giordania — *1,03* — بيرة — 13%

BIRRA E SOFT DRINK: IN EUROPA VINCE IL LUPPOLO

Consumo pro capite di birra (A), bibite analcoliche gassate (B) e bibite analcoliche non gassate (C). Dati riferiti al 2008.

73,7 CONSUMO PRO CAPITE *(litri)* — A
57 CONSUMO PRO CAPITE *(litri)* — B
15 CONSUMO PRO CAPITE *(litri)* — C

FONTE PRINCIPALE – **World Health Organization** (*Global Status Report: Alcohol Policy*)

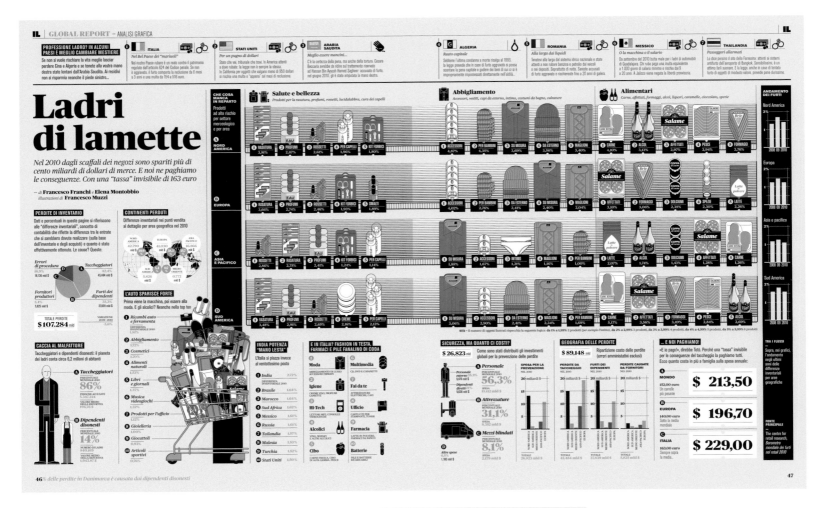

his own design toolkit. The page number has the potential to become an infographic tool as well, he notes. "At its very best, designing for editorial content is an exciting and constantly evolving research lab and launching pad for stylistic innovation. As such, one must continue to learn, experiment, and be willing to embrace new experiences with an open mind."

The tireless testing of new techniques and materials is the driving force behind Franchi's success, and certainly among the reasons why *Il Sole 24 Ore*'s executive editor recently entrusted him with the task of appointing a new team to the general newsroom. His added responsibilities include the supervision of various projects in the newspaper's print and digital edition. Franchi now coordinates a ten-strong team of in-house graphic designers and illustrators, including Giacomo

LADRI DI LAMETTE
(TOP)
For Intelligence in Lifestyle (IL)
Graphics: Francesco Franchi
Illustrator: Francesco Muzzi
Editor: Elena Montobbio

UN PAESE SENZA DATI DI FATTO
(RIGHT)
For Intelligence in Lifestyle (IL)
Illustrator: Giacomo Gambineri

Gambineri, Francesco Muzzi, and Laura Cattaneo, as well as occasional contributions from freelancers such as Spaniard Maria Corte, who illustrates the section "Fogliettone" every month, and Canadian

Raymond Biesinger whom he commissioned to illustrate the special fictional issue "RANE."

The team Franchi created at *IL Magazine* is his greatest pride and joy. "My idea was to give young and talented designers and illustrators the same opportunities that the partners at Leftloft and then the different editors-in-chief at *Il Sole 24 Ore* gave me. I was very young and they put trust in me." By offering internships and permanent positions to young illustrators and designers like Davide Mottes, Francesco Muzzi, Elsa Jenna, Laura Cantadori, Micaela Bonetti, Giacomo Gambineri, Simone Trotti, Matteo Cellerino, and Umberto Mischi, Franchi gives newcomers in the field a valuable platform. "When working at the magazine as an illustrator or a graphic designer you have a few shots every month

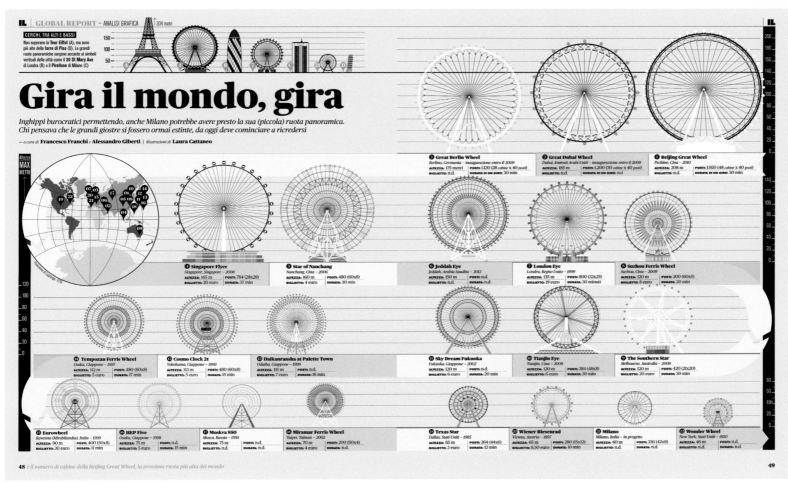

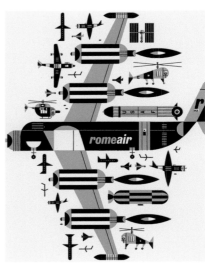

for a large readership to see your work. I think it's a good opportunity to grow if you're smart and talented." Networking is good, but to Franchi, the ability to be visible to the wider public is essential. "Designers and illustrators have to speak through their work," he says, as he does through his work and scholastic treatises.

His paradigm, treating visual elements as integral journalistic information, is now *Il Sole 24 Ore*'s newsroom policy. An open-space office facilitates the interdisciplinary approach. The atmosphere is characterized by constant exchange between illustrators, designers, and editors, and processes overlap and feed into one another, with everyone on the team contributing ideas. Franchi likes to sketch his ideas by hand first, then usually proceeds digitally, in Illustrator and InDesign. The graphic implementation,

GIRA IL MONDO
(TOP)
For Intelligence in Lifestyle (IL)
Graphics: Francesco Franchi
Illustrator: Laura Cattaneo
Editor: Alessandro Giberti

UNTITLED
(RIGHT, 2 IMAGES)
For Intelligence in Lifestyle (IL)
Illustrations: Raymond Biesinger

however, makes up only a small fraction of the process, which he breaks down into five essential steps: research, sorting information, page organization, designing, and finally the text editing. "The first

three steps make up about eighty percent of the process," he states emphatically.

Information design is a critical interpretation of data, and visual accentuation and graphic hierarchies define how

Fogliettone
Indagine su un argomento al di sopra di ogni sospetto

Generazione sprecata

Vent'anni fa nasceva la mistica della "GenX", scorciatoia per provare a vivere da artisti e rimandare il fatidico momento della maturazione. Bilancio appassionato di una rivolta giovanile schietta, poetica e disillusa

di **Stefano Pistolini**, illustrazioni di **Maria Corte**

23

Fogliettone
Indagine su un argomento al di sopra di ogni sospetto

Mia madre, Papa Francesco e io

di **Francesco Pacifico**, illustrazioni di **Maria Corte**

Storia personalissima del Papato contemporaneo e delle contraddizioni intellettuali dell'autore di questo articolo, più che del Papa

23

---

content is read and perceived. It is thus the designer's responsibility to use every communication artifact with due consideration. This is a cumbersome task, especially today when huge amounts of readily available information are transforming the media. "The dataset are getting massive and finding data is quite easy nowadays, but selecting, storing, indexing, updating, and most importantly contextualizing the information is rather difficult. Making data more accessible and manageable has thus become more crucial than ever as part of the process. There is now so much data out there in the world that we have to provide the key facts for each story, and finding the right information for each issue can be a lengthy journalistic task."

As opposed to the daily business newspaper *Il Sole 24 Ore*, the *Intelligence in Lifestyle* supplement Franchi is principally involved with is published monthly. For the sake of efficiency, his team plans ahead carefully and engages in close cooperation. "We hold the first meeting for a new issue as soon as we close the previous

UNTITLED
(4 IMAGES)
For Intelligence in Lifestyle (IL)
Illustrations: Maria Corte

one," Franchi says. Then there are about two weeks left to work on the issue. These two weeks are split among research, sorting information, page organization, design, and finally the text editing, as work is divided by the content, rather than by task. "The magazine is divided into various sections and for each one there are specific editors, designers, and illustrators," Franchi explains. Although essentially serving in the transmission of information, infographics are based on subjective editorial choices poised between design and journalism. Visual narrative elements turn facts into stories, drawing bigger pictures each with their own tone, which is why Franchi considers them far from neutral representation.

To grasp the bigger picture of Franchi's career, it would certainly be helpful to lay it out in illustration on a two-page spread, for a chronological account hardly does justice to his densely packed life. Given the solid theoretical foundation that supports Franchi's practice, it is no surprise that universities stand in line to have him lecture. Aside from holding a chair in Brand Design at the Istituto Europeo di Design in Milan, Franchi works as a visiting lecturer at Polytechnic University in Milan (Master's in Data Visualization), the Catholic University of Milan (Master's in Journalism), the Università di Lingue e Scienze della Comunicazione in Milan (Master's in Journalism), the SISSA International School for Advanced Studies

Exploring the future of news publishing and ways in which print can survive, the title seeks to outline a new, integrated approach for editorial designers, whom Franchi considers to play a pivotal role in advancing the evolution of media.

Franchi's outstanding career as a journalist and author has gained substantial momentum since 2010. In his free time beyond regular work activities or teaching commitments, he occasionally exhibits. Most recently he was part of the group show "Memory Palace" at the Victoria and Albert Museum in London. "It is indeed very hard to free up time for a private life," he says, but instead of complaining, he is already busy cooking up new ideas. Quoting Khoi Vinh, former digital design director of the *New York Times*, he talks of the contemporary world's need for a new kind of designer, the ed-ex designer (editorial experience designer), who can "combine the holistic, systems-level thinking of UX (user experience design) with the incisive storytelling instincts of editorial design." Shoulder to shoulder with Vinh, who deplores the drought in editorial experience interfaces in an extensive article on his blog, Franchi would like to delve deeper into the field of ed-ex design and contribute to its advancements. "With technology advancing at breakneck speed, and with the way we consume and digest information constantly evolving, designers are challenged to embrace new editorial formats, platforms, and visual languages." It's safe to say that he has made significant contributions already.

(Master's in Science Communication and a one-year Master's in Digital Science Journalism), and at *Il Sole 24 Ore*'s affiliated Business School.

Franchi's achievements in the field of infographics have been richly honored with numerous awards. Exploring developments and approaches in information design, he not only enjoys great international acclaim, but also the opportunity to expand his professional horizons through intercultural dialog. Having served as a judge for a number of international design awards in recent years, he has observed significant differences among countries. Aside from stylistic dissimilarities, there are considerable variations in the dynamics of design processes and workflows, he says. These observations have been explored in depth since his MA thesis, and they feed into the book project about the future of media and information graphics that he is currently working on. "I am building on the ideas I introduced in my dissertation and combining them with the professional experience I have gained since I wrote it."

Hafen

CO$_2$

ÖL/GAS

CO$_2$

CO$_2$-EINLAGERUNG

Öl-/Gasfeld

Jan Schwochow

"YOU FEEL LIKE AN ARCHAEOLOGIST OR A DETECTIVE AT TIMES. WE MUST RESEARCH EVERY CASE PATIENTLY, AND IN DETAIL."

Jan Schwochow loves to engage with data and information of all sorts. Inconceivable for many, he even enjoys collecting it, organizing columns of figures, and drawing up facts in Excel sheets. Working at the crossroads between graphic design, illustration, and journalism, he mostly identifies with the latter. Aesthetic appearance is a nicety, he says. Most importantly, he wants to supply new insights. Following that mission, Schwochow has created a 15-strong data visualization task force called Golden Section Graphics.

Looking back on over 20 years of experience in the field of infographics, Schwochow's strong journalistic orientation stems from his longstanding work relationship with the German weekly Stern. He first joined the magazine for a temporary design job back in 1990, two years before he began to study. His earliest works

published in Stern had fairly little to do with infographics. They were, quite simply, illustrations, produced shortly before Stern's graphic department had switched to computers. One, portraying Milli Vanilli at the time of the pop stars' big playback scandal, was a collage. Another, a rather atmospheric opener for an article dealing with the Second Gulf War, was composed and modified with the help of a color copier. Others were caricature-like drawings. Schwochow's very first computer illustration, a refrigerator that can order its contents itself, which accompanied an article on what were then highly futuristic domestic robots, was published in Stern in 1993. The first digital 3D-infographic, the Pyramid of Cheops in cross section, would follow that same year.

Following his first short temporary employment at Stern, Schwochow's career

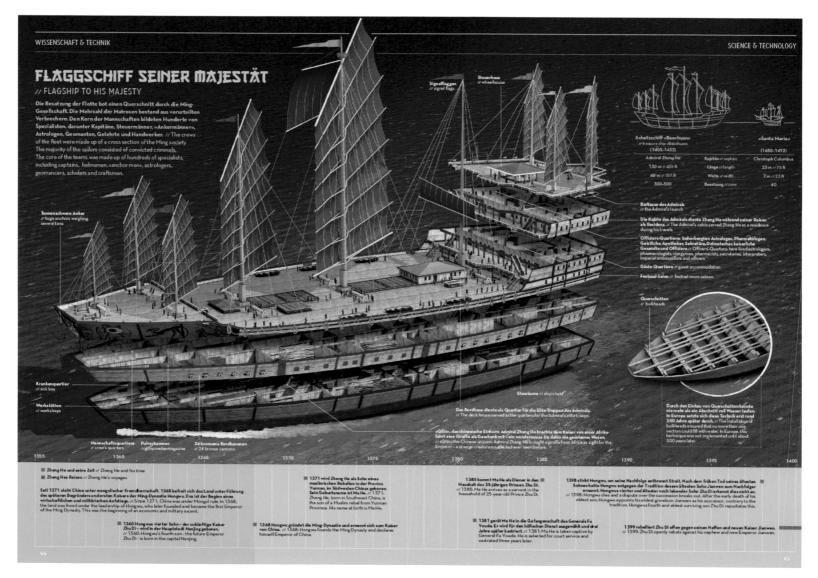

took off at action-packed pace. He started out as a freelance designer and enrolled for communication design at the Hamburg University of Applied Sciences. In 1994, during his studies, he co-founded the digital communications agency DDD design, which he led and art directed until 1997. Right after graduation, he co-founded another web agency, Ahrensburger online GBR, and remained active associate, art director, and editor for the two years that the company existed. In 1999 a permanent position followed in *Stern*'s graphic department, which he suspended in 2001 to become art director for information graphics at a Hamburg-based publisher called Milchstrasse. In 2002, back at *Stern*,

CHINESE ADMIRAL ZHENG HE
(TOP)
For In Graphics magazine,
Golden Section Graphics

CSS TECHNOLOGY
(PAGE 106)
3D-Rendering Cinema 4D/Photoshop
Client: Muehlhausmoers Corporate
Communications/Vattenfall

he was promoted to head of the magazine's infographics department and art director of infographics, a position he would hold until 2004, when he moved to Berlin to work for the weekly newspaper *Welt am Sonntag*. Concurrently, he put together an information graphics department for the creative agency KircherBurkhardt, which he headed for the following two years. Golden Section Graphics arose in 2007 from the wealth of expertise gathered over all these years.

"When I started the company I benefited greatly from my many years of prominence in the media industry—commissions just came, and it has remained so until today." It would not take long until

Golden Section's graphics were acclaimed by renowned publications and business clients alike. Schwochow and his team have visualized subject matters as diverse as the discovery of the famous iceman Oetzi, tobacco production processes, the combat tank Leopard 2 A6, and the events at the nuclear power plant in Fukushima following the earthquake and the tsunami in March 2011. Adopting the ambitious journalistic standard of in-depth articles, examples like the above represent editorial contributions in their own right. They certainly tell their very own stories, in that they string together multiple images in a row, or employ visual and verbal content as closely entwined elements reminiscent of a comic. Naturally, Schwochow does not consider himself a visual storyteller over an illustrator. But in fact, he and his team at Golden Section Graphics are Germany's pioneers in visual storytelling.

To speak of genres may be out of place here, but Schwochow's words evoke a sense of adventure and murder mystery. "You feel like an archaeologist or a detective at times. We must research every case patiently, and in detail. Firstly, to understand the subject matter ourselves. Secondly, in an effort to detect a new aspect to it and present that to the reader." His approach is investigative and one of scientific precision. "I am an enthusiastic advocate of accuracy. I have a distinct

sense of justice and want to understand facts and circumstances that surround me everyday." Schwochow's graphics are not visual commentaries, but reports of matter-of-fact objectivity, not there to persuade, but to aid decision-making. He seeks to process information in a way that encourages readers to form their own opinions.

First comes the information, then the visualization. "The second step, the graphic or illustrative transfer of knowledge, is no less important than the first," Schwochow notes, but it depends on step one as its solid foundation. "Well-researched facts and exciting stories make developing a good infographic a whole lot easier." What

makes an infographic good? "A good infographic should work equally well for everyone and, in the first instance, answer one question. For example: How does a steam engine work? The graphic should explain the issue in question factually, and in the best possible way, but also present it attractively enough to encourage the viewers to dedicate their time, for we call on his attention all too often, asking him to engage in complex issues." Schwochow begins his work with an initial set of questions: Who am I addressing? What is my task? What query is there to be answered? What problem to be solved? If he cannot find answers to these questions, Schwochow is forced to speculate,

EVONIK – EVERY DAY
BIOTECHNOLOGY
3D-Rendering Cinema 4D/Photoshop
Client: Redaktion4/Evonik

which he aims to avoid. If unavoidable, he does his best to distinguish fact and guess clearly, by means of his design toolkit. "As a graphic designer, I always have the opportunity to mark eventualities, like with dotted lines and the remark 'alleged route of the perpetrator.'"

"The visual should guide the reader through the topic. Important elements must be highlighted, insignificant ones designed unobtrusively. The structure must be clearly evident, the use of text, form, and color must be implemented reasonably.

Minor information should rather be left out, for the famous principle of 'less is more' applies here as well." Certainly, "less is more" must not be mistaken with all-around simplification. "A complex issue, like for instance the urban water cycle, cannot really be simplified, while a plain statement à la 'the water is cold and the sun hot' can obviously be visualized with very simple means. Each new task requires careful inspection and potentially a whole new approach and visual solution. Commissions can be so very different."

Schwochow explains the typical process: "Generally speaking, we start by gathering as much information as possible about the topic, to get an idea. Then we sort this information and make sketches or visualize the data with different graph types to reveal particular statements. This is usually done using Excel and Adobe Illustrator. Obviously, the internet plays an important role in today's research work. It offers plenty of interesting sources, which would previously have been inaccessible, or possible only at the cost of much time

and effort. The danger is that there is also a lot of wrong or diluted information. We often need to question the reliability of online sources. New media communicate faster and unfortunately often factually wrong. The internet, especially sites like Wikipedia, stores all this data and we have to dig through the garbage and filter out useful bits and pieces."

That filtering is Golden Section's specialty, and they call it data mining. "Tasks like these are becoming more common as the world's vast amounts of data are increasing rapidly, every second, every day," Schwochow says. With data mining, he and his colleagues refer to the extraction of valuable content from a heap of raw data. That heap can consist of numbers, but this is just one of many possibilities. Schwochow has, for example, over the course of two years, documented around 150 kilometers of the Berlin Wall in very detailed aerial photos. One of his employees once watched all the James Bond movies, twice even, and gathered a huge amount of data of all kinds. The result was a series of entertaining statistics, revealing new insights. Among other things, when and how often Bond famously said, "A martini please—shaken, not stirred!"

Golden Section Graphics' keen ambition to develop self-generated content gave strong impetus to *In Graphics*, an independent, biannual publication featuring topics from politics and economics to culture and entertainment, solely in the form of infographics. "Economically, the magazine is not yet worthwhile, especially not through sales, and there is virtually

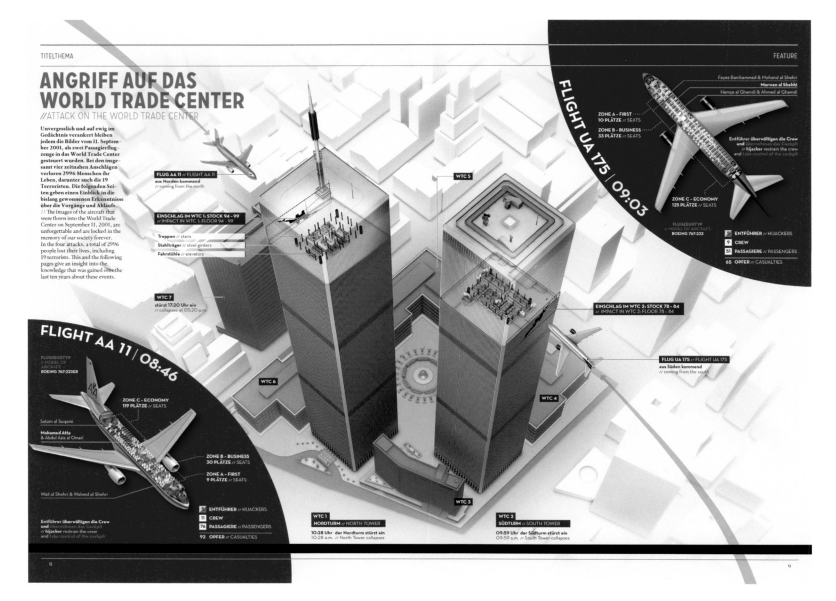

ANGRIFF AUF DAS WORLD TRADE CENTER
// ATTACK ON THE WORLD TRADE CENTER

Unvergesslich und auf ewig im Gedächtnis verankert bleiben jedem die Bilder vom 11. September 2001, als zwei Passagierflugzeuge in das World Trade Center gesteuert wurden. Bei den insgesamt vier zeitnahen Anschlägen verloren 2996 Menschen ihr Leben, darunter auch die 19 Terroristen. Die folgenden Seiten geben einen Einblick in die bislang gewonnenen Erkenntnisse über die Vorgänge und Abläufe.
// The images of the aircraft that were flown into the World Trade Center on September 11, 2001, are unforgettable and are locked in the memory of our society forever. In the four attacks, a total of 2996 people lost their lives, including 19 terrorists. This and the following pages give an insight into the knowledge that was gained over the last ten years about these events.

FLUG AA 11 // FLIGHT AA 11
aus Norden kommend
// coming from the north

EINSCHLAG IM WTC 1: STOCK 94 - 99
// IMPACT IN WTC 1: FLOOR 94 - 99

Treppen // stairs
Stahlträger // steel girders
Fahrstühle // elevators

WTC 5

WTC 7
stürzt 17:20 Uhr ein
// collapses at 05:20 p.m.

FLIGHT AA 11 | 08:46
FLUGZEUGTYP // MODEL OF AIRCRAFT: BOEING 767-223ER

Satam al Suqami

Mohamed Atta & Abdul Aziz al Omari

ZONE C - ECONOMY
119 PLÄTZE // SEATS

ZONE B - BUSINESS
30 PLÄTZE // SEATS

ZONE A - FIRST
9 PLÄTZE // SEATS

Wail al Shehri & Waleed al Shehri

Entführer überwältigen die Crew und übernehmen das Cockpit // hijacker restrain the crew and take control of the cockpit

5 ENTFÜHRER // HIJACKERS
11 CREW
76 PASSAGIERE // PASSENGERS
92 OPFER // CASUALTIES

WTC 6

EINSCHLAG IM WTC 2: STOCK 78 - 84
// IMPACT IN WTC 2: FLOOR 78 - 84

WTC 4

FLUG UA 175 // FLIGHT UA 175
aus Süden kommend
// coming from the south

WTC 3

WTC 1
NORDTURM // NORTH TOWER
10:28 Uhr der Nordturm stürzt ein
10:28 a.m. // North Tower collapses

WTC 2
SÜDTURM // SOUTH TOWER
09:59 Uhr der Südturm stürzt ein
09:59 a.m. // South Tower collapses

FLIGHT UA 175 | 09:03

Fayez Banihammad & Mohand al Shehri
Marwan al Shehhi
Hamza al Ghamdi & Ahmed al Ghamdi

ZONE A - FIRST
10 PLÄTZE // SEATS
ZONE B - BUSINESS
33 PLÄTZE // SEATS

Entführer überwältigen die Crew und übernehmen das Cockpit // hijacker restrain the crew and take control of the cockpit

ZONE C - ECONOMY
125 PLÄTZE // SEATS

FLUGZEUGTYP // MODEL OF AIRCRAFT: BOEING 767-222

5 ENTFÜHRER // HIJACKERS
9 CREW
51 PASSAGIERE // PASSENGERS
65 OPFER // CASUALTIES

no advertising," Schwochow says. "The main financial benefit comes through reprinting rights." *Die Zeit*, for example, often publishes infographics that have previously appeared in *In Graphics*. "Most importantly, however, the magazine enables us to publish self-generated content, themes that other publications do not have the room or courage to commission. Many things that we have done and will be doing at Golden Section Graphics are absolutely uneconomical or simply do not have the primary goal to bring in money, because we want to have fun!" Schwochow does his best to keep hierarchies flat and maintain an amicable atmosphere within

9/11
(THIS PAGE)
For In Graphics magazine, Golden Section Graphics

DEUTSCHE BANK GREENTOWERS
(RIGHT PAGE)
Client: Behnken & Prinz

the company. "The human aspect of cooperation is very important to me; people should fit together and enjoy their work as a team."

Good organization is essential, especially when it comes to complex collaborative projects. "Infographic designers are generally rather loners, even in newsrooms they rarely work in teams, which I think is a shame. At Golden Section Graphics that is different. Each employee can have different areas of expertise, such as illustration, 3D, or someone can write very well. I believe that everything should come together in visual communication—the media, the concept, the images,

the text, and eventually the infographics. Only in view of the communication goal can I choose the appropriate tool from the toolbox." Schwochow's collaborative approach seems to point the path toward the future, requiring information design and the information designer to become ever more flexible. "Take the example of cartography," Schwochow says. "That used to be an independent profession. Today we have to be strong in their capacity, too, and know how to deal with projections and simulations of earth's surface. That requires a great deal of know-how and basic understanding of the relevant technologies. 3D-graphics call for the ability to

think in spatial terms, multimedia ones for skills in HTML, Flash-Animation, and specialist 3D-software. At Golden Section Graphics we also write the copy of our visualizations ourselves, which calls for a thorough command of grammar and spelling." Schwochow did not learn any of these things during his studies, but instead either taught himself, peu à peu, over time, or in collaboration with specialists from his team.

Albeit keeping the hierarchies as flat as possible, there are art directors who take responsibility for individual projects. Golden Section Graphics always has several projects on the go. "Sketches and intermediate drafts are very important in the daily routine, not only internally, in consultation with the art director or me. They make the communication with the customer a lot easier too. Pencil sketches still have the necessary degree of abstraction and the customer can—given appropriate powers of imagination—still significantly influence the graphic. Once we are in the actual implementation process, revisions mean additional expenditure and unnecessary costs." Knowing that clients like to keep changing things until the end, Schwochow has established two to three rounds of agreements and sets binding timing in advance. He also calls in project managers, who facilitate complex workflows, especially when it comes to large-scale projects. "We are currently working on a project for which we need to create 1,000 infographics over the course of 2.5 years. That means around five graphic designers working on a daily basis to deliver an average of two finished graphics a day. That's a big challenge, especially as we do the research, text captions, and prepress work all ourselves. So both internal processes and the customer contact must run smoothly. In the case of the 1,000-graphics project, we have agreed upon a workflow to be maintained by both sides. Would there be chaos on the customer's side, we could try as we might but the project would simply fall apart and be uneconomical."

HISTORIC OLYMPIA
For In Graphics magazine, Golden Section Graphics

Economic efficiency appears to be a sore point in infographics. For although the demand is great and growing, fees generally fall far short of labor costs. "Clients tend to compare infographics to photographs or illustrations which are, in general, less time-consuming to produce." Free low-cost competitors further spoil prices. Schwochow once told the German magazine *Page* that he and his team happen to end up with the same hourly wage as their cleaner, and that his own income is now far from what he had last earned at *Stern*. Be that as it may, rather than complaining, he praises his independence and the great variety that working with Golden Section Graphics offers. Besides the usual business of around 100 annual commissions, he and his colleagues do not only produce *In Graphics,* but also a fine selection of posters and books. Most recently, Schwochow co-edited the infotainment tome *Deutschland Verstehen* (Understanding Germany), which reveals topical facts, features, and anecdotes on the country and its people in the illustrative language of infographics. In late 2014 Schwochow will start teaching at AID, the new Academy for Illustration and Design in Berlin. Together with his colleague Dirk Aschoff, who joined the team of Golden Section Graphics in 2011, he will pass on his expertise in visual storytelling and research to a new generation of students, placing particular importance on the development of journalistic skills such as research and source comparisons.

All entrepreneurial freedom bears the heavy responsibility of ensuring a stable commissions situation to pay Golden Section's eleven permanent and four freelance employees. Schwochow knows about the importance of visibility. "Since the company was founded, I have sought to appear in many publications, hold lectures, and simply be present on a widely scattered scale. We have also received a number of awards. Googling infographics in the German-speaking area, but also internationally, one will forcibly pretty quickly come across Golden Section Graphics and Jan Schwochow."

Golden Section does not, as a matter of principle, take part in unpaid pitches, nor do they actively recruit customers. There is no particular reason to do so. "*In Graphics* and the book *Deutschland Verstehen* are the best business cards we could possibly wish for."

Archived chronologically on his personal website, Schwochow's works—from the early 1990s *Stern* illustrations to recent elaborate pieces by Golden Section Graphics—not only chronicle his own professional progression, but also aptly demonstrate the advances digital technologies have brought to the field of infographics as a whole. "Today, the computer helps us tremendously—he is a loyal companion and accelerates work

ÖTZI
For In Graphics magazine,
Golden Section Graphics
Illustration: Golden Section
Graphics / Fabian Rüdy

processes. There are great tools that visualize complex data sets in seconds. This was not possible earlier. Nevertheless, we still do a lot of sketching by pencil and the best tool is still and always will be our brain. In the end, it is the idea that counts—style or medium are secondary. I'm not so sure that interactive graphics are really that much of a help. In my view, any interaction with a user must follow a clear communication objective. There is a lot of playful stuff and unnecessary bling-bling out there which no one actually needs. I am a very tactile person. I like books and we are working in that field a lot. Print graphics are important." At Golden Section Graphics they still generate the lion's share of revenues.

"Two-dimensional print graphics are indeed often complex enough, thus very time-consuming and expensive. An online version of a print graphic, animation, or interaction would require much more effort which most customers are not willing to pay for. We certainly like to work for all kinds of media and would love to become more involved in the field of exhibition design, fitting whole exhibition spaces with information graphics. In the end, we really do not care about the medium. We just like to tell visual stories."

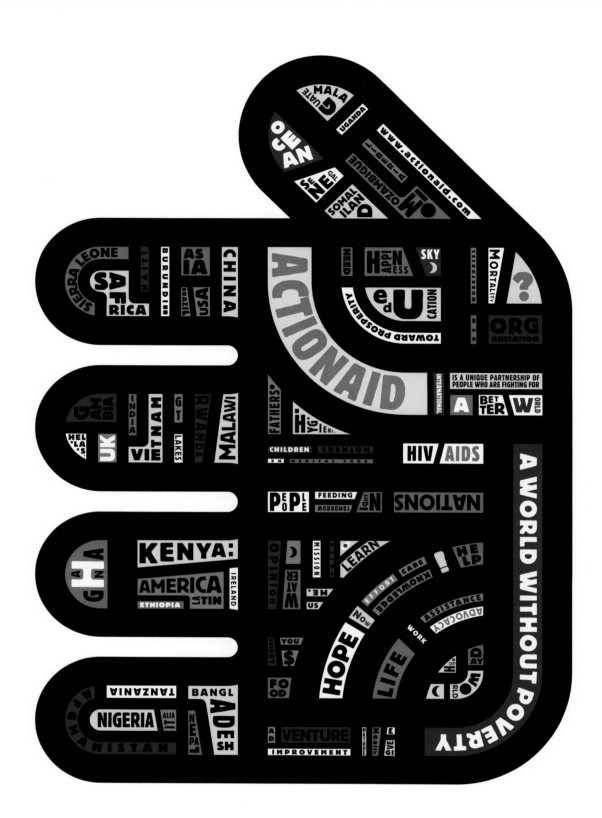

www.actionaid.org

act:onaid
international

Peter Grundy

"THE BACKBONE OF MY WORK IS NOT JUST TO CONVEY EXISTING INFORMATION, BUT TO HAVE OPINIONS AND ILLUSTRATE THOSE."

PLACE AND DATE OF BIRTH
Worcester, United Kingdom; 1954

COUNTRY OF RESIDENCE
United Kingdom

FAMILY STATUS
Married, 1 dog

EDUCATION / DEGREE
BA, Bath Academy of Art,
MA, Royal College of Art

ACTIVE IN THE FIELD OF ILLUSTRATION SINCE
1980

BREAKTHROUGH PROJECT
Shell Scenarios 2000–2010

KEY CLIENTS
Shell International, World Economic Forum,
Osborne Clarke, Guardian Newspapers

MOST RENOWNED PROJECTS
G2 Graphic, New energy future campaign,
Bodyparts diagram, Grundini book

COMMISSIONS PER YEAR
100–120

AVERAGE TURNAROUND TIME PER COMMISSION
1 day to 6 months

WORKSPACE
Home studio

EMPLOYEES
As Grundy & Northedge 5,
as Grundini none

AGENTS
Debut Art

HOW MUCH COMMISSION DO YOUR AGENTS TAKE
30%

TEACHING POSITIONS
Lectures at most British colleges

AWARDS
Various Design & Art Director awards and
Association of Illustrator awards over 30 years

MEMBER ASSOCIATIONS
D&AD and AOI

GALLERIES
None

Here within the chapter on infographics, it should be noted that Peter Grundy is no visual journalist. If he was, he would be Gonzo, inasmuch as his approach to accuracy is imbued with subjectivity and emotion. A sense of caricature-like simplification and abstraction fills his graphics with personality and life. Grundy is an illustrator who visualizes data with a twinkle in his eye. He has no fear in taking a clear stance, and his great talent turns everything he touches into accessible chunks of information. Enjoyable ones, even. His work is simple and thoroughly stripped down to the core, pictorial, and playful. He seems to be telling us not to take the world so seriously all the time, with all the weight we already bear.

One of Grundy's early data visualizations appeared in *Blueprint Magazine* in 1990, headlined "Doughnut London—Three decades that saw a city explode." He and his former business partner Tilly Northedge had illustrated London's expansion and Britain's industrial decline in a diagram of circular shape, vaguely reminiscent of a giant doughnut. It consisted of evenly colored shapes and pictograms, and some explanatory text. "It was the first piece of work whereby we wrote, designed, and illustrated a major infographic with total creative freedom," Grundy recalls. The piece, he said, laid the foundation for how he and Northedge would approach data visualization for decades to come. "We gathered information, had an opinion, and illustrated that in a visually exciting way that engaged the reader. Tell that to the traditionalists who thought it [infographics] was all about choosing colors to go in pie charts and deciding what size the

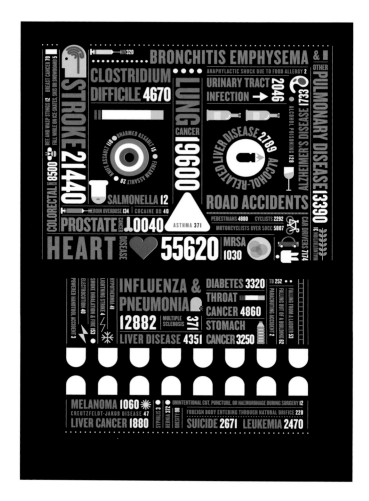

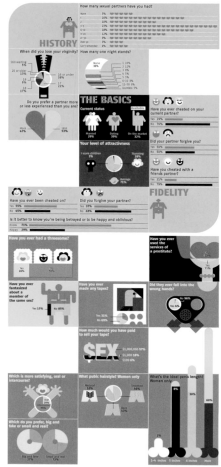

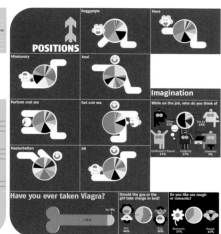

typeface was, and you'll understand some of the reception we received." These traditionalists would later denounce Grundy & Northedge's data visualizations as "cumbersome, wasteful, and lacking in logic, economy, and accuracy."

Grundy's readiness to defy such criticism with confidence and break with tradition in favor of subjectivity and experimental abstraction can be traced back to his days as a student at the Royal College of Art in London. Having graduated from the Bath Academy of Art in 1976, he attended the RCA's graphic design program, which was known to foster unconventional approaches. "Whereas Bath was a very traditional art college, the RCA in the 1970s was anything but. There I was taught by Lou Klein, a New York advertising guru who told us to forget everything we had learned previously and start again. His teaching philosophy was about ideas.

DEATH
(LEFT)
Client: Men's Health magazine, 2007
Art Direction: Kerem Shefik

MAXIM SEX SURVEY
(RIGHT)
Client: Maxim magazine, 2007
Art Direction: Craig Brooks

ACTIONAID POSTER
(PAGE 116)
Client: ActionAid, 2004

The first project we got was, 'a black man sees a white man for the first time, what happens next.' Our solutions were not to be visualized at all. Instead we got a one-minute phone call to Klein, when we were expected to explain our idea."

Lou Klein's way of thinking would play a major part in Grundy's career. He had met Tilly Northedge while still at RCA, and the two of them started a design group called Grundy & Northedge in 1980. Information design was not very popular at that time, and would not be for years to come. In 1996 Hugh Aldersey Williams, the then editor-at-large of *Graphis* magazine, referred to the lack of recognition in a feature on Grundy & Northedge: "The humble basic communication of information has never had the glamour of other areas of design," he wrote. "The creation of a poster casts the designer as an artist. Bringing into being a

corporate identity for some giant multinational company showcases the designer as a business strategist. But the design of a map for a housing project or a set of instructions for how to tie a bowtie—what sort of designer does jobs like these?"

Grundy & Northedge did such a job, not least triggered by what they considered the scarce quality of the field. "I think the total lack of good people doing information design in 1980 turned Tilly Northedge and I to this area." Also, information design was more about explaining than selling, which was more interesting to them at the time. The notion of infographics as a social contribution has motivated Grundy from the beginning, much more than financial incentives. "In 1980 the money offered was poor, because the area of work was new and regarded as unnecessary most of the time. Today, clients have accepted the value of providing information to an audience or customer as 'added value.' This was not accepted in the 1980s."

The way Grundy and Northedge played out their information design dream was characterized by a very graphic approach. "This was a very simple way of drawing that followed the creation of iconography and typography taught to us in the 1970s. It was a world without computers and therefore our tools were ruling pens, rulers, and paint, all things in fact found in a geometry set. Our drawings were very mechanical and simple and used form and color as the main ingredients to create elegance." When they started using computers in the early 1990s their work didn't look any different. "The computer software did what we had been doing for a decade previously with our geometry set."

Although the approach was rather graphic in form, Grundy & Northedge soon worked as illustrators, rather than designers. The shift was motivated by necessity. "It was all about budgets," Grundy says. "In 1989 the studio system was adopting the ad agency model, that is, people with defined roles. Designers had ideas, then got

GATWICK AIRPORT USER GUIDE
Client: Honey Creative, 2011
Art Direction: John Madden

in the best illustrator, photographer, and copywriter to realize that idea. This works fine so long as there's a budget to support that, but with information design the work was mainly in publishing and the money was low, so we found ourselves in a position where we not only had to come up with ideas, but find a way of making the images to go with them."

The very simple way of drawing that Grundy and Northedge developed for this was, as Grundy puts it, within their limited illustration capability. It would become the undoubtedly recognizable

Grundy & Northedge brand, which enriched the design scene for two and a half decades. When Tilly Northedge retired in 2006, Grundy changed the studio's name to Grundini, but remained true to what one might be inclined to speak of as the Grundy & Northedge style. Grundy avoids the term in context of his work. "Style isn't important at all in information design or any other area of illustration for that matter. It's the idea that is important. The most important part of a Grundy image is the idea. Style is simply the way the idea is communicated."

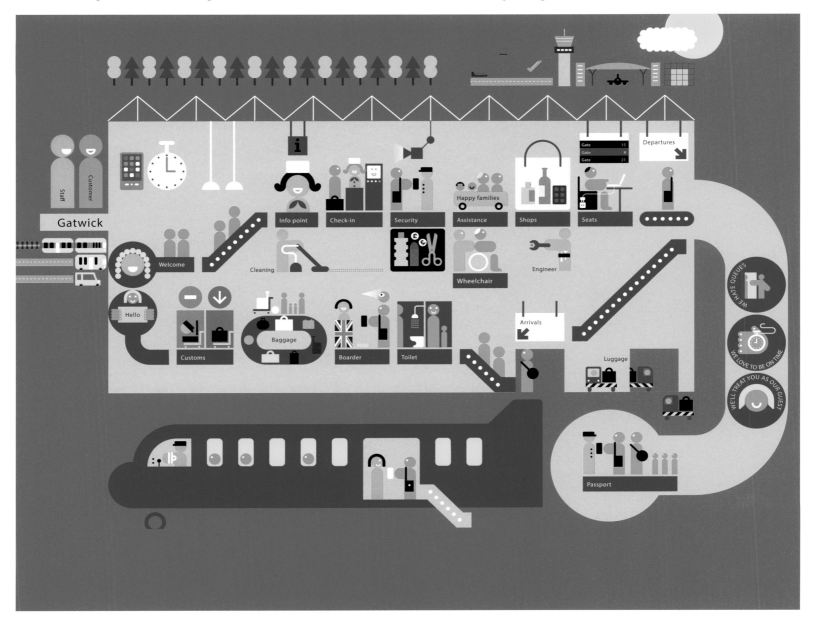

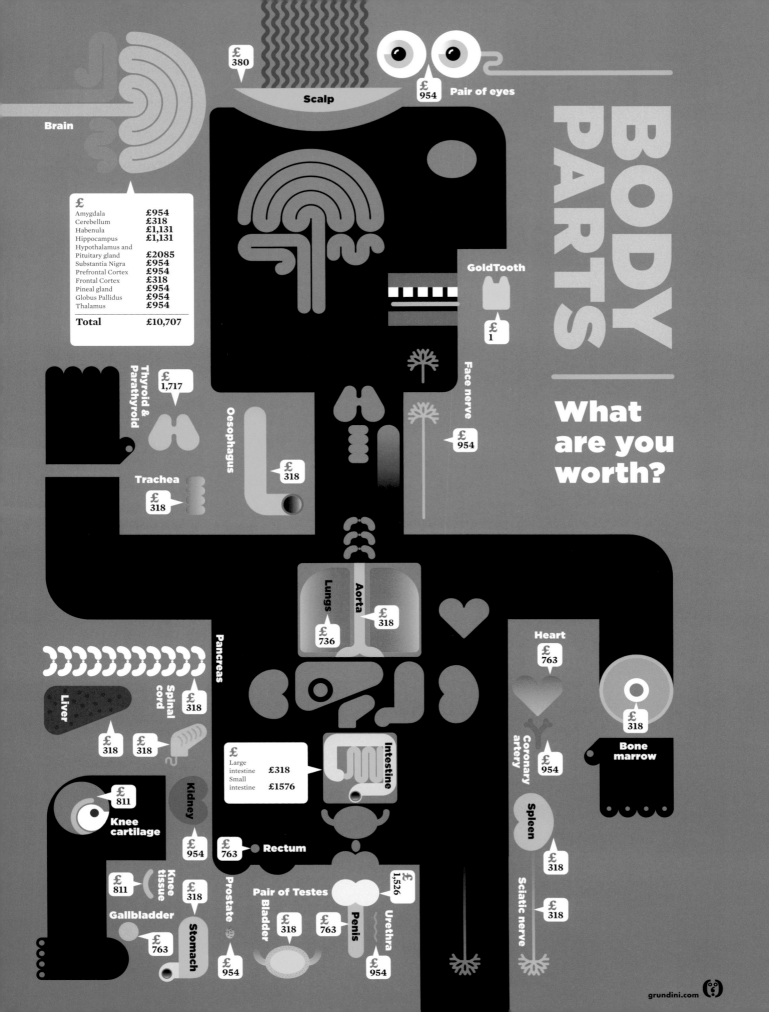

BODY PARTS

What are you worth?

Brain

£ 380 — Scalp

£ 954 — **Pair of eyes**

£	
Amygdala	£954
Cerebellum	£318
Habenula	£1,131
Hippocampus	£1,131
Hypothalamus and Pituitary gland	£2085
Substantia Nigra	£954
Prefrontal Cortex	£954
Frontal Cortex	£318
Pineal gland	£954
Globus Pallidus	£954
Thalamus	£954
Total	**£10,707**

GoldTooth — £ 1

Face nerve — £ 954

Thyroid & Parathyroid — £ 1,717

Oesophagus — £ 318

Trachea — £ 318

Lungs — £ 736

Aorta — £ 318

Heart — £ 763

Bone marrow — £ 318

Pancreas

Spinal cord — £ 318

Liver — £ 318

Coronary artery — £ 954

Spleen — £ 318

£	
Large intestine	£318
Small intestine	£1576

Intestine

Sciatic nerve — £ 318

Knee cartilage — £ 811

Kidney — £ 954

Rectum — £ 763

Knee tissue — £ 811

Prostate — £ 318

Pair of Testes — £ 1,526

Gallbladder — £ 763

Stomach — £ 954

Bladder — £ 318

Penis — £ 763

Urethra — £ 954

grundini.com

Grundy develops ideas through reading and talking, sketching, note-making, or just plain thinking, smoothly switching back and forth between these techniques until he arrives at a witty solution. Usually, that amounts to around 40% of the overall time he takes for a project, leaving around 60% for the actual illustration. That is, since Grundy and Northedge crossed over from pencils and paint to computers in 1994, exclusively drawing in Adobe Illustrator.

Having spent a quarter of a century developing a way of thinking and drawing that simplified complicated things, Grundy is quite clear about what sets his approach apart from infographic design, in the traditional sense. "The backbone of my work is not just to convey existing information, but to have opinions and illustrate those." He refers to the G2 project, a weekly graphic spread for the *Guardian*, for which he and Northedge visualized various social and political issues like the arms trade, health and fitness, or childcare in the U.K. Aside from facts, each spread contained statistical information. "The big picture was in each case our opinion on the world and how it looked."

Over the years, Grundy, first in collaboration with Northedge and then on his own as Grundini, has illustrated things as diverse as the workings of nuclear reactors, waste cycles, the mazy interior structure of the Victoria and Albert Museum, the meeting of the G5, and the achievements of famous British physicists, imbuing them with a light and very personal dimension. "I seek in every idea a visual metaphor, often using humor that brings the information closer to the reader," he says. Humor has proven an effective strategy for Grundy, but must be treated with due caution. "If humor plays a decisive role in your ideas, the messages can easily become obscured," Grundy notes, in particular view of international projects.

In the 1990s, when emails and file transfers changed everything, Grundy began working for people all over the world. He describes how the digital revolution

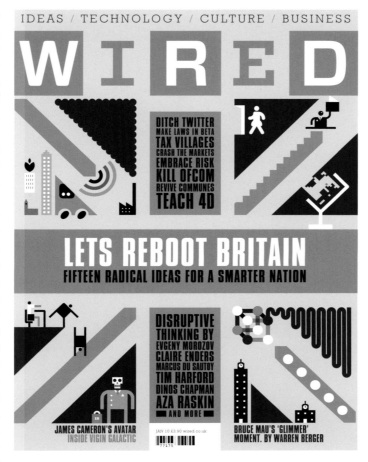

BODY PARTS DIAGRAM
(LEFT PAGE)
Client: Esquire magazine, 2007
Art Direction: Alex Breuer

REBOOT BRITAIN
(TOP)
Client: Wired UK, 2009
Art Direction: Steve Peck

CR COVER
(BOTTOM)
Client: Creative Review, 2011
Art Direction: Paul Pensom

has not only expanded his customer base, but also changed his working process. "In the 80s and 90s I spent more time with clients. There was no email, there were meetings and phone calls. When offered work, I went to the client and took a brief. A week later I would go back with an idea, and when approved, I would do the artwork which again I would deliver by hand." Today, personal contact is rare. "In fact I have regular clients whom I don't ever see, I'm not even sure what they look like. Perhaps they don't know what I look like! This is a shame and I do try and visit people whenever possible. However, I have become experienced at communicating with people over the years and the global environment has not become an issue as of yet, although I do hate conference calls."

Grundy & Northedge grew on an international level throughout the 1990s, and in addition to the editorial clientele,

they gained advertising, corporate, and institutional commissioners who took a liking to their visual language. They started to work for the World Bank, the UN, and other non-profit organizations. In 2001 Alan Fletcher introduced Grundy to Shell Scenarios, a research platform that the energy and petrochemical giant set up to explore alternative views on the future of economics, energy supply and demand, geopolitical shifts, and social change, and a project that merged information design and corporate communications to create plausible stories around the Shell brand.

There was initially a temptation to grow, like other studios, but because of the very individual nature of their work—they employed five people as assistants over the years—they chose not to expand their business beyond that. This was mainly due to the fact that they considered it difficult to delegate illustration, which had become the core of the "G&N offer." Indeed, working together creatively is not always easy, and even seeming dream teams like Grundy and Northedge don't just fall from heaven. "Northedge and I spent many years finding our space together," remembers Grundy. "Usually business partners are two (or more) different people. Often a creative and a business partner. Tilly Northedge and I were not like that, we were both creative, and initially there were tensions that arose from two people that really believed in a mission. However, looking back, we did have different roles. I was the intuitive one whereas Tilly Northedge was the

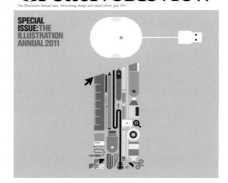

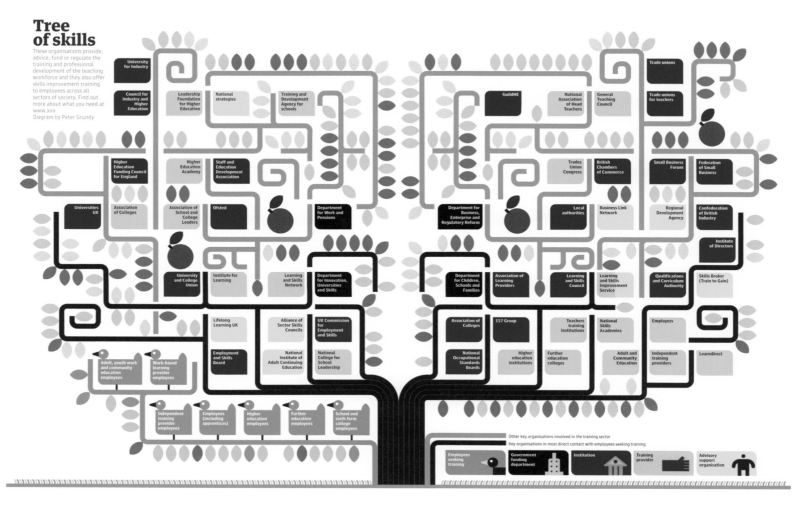

Tree of skills

These organisations provide, advice, fund or regulate the training and professional development of the teaching workforce and they also offer skills improvement training to employees across all sectors of society. Find out more about what you need at www.xxx

Diagram by Peter Grundy

logical one, but I guess we didn't know that at the time."

Looking back on 26 years of the two working together, one of their RCA colleagues, Phil Wong, associate at Carter Wong Design London, described the "unlike bedfellows" in an article that appeared in the October 2006 edition of *Design Week*. "Peter Grundy is the extrovert and takes centre stage while Tilly Northedge, precise and considered, is content to be in the background. Or perhaps it is a status quo formed by years of interaction, for it was not always so. After a Grundy-dominated meeting in the infancy of the partnership Northedge asked, 'Next time can I say something?'"

Extroversion and proactivity are benefits in business. Grundy has drawn

LIFE LONG LEARNING DIAGRAM
(THIS PAGE)
Client: The Guardian, 2009
Art Direction: Richard Doughty

TREE OF EXTINCTION DIAGRAM
(RIGHT PAGE)
Client: Audubon magazine, 2010
Art Direction: Kevin Fisher

on it until now, working on his own as Grundini. "I must have shown portfolios to over 1,000 people since leaving the RCA in 1979. Today I have a reputation which I've carefully built over the years by events, printed materials, and articles during the Grundy & Northedge years." He claims to not be much of a networker. "But I do have a very good website." The site is relatively new, content-managed, and entertainingly informative as one might expect. "It is estimated that there are 217.6 billion Lego bricks in the world. That's 62 for every man, woman, and child alive today," the "Bimonthly Look at Life," a web exclusive, reveals. In 2007, Grundy produced a print publication showcasing his work, with a focus on the Grundini years. "It is a book of pictures, some real

jobs, others personal, divided into five themes, with the invention of allowing me to stop the past, have a breather, and start the future."

With Grundini, Grundy has stopped doing large projects to focus on smaller ones instead. "Why? Because large projects are about 20% creative and 80% management, and I find the latter boring." Small, especially self-initiated projects may have no immediate commercial gain, but he appreciates them for providing priceless freedom to come up with fresh ideas, uncontaminated by client, time, and commercial constraints. "It's projects like the Grundini book, the most expensive therapeutic exercise I've ever done, that lay seeds that I can develop in future jobs." Grundy also mentions his 2003 "Squarehead" exhibition

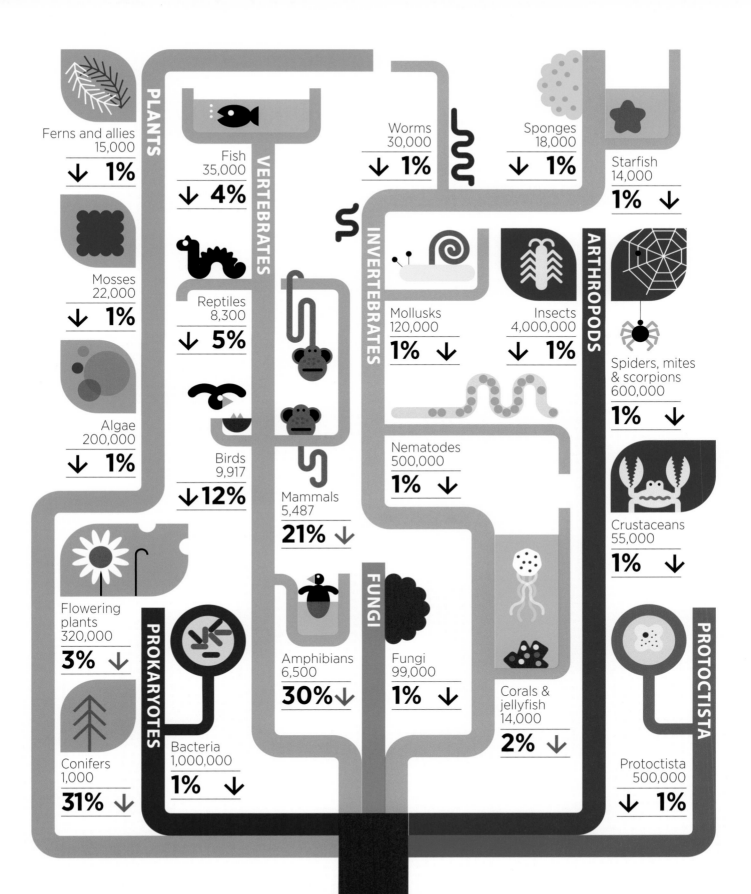

PLANTS

Ferns and allies
15,000
↓ **1%**

Mosses
22,000
↓ **1%**

Algae
200,000
↓ **1%**

Flowering plants
320,000
3% ↓

Conifers
1,000
31% ↓

VERTEBRATES

Fish
35,000
↓ **4%**

Reptiles
8,300
↓ **5%**

Birds
9,917
↓ **12%**

Mammals
5,487
21% ↓

Amphibians
6,500
30% ↓

INVERTEBRATES

Worms
30,000
↓ **1%**

Mollusks
120,000
1% ↓

Nematodes
500,000
1% ↓

Fungi
99,000
1% ↓

Corals & jellyfish
14,000
2% ↓

Sponges
18,000
↓ **1%**

ARTHROPODS

Starfish
14,000
1% ↓

Insects
4,000,000
↓ **1%**

Spiders, mites & scorpions
600,000
1% ↓

Crustaceans
55,000
1% ↓

FUNGI

PROTOCTISTA

Protoctista
500,000
↓ **1%**

PROKARYOTES

Bacteria
1,000,000
1% ↓

TREE OF EXTINCTION

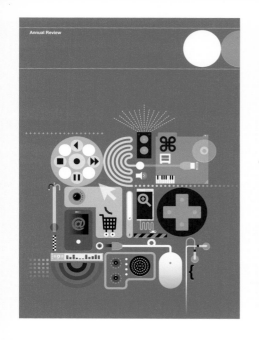

How to save 49p a day.

✗ No. you're in the wrong position.

✓ That's better.

How to find 49p a day.

✗ Cuddling will not generate funds.

✓ Now you're on your way..

How to make 49p a day.

✗ Something not right here.

✓ That's walking.

in this context, which featured a series of art prints based on typographic ideas. "The financial contributions I've made over the years to produce these 'things' is considerable but worth it."

Grundy does not do pitches anymore. He and Northedge used to, back in the Grundy & Northedge days, but rarely won any. "In my experience, the sort of people and companies who seek tenders are the first to be scared off by an uncompromisingly distinctive approach. One of the advantages of a good website is it means people have usually made the decision to use me before they get in touch." Grundini is a limited company, but requires careful organization, which Grundy does himself with the assistance of an accountant. He claims to be good with money. "One of the most important things to understand in this business is the value of an illustration. It's not just the process to answer a brief and do a picture, it's the extent that the picture is used by a client and the value it is to a client. For instance, an icon produced for a magazine with a single

OSBORNE CLARKE COVER SET
(LEFT PAGE)
Client: Osborne Clarke, 2008–13
Art Direction: Maryanne Beavers

BT INTERNET CAMPAIGN
(THIS PAGE)
Client: BTinternet. AMV, 2003

publication is low value financially, but an icon produced as part of a brand identity with multiple use is high value financially." Grundy is represented by Debutart, and he praises his agents for their helpfulness over the last 10 years, especially in building up his advertising work. He promotes his new, more independent way of working very actively and effectively by himself, with things like the website or Grundini, the book. "It turned off some clients, but turned on a whole load more, and brings me neatly to the present day, where I'm still explaining complicated things using a simple, visual language with fun ideas."

He does so indeed, and spares no effort. "When I was at the RCA, I remember a piece of advice given by a tutor. He said this business requires 'total commitment' and I've remembered that ever since." If Grundy turns down work, it is rarely to free up time for leisure. "Both my wife and I are creative, so we understand and manage." Instead, he takes the liberty to focus on what he is best at. "Clients who

come along with a fully rounded idea of what they want regard the illustrator as some sort of stylist. My offer is the idea, that is what people pay for. They get the picture for free!"

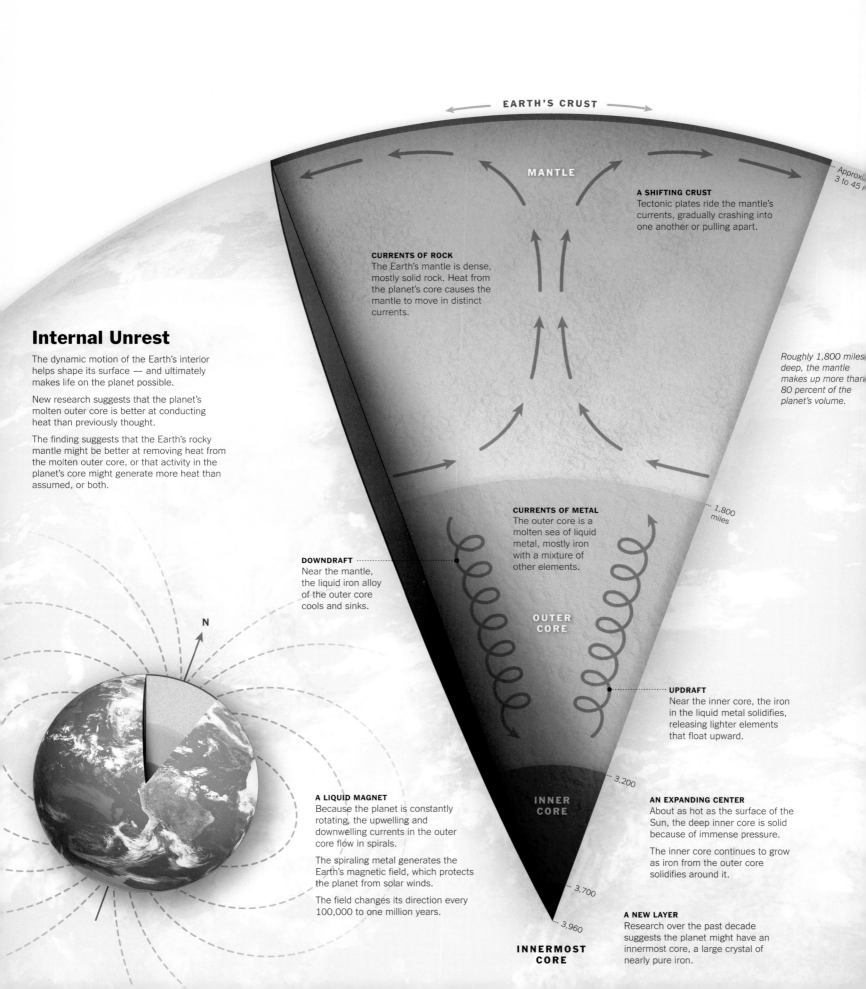

EARTH'S CRUST

MANTLE

Internal Unrest

The dynamic motion of the Earth's interior helps shape its surface — and ultimately makes life on the planet possible.

New research suggests that the planet's molten outer core is better at conducting heat than previously thought.

The finding suggests that the Earth's rocky mantle might be better at removing heat from the molten outer core, or that activity in the planet's core might generate more heat than assumed, or both.

A SHIFTING CRUST
Tectonic plates ride the mantle's currents, gradually crashing into one another or pulling apart.

CURRENTS OF ROCK
The Earth's mantle is dense, mostly solid rock. Heat from the planet's core causes the mantle to move in distinct currents.

Approxi...
3 to 45...

Roughly 1,800 miles... deep, the mantle makes up more than... 80 percent of the planet's volume.

CURRENTS OF METAL
The outer core is a molten sea of liquid metal, mostly iron with a mixture of other elements.

... 1,800 miles

DOWNDRAFT
Near the mantle, the liquid iron alloy of the outer core cools and sinks.

OUTER CORE

UPDRAFT
Near the inner core, the iron in the liquid metal solidifies, releasing lighter elements that float upward.

... 3,200

N

INNER CORE

A LIQUID MAGNET
Because the planet is constantly rotating, the upwelling and downwelling currents in the outer core flow in spirals.

The spiraling metal generates the Earth's magnetic field, which protects the planet from solar winds.

The field changes its direction every 100,000 to one million years.

AN EXPANDING CENTER
About as hot as the surface of the Sun, the deep inner core is solid because of immense pressure.

The inner core continues to grow as iron from the outer core solidifies around it.

... 3,700

... 3,960

INNERMOST CORE

A NEW LAYER
Research over the past decade suggests the planet might have an innermost core, a large crystal of nearly pure iron.

Jonathan Corum

PLACE AND DATE OF BIRTH
Boston, Massachusetts, United States; 1973

COUNTRY OF RESIDENCE
United States

FAMILY STATUS
Married, 1 son

EDUCATION/DEGREE
BA in Art and East Asian Studies, Yale University

ACTIVE IN THE FIELD OF ILLUSTRATION SINCE
1995

BREAKTHROUGH PROJECT
Online work at style.org

KEY CLIENTS
The New York Times, The Font Bureau

MOST RENOWNED PROJECTS
Kepler's Tally of Planets (2013), Guantánamo Detainees (2011), Lunge Feeding (2007), Estimating the Airspeed Velocity of an Unladen Swallow (2003)

COMMISSIONS PER YEAR
100 graphics a year for the New York Times, a handful of freelance projects through 13pt freelance studio

AVERAGE TURNAROUND TIME PER COMMISSION
Most of the graphics for the New York Times are finished in a few days, freelance projects can take longer, depending on the type of work

WORKSPACE
During the week at the New York Times Building; 13pt is a home studio

EMPLOYEES
None

AGENTS
None

HOW MUCH COMMISSION DO YOUR AGENTS TAKE
None

TEACHING POSITIONS
None

AWARDS (SELECTION)
16 awards from the Society for News Design and 8 medals from Malofiej, including Best in Show; National Design Award for communication design with the New York Times graphics desk (2009)

MEMBER ASSOCIATIONS
None

GALLERIES
None

"I TRY TO APPLY COMMON SENSE, WITH A FOCUS ON CLARITY AND SIMPLICITY. I TRY NOT TO HAVE A FIXED STYLE BEYOND THAT. IF I'M SUCCESSFUL THE RESULT WILL HOPEFULLY BE ELEGANT. IF I'M NOT SUCCESSFUL, THE RESULT WILL HOPEFULLY BE AT LEAST UNDERSTANDABLE."

The *New York Times* building has conference rooms and work rooms of different sizes, each labeled with a small glass plate. At the top of each plate there is a cryptic room code in white type and numbers: "02E3-251." Below it: either "Conference Room," "Team Room," or "Work Room." When people organize meetings at the *Times*, they send emails like "We're meeting in Medium Conference Room 02P5-345/8AV HQ 02FL, and when I figure out exactly which room that is, I'll let you know."

Jonathan Corum, information designer at the *Times*, has observed the situation with interest, and considered it in preparation for a talk he held at the Tapestry Conference in March 2013, a relatively new event designed to advance interactive online storytelling with data. Cut out of the final talk due to time limitations, he revisits the consideration on his website: "The design is by Pentagram, and it looks good—so what's the problem? The problem it that, after more than 5 years in the building, nobody knows what the code means. Most people realize that the first two digits show the floor number—these photos are all from the 2nd floor—but that's about it."

Corum's specialty is in making information clear and accessible to the broadest possible public. Design, to him, is most importantly a means to communicate efficiently, and unmistakably. And so, he considers the *Times*' office signage a great example of how the ensemble of "overwhelming detail" and "oversimplification," with nothing in between, can end up rather meaningless. "Keep in mind that 16 digits are enough to distinguish my credit card number from the tens of millions of other cards out there, but these 16 characters don't contain enough legible information to locate a conference room." He tells of employees solving the problem by talking about rooms in relation to internal landmarks. "We're in the room with the folding divider below the Page One conference room," and other such descriptions are used.

To Corum, good design makes periphrases obsolete. He advocates clarity and user-friendly form, which is why he would take great pleasure in redesigning

benefit from a new tax form redesigned by Corum. Thus far, millions benefit from Corum's infographics, more than 1,000 of which have appeared in the *New York Times,* mostly in the Science section that he coordinates. "My work has not appeared in galleries, but my graphics on newsprint have been used as packing material, to house train puppies, and to line bird and hampster cages across the country," Corum

visualized glaciers melting and respective prognoses. On the lighter side, he's created an alleged formula to predict how soon celebrity marriages blow up, or the fastest solution to solve a Rubik's Cube. Taking great pleasure in the variety of his work, he is constantly trying to research and understand new material, to then find an elegant way to explain it. His graphics for the *Times* have won 16 awards from the Society

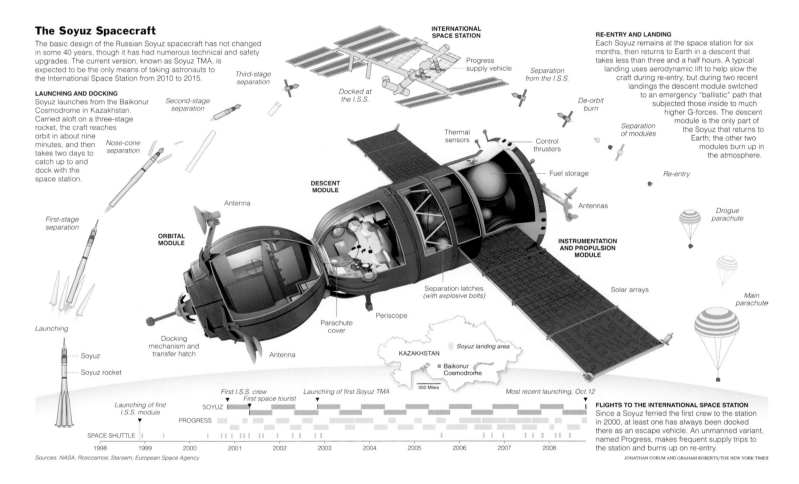

The Soyuz Spacecraft

The basic design of the Russian Soyuz spacecraft has not changed in some 40 years, though it has had numerous technical and safety upgrades. The current version, known as Soyuz TMA, is expected to be the only means of taking astronauts to the International Space Station from 2010 to 2015.

LAUNCHING AND DOCKING
Soyuz launches from the Baikonur Cosmodrome in Kazakhstan. Carried aloft on a three-stage rocket, the craft reaches orbit in about nine minutes, and then takes two days to catch up to and dock with the space station.

INTERNATIONAL SPACE STATION

RE-ENTRY AND LANDING
Each Soyuz remains at the space station for six months, then returns to Earth in a descent that takes less than three and a half hours. A typical landing uses aerodynamic lift to help slow the craft during re-entry, but during two recent landings the descent module switched to an emergency "ballistic" path that subjected those inside to much higher G-forces. The descent module is the only part of the Soyuz that returns to Earth; the other two modules burn up in the atmosphere.

Third-stage separation · Second-stage separation · Nose-cone separation · First-stage separation · Launching · Soyuz · Soyuz rocket · ORBITAL MODULE · Antenna · Docking mechanism and transfer hatch · Antenna · DESCENT MODULE · Parachute cover · Periscope · Separation latches (with explosive bolts) · Thermal sensors · Control thrusters · Fuel storage · Progress supply vehicle · Docked at the I.S.S. · Separation from the I.S.S. · De-orbit burn · Separation of modules · Antennas · INSTRUMENTATION AND PROPULSION MODULE · Solar arrays · Re-entry · Drogue parachute · Main parachute

KAZAKHSTAN · Soyuz landing area · Baikonur Cosmodrome · 300 Miles

First I.S.S. crew · First space tourist · Launching of first Soyuz TMA · Most recent launching, Oct.12 · Launching of first I.S.S. module · SOYUZ · PROGRESS · SPACE SHUTTLE

1998 1999 2000 2001 2002 2003 2004 2005 2006 2007 2008

FLIGHTS TO THE INTERNATIONAL SPACE STATION
Since a Soyuz ferried the first crew to the station in 2000, at least one has always been docked there as an escape vehicle. An unmanned variant, named Progress, makes frequent supply trips to the station and burns up on re-entry.

Sources: NASA; Roscosmos; Starsem; European Space Agency

JONATHAN CORUM AND GRAHAM ROBERTS/THE NEW YORK TIMES

the U.S. tax forms. "Every year when I'm doing my taxes I think: I'm a college-educated designer and I can barely make any sense out of this." Tax forms are seen by tens of millions of Americans each year and are the cause of much frustration, in part because the design is terrible and the writing is extremely complicated.

There is every reason to believe that tens of millions of U.S. citizens would

THE SOYUZ SPACECRAFT
(TOP)
Jonathan Corum with Graham Roberts for the New York Times, 2008

INTERNAL UNREST
(PAGE 126)
Jonathan Corum with Frank O'Connell for the New York Times, 2012

says. Most importantly, it has made the world a bit more understandable.

As part of his position at the *Times,* which he has held since 2005, Corum designs roughly 100 graphics a year. He has illustrated sun storm forecasts, examined spacesuit collections, explained procedures of Mars missions, highlighted genome sequencing methods in cancer treatment, and

for News Design and 8 medals from the international Malofiej competition, including "Best in Show." In 2009, the *Times* graphics desk received a National Design Award for communication design. Corum takes it with modesty. "I don't think I'm famous enough for my career to have milestones!"

Corum was set on the path to his career during high school, when his father gave him Edward Tufte's first two books on information graphics, The *Visual Display of Quantitative Information and Envisioning Information*. "I was wondering if I should apply to art school at the time. But then, those books made so much sense to me, and included such elegant combinations of maps and charts and illustrations, that I knew I wanted to be a designer." Not knowing where to study with a focus on information graphics he enrolled in graphic design and Japanese art history at Yale. After graduation he got a job at the digital type studio and foundry Font Bureau, where he drew type and worked on a variety of TrueType hinting projects. "I kept meaning to go back to graduate school in design, but never stopped working."

In 1998, Corum established 13pt, an information design studio. He has been

ORBITAL MECHANICS
(RIGHT)
Jonathan Corum for the
New York Times, 2010

DRIVING GALAXIES APART
(BOTTOM)
Jonathan Corum for the
New York Times, 2008

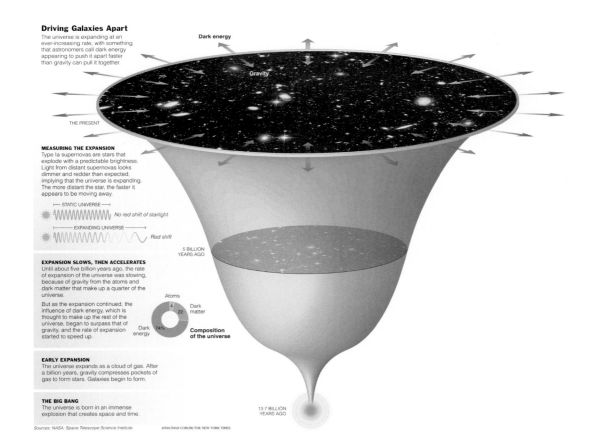

senior designer at the design firm Interactive Bureau, and design director at Online Retail Partners, a company that assists retailers wanting to set up successful e-commerce businesses, where he oversaw the information and interaction design of various web-based projects. He believes that it was not least the comprehensive body work that had accumulated in his online portfolio at style.org that got him the attention of the *New York Times*' editors who would offer him the position as Graphics Editor. In retrospect, the short detour through type design and the long detour through information architecture and web design appear as important stages of Corum's professional development. "I think type design was very good training for the eye and the hand, and web design was good training for thinking about and designing for someone else, instead of myself. So in a way, both of those disciplines have carried over into my current work as an information designer."

In fact, the term "information design" comes close to covering the types of work Corum has done in the past, it encompasses type design and web design, as well as his current role at the *New York Times*.

Frozen Carbon

Perennially frozen ground, known as permafrost, underlies nearly a quarter of the Northern Hemisphere and stores a huge amount of carbon.

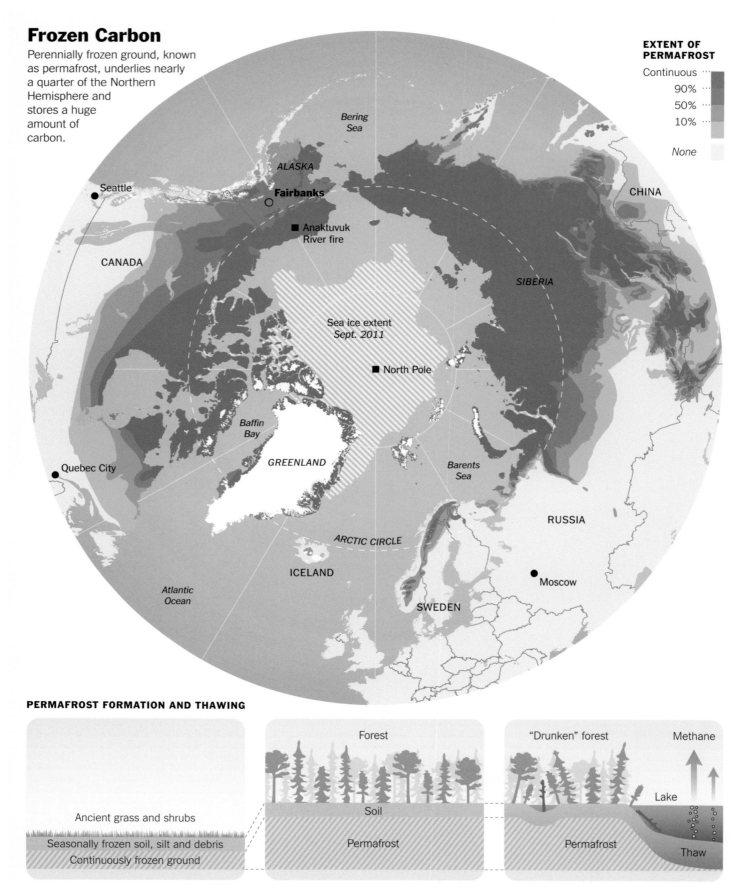

EXTENT OF PERMAFROST

Continuous
90%
50%
10%

None

Bering Sea

ALASKA
Seattle
Fairbanks
■ Anaktuvuk River fire

CHINA

CANADA

SIBERIA

Sea ice extent
Sept. 2011

■ North Pole

Baffin Bay

GREENLAND

Barents Sea

Quebec City

RUSSIA

ARCTIC CIRCLE

ICELAND

Moscow

Atlantic Ocean

SWEDEN

PERMAFROST FORMATION AND THAWING

Ancient grass and shrubs

Seasonally frozen soil, silt and debris
Continuously frozen ground

Forest

Soil

Permafrost

"Drunken" forest
Methane

Lake

Permafrost

Thaw

ANCIENT PLANTS removed carbon from the atmosphere by absorbing carbon dioxide. When the plants died, much of their stored carbon was trapped and frozen in layers of soil and glacial silt.

OVER THOUSANDS OF YEARS the layers of soil and debris built up to form a deep layer of continuously frozen ground, called permafrost, which now contains twice as much carbon as the entire atmosphere.

CARBON ESCAPES when organic material in permafrost thaws and decomposes. Carbon dioxide is released in aerated areas, but in lakes and wetlands carbon bubbles up as methane, an especially potent greenhouse gas.

Sources: National Snow and Ice Data Center; BioScience; National Research Council Canada; NASA

JONATHAN CORUM/THE NEW YORK TIMES

"I try to focus on explaining information simply and clearly, regardless of the medium," Corum explains. He does not consider himself an illustrator, as illustration is only one aspect of his work. "I try to merge illustration, maps, charts, design, and annotation into coherent graphics, not keep them separate."

Essentially, what Corum does is translate. "Scientists usually speak at a very high or advanced level to an audience of their peers, and I try to translate what they are saying for a more general audience. In doing that translation, I don't hesitate to take ideas or parts of graphics from the scientist and then redraw or collage them in a more common-sense way. Some people use the term 'visual journalist,' but I think I'm more of a designer than a true journalist." Corum is usually not coming up with content, but trying to explain it more simply.

A good infographic, to Corum, should explain and should let the information come forward. "The design itself should disappear." Corum distinguishes between his approach and that of data visualization. "The terms are not well defined, but I often think that 'data visualization' puts an emphasis on representing the data in a striking way, but with less of an emphasis on explaining the data. I'm less interested in visualization than in conveying understanding. I try to focus on the information that I'm trying to explain, instead of focusing on making something that looks cool."

The core, again, is to make content accessible to the audience, and in that lies what Corum considers the most common error of his trade. "I think some people who design visualizations and information graphics don't think very much about the person on the receiving end who will be looking at the graphic. It's easy to fall in love with an early sketch or a striking image, and not question whether it's really the best way to explain the information. I strongly feel that you should not design for yourself, but should design for your audience. Depending on what kind of

THE H1N1 SWINE FLU VIRUS contains a mixture of genes from human, avian and swine influenzas.

Like all flus the virus is mutating rapidly, but it currently lacks several genes thought to increase lethality.

VIRUS — RNA

H1 Hemagglutinin
N1 Neuraminidase

Human

Avian

American swine

Eurasian swine

artist or designer you are, you might have a reader, viewer, listener, or user. Keeping that audience in mind at all times can help you avoid some of the pitfalls of designing for yourself."

In accordance with his service-oriented approach, Corum values practicality

over style. "I try to apply common sense, with a focus on clarity and simplicity. I try not to have a fixed style beyond that. If I'm successful the result will hopefully be elegant. If I'm not successful, the result will hopefully be at least understandable. A client once said I have a 'distinctive, radically clear style' and I thought that was a very high compliment."

If that is his style, he developed it by aggressively deleting and simplifying things. "I try to take away as much as possible without changing the meaning of the graphic. Simplifying and editing are important activities, but I try to keep everything in the world of facts. In some cases, like the drawing of a cell, I might need to dramatically simplify everything, or resort to metaphor, but I try to have scientists look at my work and make sure that I'm not designing fiction."

Stepping aside to elucidate the subject matter, Corum aims to design a framework for the information that is as clean and objective as possible. He tries not to introduce his own opinions or thoughts about the topic, but instead susses out its central idea, translating it to a new audience by eliminating scientific jargon or technical terms. He is not promoting or criticizing this core idea, just trying to explain it more simply.

In a recent talk, Corum declared: "If you spend more time editing your graphic than you do creating it, you're doing

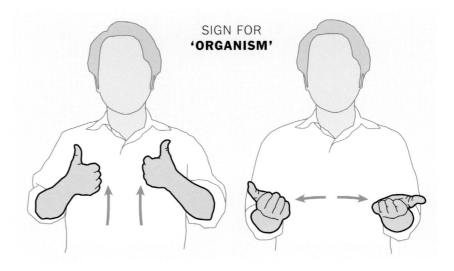

SIGN FOR
'ORGANISM'

something right." That is the strategy that defines his workflow. If the graphic is based on a report or scientific paper, he usually starts by reading the paper and looking for background material or related papers by the same authors. Once he believes he has a good understanding of what the science is, he tries to find the central idea or core piece of information that needs to be conveyed to the readers.

"From there it becomes more of a traditional design problem." Corum does sketches by hand, then goes on to mainly

FROM MICROBES TO CRUDE
Jonathan Corum for the New York Times, 2010

work in Adobe Illustrator. "Putting something down on paper usually doesn't take very long, but I want it to be the right thing. And so I often spend more time researching than designing, and then more time editing and simplifying the final graphic. I try to understand more about the topic than what I actually put into the graphic."

The path may be long, but time is usually short. At the *Times,* there are two kinds of deadlines: breaking news or daily graphics that will appear in the paper the following day, which might

require a late night of work; and long-term projects that might not appear for several weeks. Corum is one of the few people on more of a weekly schedule, because the Science section comes out once a week. "That gives me a fairly regular work schedule, and gives me the luxury of being able to set a graphic aside at night and look at it with fresh eyes the next morning. With daily graphics or breaking news you are usually rushing to finish and usually don't have a chance to see it again with fresh eyes."

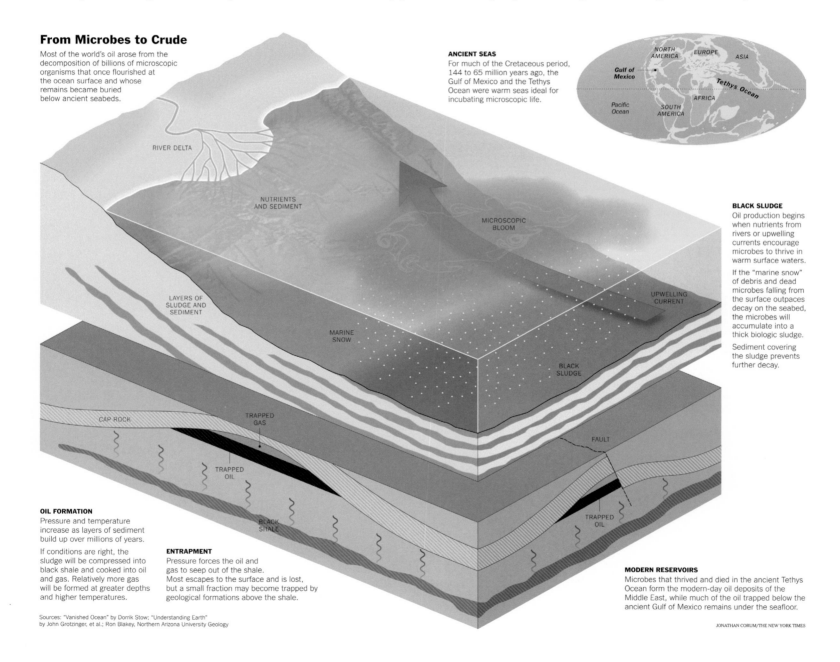

From Microbes to Crude

Most of the world's oil arose from the decomposition of billions of microscopic organisms that once flourished at the ocean surface and whose remains became buried below ancient seabeds.

ANCIENT SEAS
For much of the Cretaceous period, 144 to 65 million years ago, the Gulf of Mexico and the Tethys Ocean were warm seas ideal for incubating microscopic life.

BLACK SLUDGE
Oil production begins when nutrients from rivers or upwelling currents encourage microbes to thrive in warm surface waters.

If the "marine snow" of debris and dead microbes falling from the surface outpaces decay on the seabed, the microbes will accumulate into a thick biologic sludge.

Sediment covering the sludge prevents further decay.

OIL FORMATION
Pressure and temperature increase as layers of sediment build up over millions of years.

If conditions are right, the sludge will be compressed into black shale and cooked into oil and gas. Relatively more gas will be formed at greater depths and higher temperatures.

ENTRAPMENT
Pressure forces the oil and gas to seep out of the shale. Most escapes to the surface and is lost, but a small fraction may become trapped by geological formations above the shale.

MODERN RESERVOIRS
Microbes that thrived and died in the ancient Tethys Ocean form the modern-day oil deposits of the Middle East, while much of the oil trapped below the ancient Gulf of Mexico remains under the seafloor.

Sources: "Vanished Ocean" by Dorrik Stow; "Understanding Earth" by John Grotzinger, et al.; Ron Blakey, Northern Arizona University Geology

JONATHAN CORUM/THE NEW YORK TIMES

The Battle of Agincourt

An army led by King Henry V of England defeated a French force near the village of Agincourt on Oct. 25, 1415. Medieval reports describe the French Army as being much larger.

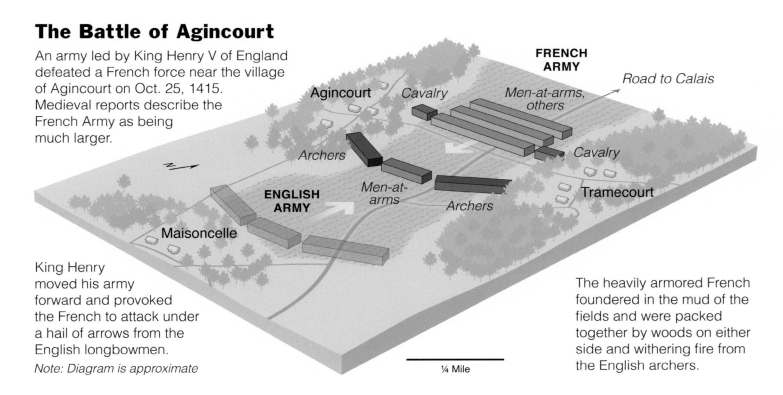

FRENCH ARMY

Road to Calais

Agincourt

Cavalry

Men-at-arms, others

Archers

ENGLISH ARMY

Men-at-arms

Cavalry

Archers

Tramecourt

Maisoncelle

King Henry moved his army forward and provoked the French to attack under a hail of arrows from the English longbowmen.

Note: Diagram is approximate

¼ Mile

The heavily armored French foundered in the mud of the fields and were packed together by woods on either side and withering fire from the English archers.

Corum tries to come in a little early to begin the day with a block of uninterrupted time. "I only listen to music while working, quietly playing Scottish bagpipe tunes. Music with lyrics can be a distraction. Solo bagpipe music has great rhythm, a great history, and no lyrics. I also try to minimize popups, messages, and other distractions on my computer. Blocks of uninterrupted work are the most satisfying and productive for me." Having had some of those, he usually manages to leave a little earlier at night.

Corum still runs 13pt, the information design studio that was his full-time job for years before he joined the *Times*. The studio is just him, working from his home office whenever he finds the time and with no agent, getting all his commissions from word of mouth. "I love the flexibility, and working on my own taught me how to be efficient," Corum notes. "The biggest change in coming to the *Times* was having other people around, and having other people who knew so much more about different topics than I did." The graphics desk at the *Times* is a team of about 25 people.

THE BATTLE OF AGINCOURT (DETAIL)
(TOP)
Jonathan Corum for the New York Times, 2009

WIRED TO COUNT
(BOTTOM)
Jonathan Corum for the New York Times, 2009

Wired to Count

A sliver of the parietal cortex is particularly active in judging quantity.

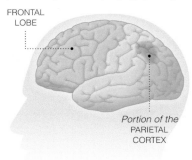

FRONTAL LOBE

Portion of the PARIETAL CORTEX

There are a few people like Corum, who coordinate a single section of coverage (e.g. Science, National, Metro), and a number of people who specialize in a particular technology, like 3D rendering or online map development. "People on the desk have a wide range of skills and come from different academic and personal backgrounds," Corum says. "That leads to a lot of collaboration."

While most of his *Times* graphics are finished in a few days, many of Corum's freelance projects take a lot longer. Fitting his freelance work into spare moments and weekends at home, he cut back on his 13pt work quite a lot in 2012, when his son was born. "I've been using this year as a sort of self-imposed sabbatical from freelance design, and have been spending my spare time learning some new programming and visualization languages. It has been very interesting to watch my son learn. When he started crawling and walking I was of course happy, but when at 11 months he started matching foam letters by shape and color and using spatial logic, I was even more proud."

However rare his spare moments at home, Corum seizes them to work on free design projects. Whenever time allows, he posts experiments or short pieces explaining his work on his website. But he probably does not write enough "to ever be well known," he believes. "I am a very poor networker and self-promoter. For me the enjoyment comes with practice, and I would rather practice design than talk or write about it. I'm happy not being famous or an 'infographics guru' or something like that."

PLACE AND DATE OF BIRTH
Madrid, Spain; 1970

COUNTRY OF RESIDENCE
United States

FAMILY STATUS
Married

EDUCATION / DEGREE
BA in Journalism

ACTIVE IN THE FIELD OF ILLUSTRATION SINCE
1991

BREAKTHROUGH PROJECT
None in particular

KEY CLIENTS
National Geographic; Clients of 5W Infographics include the New York Times, Exxon Mobil, Le Monde, Scientific American, Smithsonian Magazine, Reader's Digest, Sports Illustrated, BBDO, Rolling Stone, Paris Match, Bonnier Group, and many others

MOST RENOWNED PROJECTS
The Terracotta Army (National Geographic), 50 Years of Exploration (5W for National Geographic)

COMMISSIONS PER YEAR
N/A

AVERAGE TURNAROUND TIME PER COMMISSION
8 months to over 1 year from conception to final at National Geographic, around 2 weeks at 5W

WORKSPACE
Shared office at National Geographic; studios in Madrid and New York with 5W Infographics

EMPLOYEES
National Geographic has over 20 people and multiple freelancers creating graphics, maps, and art for all platforms. 5W has no employees, just consultants and freelancers.

AGENTS
None

TEACHING POSITIONS
Since 2000: Instructor for the "Show, Don't Tell" infographics workshop at the Malofiej convention at the University of Pamplona, Spain; Visiting teacher at the University of Hong Kong in Shanghai, National Chiao Tung University in Taiwan

AWARDS (SELECTION)
Pulitzer Prize finalist with a team of reporters of the New York Times (2001); more than 50 Awards from Society of News Design, Society of Publication Design, Malofiej and American Institute of Graphics Arts

MEMBER ASSOCIATIONS
Society of News Design, Guild of Natural Science Illustrators

GALLERIES
5wgraphics.com; juanvelascoblog.com

Juan Velasco

"THERE IS NO ROOM FOR FICTION IN INFOGRAPHICS. ONLY FOR FACTS. CREATIVITY IS GOOD AS LONG AS IT'S AT THE SERVICE OF INFORMATION. HAVING SAID THAT, THERE IS NO REASON AN INFOGRAPHIC CAN'T BE BEAUTIFUL AND TRULY CREATIVE IN EXPLAINING INFORMATION."

"We are in the age of big data," states Juan Velasco. "Everything is being measured and quantified and ever more raw information is available and accessible to more people." Naturally, there is a growing need to make sense of it all, to organize and edit information to become more accessible to the public. And so, the field of infographics is expanding and flourishing, "even in print, despite the print media crisis in Western countries," Velasco says. Art directing the graphics department at *National Geographic,* a magazine renowned for featuring high standard infographics, he knows first-hand.

Illustrated infographics can get where text and photographs cannot. "They can reveal patterns hidden in data sets or in geography. They can see the very small (atoms) and the very large (space), the very abstract (visualizing processes), what

is inside (cutaway and cross sections), or what is no longer alive (like a reconstruction of a dinosaur or an extinct hominid). Graphics synthesize and help in understanding complex information by making it visual, linear, and simplified." Compared to traditional illustration, the approach of infographic design is more literal than conceptual. The raison d'être of explaining very specific matters clearly limits the possibility of conceptualizing and abstracting. The challenge, to Velasco, is to come up with brilliant concepts within those limits. "I enjoy that challenge more than complete creative freedom."

Velasco loved to draw when he was little, but did not intend to become an illustrator. "It was probably because I didn't feel I was too talented at it since both of my brothers and my father were better artists." Velasco's father was a journalist,

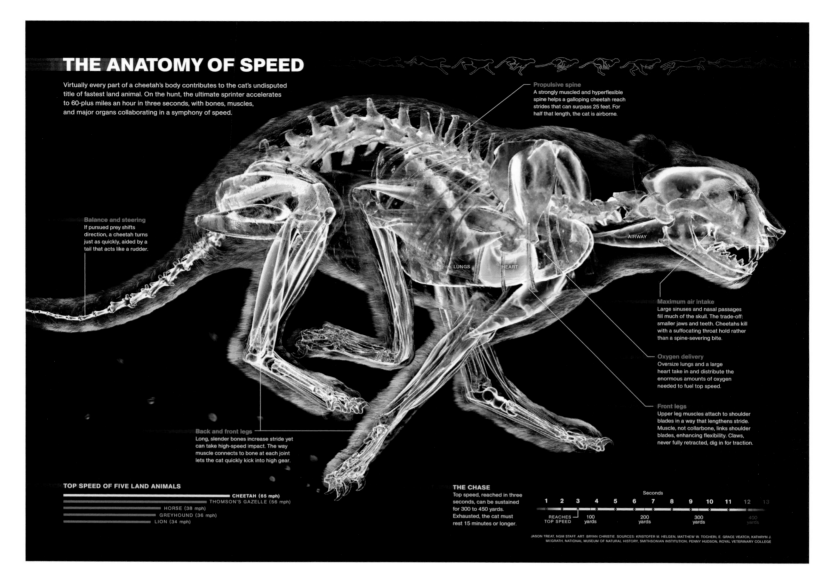

THE ANATOMY OF SPEED

Virtually every part of a cheetah's body contributes to the cat's undisputed title of fastest land animal. On the hunt, the ultimate sprinter accelerates to 60-plus miles an hour in three seconds, with bones, muscles, and major organs collaborating in a symphony of speed.

Propulsive spine
A strongly muscled and hyperflexible spine helps a galloping cheetah reach strides that can surpass 25 feet. For half that length, the cat is airborne.

Balance and steering
If pursued prey shifts direction, a cheetah turns just as quickly, aided by a tail that acts like a rudder.

AIRWAY

LUNGS   HEART

Maximum air intake
Large sinuses and nasal passages fill much of the skull. The trade-off: smaller jaws and teeth. Cheetahs kill with a suffocating throat hold rather than a spine-severing bite.

Oxygen delivery
Oversize lungs and a large heart take in and distribute the enormous amounts of oxygen needed to fuel top speed.

Front legs
Upper leg muscles attach to shoulder blades in a way that lengthens stride. Muscle, not collarbone, links shoulder blades, enhancing flexibility. Claws, never fully retracted, dig in for traction.

Back and front legs
Long, slender bones increase stride yet can take high-speed impact. The way muscle connects to bone at each joint lets the cat quickly kick into high gear.

TOP SPEED OF FIVE LAND ANIMALS
CHEETAH (65 mph)
THOMSON'S GAZELLE (56 mph)
HORSE (38 mph)
GREYHOUND (36 mph)
LION (34 mph)

THE CHASE
Top speed, reached in three seconds, can be sustained for 300 to 450 yards. Exhausted, the cat must rest 15 minutes or longer.

Seconds
1 2 3 4 5 6 7 8 9 10 11 12 13

REACHES TOP SPEED   100 yards   200 yards   300 yards   400 yards

JASON TREAT, NGM STAFF. ART: BRYAN CHRISTIE. SOURCES: KRISTOFER M. HELGEN, MATTHEW W. TOCHERI, E. GRACE VEATCH, KATHRYN J. MCGRATH, NATIONAL MUSEUM OF NATURAL HISTORY, SMITHSONIAN INSTITUTION; PENNY HUDSON, ROYAL VETERINARY COLLEGE

---

a writer, and a well-known illustrator in Spain, so art and writing were always present in his life while growing up. Initially he wanted to write for newspapers, so he studied journalism at the Complutense University in Madrid. Still, he loved to draw. When he discovered the possibility to combine both in the field of infographics, which was still largely without regard then, he thought this was it for him—working with information and revealing the stories and patterns hidden by its complexity in drawings.

As infographics did not exist as a subject in journalism schools then—it rarely did until now—Velasco experimented on his own as well as he could. When his

THE ANATOMY OF SPEED
(THIS PAGE)
Bryan Christie, National Geographic

A NEW ANCESTOR FOUND
(PAGE 134)
John Gurche, National Geographic Stock

brother Samuel got a job as a staff illustrator at the daily newspaper *El Mundo*, he was taken onboard as an intern. "I was 21, still in college. *El Mundo* was one of the pioneers in modern infographics during the early 1990s, and the work we were doing won numerous international awards."

Velasco started assisting the sports section in visualizing the stats and ratings for football matches. That was done in PageMaker then, only he had to use the Macs in the graphics department and sit there. "They had this amazing computer and drawing software that I wanted to get my hands on. Eventually, one day they let me do a 2-column fever chart about the bad results under Spain's new football

coach. I drew his caricature sliding down along the line of the chart. Needless to say, it was incredibly bad."

Somewhere during his five years at *El Mundo*, Velasco's infographics got incredibly good. He would not have been offered a job at the acclaimed graphics department of the *New York Times* if they hadn't. Having moved to the U.S. to freelance for them, he was soon hired as a full-time member of the team. As he told John Grimwade, a frequent collaborator and former colleague at the *Times* in an interview, he experienced the new environment as somewhat intimidating in the beginning.

"You could look in any direction and see a couple of Pulitzer winners typing away. I was really lucky to be hired by Charles Blow, who somehow saw some talent in me despite my pitiful English and my being used to different standards in information research. People there were really patient, encouraging, and friendly. At this time, the *New York Times* had a real dream team in infographics with people like Charles himself, Archie Tse, Frank O'Connell, Mika Grondahl, Andrew Phillips, and many others. With such talent around, I remember my frequent amazement at not being fired early on. Perhaps because I am kind of quiet they didn't notice me as much, so I kept cranking on and building my skills as fast as I could. It was the best school of journalism and infographics I could ever imagine."

A firm part of the *New York Times* infographics team from 1996 to 2001, first as a Graphics Editor and later Graphics Art Director, Velasco moved on to start his own company, 5W Infographics, in 2002, together with his brothers. He remembers how nerve-wracking the absence of the fixed income was in the beginning. "I had spent my evenings freelancing while still working at the *Times* (which was exhausting) to get some cushion savings and to get clients. But I didn't have any financing or any clients that I could count on to provide steady income. It was all one-shot assignments and never knowing where the next job would come from. But slowly, it did work for me."

5W didn't have a website back then, and most clients were acquired through mailings. "We sent work samples to designers and art directors. We looked at magazines' addresses and staff names at Barnes and Noble and sent them work. The response rate was quite low as with any direct marketing, but eventually you get some assignments, and then other people see your work published, you meet people, start networking. It's a long and constant effort. Making a website made things a bit easier later on, but most work still comes by word of mouth or people seeing your work somewhere. People would just email us or call us on

the phone with graphics assignments, mostly for magazines and newspapers." After a while, 5W started to get frequent commissions for the *National Geographic,* and eventually they offered Velasco a full-time job as Graphics Director. He became the publication's Art Director in 2008, a position he still holds today.

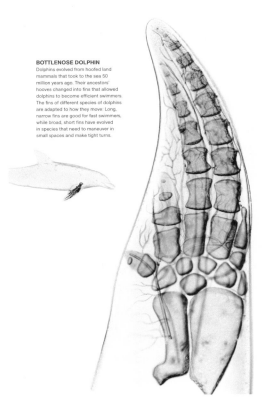

BOTTLENOSE DOLPHIN
Dolphins evolved from hoofed land mammals that took to the sea 50 million years ago. Their ancestors' hooves changed into fins that allowed dolphins to become efficient swimmers. The fins of different species of dolphins are adapted to how they move: Long, narrow fins are good for fast swimmers, while broad, short fins have evolved in species that need to maneuver in small spaces and make tight turns.

DOMESTIC CAT
Cat hands grow narrow, curved claws. Most of the time ligaments running over the top of a cat's hands keep the claws retracted inside sheaths. To catch prey, a cat pushes off its hind legs and stretches out its arms. Muscles along the top and bottom of its hands contract, which draws the claws out like switchblades. The claws sink into the prey, the cat shifts its weight to its hind legs, and the hands draw the prey to the cat's mouth.

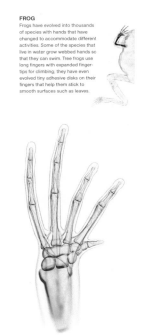

FROG
Frogs have evolved into thousands of species with hands that have changed to accommodate different activities. Some of the species that live in water grow webbed hands so that they can swim. Tree frogs use long fingers with expanded fingertips for climbing; they have even evolved tiny adhesive disks on their fingers that help them stick to smooth surfaces such as leaves.

THE COMMON HAND
Bryan Christie, National Geographic

Looking back at his career, Velasco is very clear about how his skillset has developed in its various stages: "*El Mundo* was my school in terms of design, illustration, and working in a fast-deadline environment. We were producing multiple graphics and illustrations on a daily basis. At the *New York Times*, I learned how to be a reporter. The graphics editors at the *New York Times* do their own research (and it's held to very high standards) and writing. I learned about doing interviews, working in the field, analyzing data, etc. With 5W, I learned about the realities, rewards, and hardships of the freelancing business. Finally, at *National Geographic* I have learned a lot about management,

the magazine business, cartography, and the challenges of art directing some of the best illustrators in the world."

All feed into his current practice and his understanding of visual journalism. "My job is to tell and explain relevant stories, to turn on the light for readers and help them understand complex information in a visual way that goes where the written language or the camera lens can't go." As varied as his topics are, Velasco appreciates how his work takes him "from the highest demands of scholarly research to the fine craft of writing to the pleasures of artistic creativity, sometimes all during the same day! Every story is different and I also enjoy the fact that you have to become an expert in very little time, learning a lot on a variety of topics: history, wildlife, archaeology, paleoanthropology, geopolitics, climate science… Nearly all topics I work on are exciting in one way or another. Science and art, truth and expression mix to elevate storytelling." Velasco says he is very alert to not

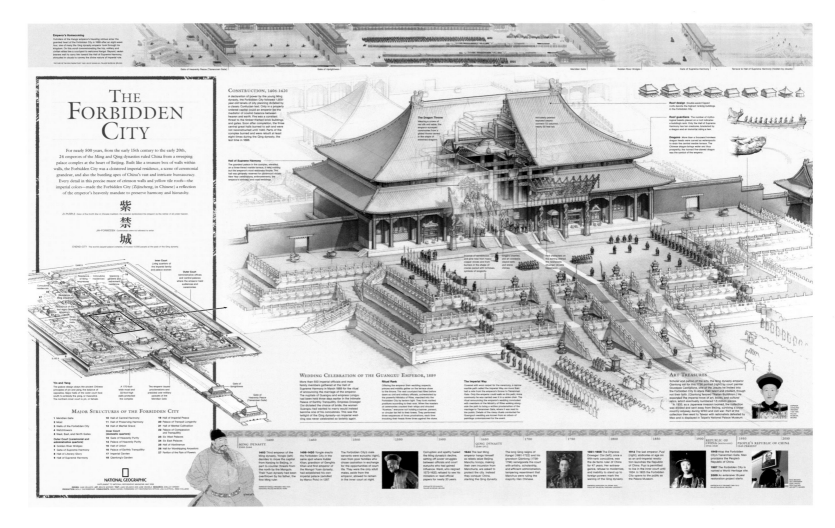

being carried away by imagination. "As a visual journalist, you need a good deal of curiosity and interest about the world and its current events, but also a commitment to accuracy and truthfulness."

Many of the infographics Velasco works on at *National Geographic* are heavily illustrated, and he considers his practice a pathway of illustration. However, he clearly draws distinctions. "Infographics need to be visually engaging and beautiful, but demand multiple skills that go beyond graphic design and illustration." They require research, a fine grasp of complex contexts, analytical thinking, the ability to communicate clearly in both images and words, focus, a structure and balance of information, creation of visual flows and hierarchies, and the ability to work with color as information. Abstraction and simplification

THE FORBIDDEN CITY
(LEFT PAGE)
Jon Foster, National Geographic Stock

THE FORBIDDEN CITY
(THIS PAGE)
Bruce Morser, National Geographic Stock

are almost always necessary to make stories approachable, but visual journalism cannot afford to be lost in translation or interpretation. Velasco is most importantly bound to representing information objectively. "There is no room for fiction in infographics. Only for facts. Creativity is good as long as it's at the service of information. Having said that, there is no reason an infographic can't be beautiful and truly creative in explaining information."

Authorship in information graphics comprises various editorial choices, which is why style lies in the visual, the writing, and the editing. "Many people are technically excellent, but it's much harder to have a unique voice in a field where artistic expression is necessarily limited by the need for accuracy and simplicity. Those who can do both, and those who can display complex data and complex

cartography with style, elegance, simplicity, and clarity are rare."

Velasco cherishes rich and sophisticated visuals that engage readers while keeping the storytelling very simple, clean, and explanatory. "I like short but very well edited text that makes you learn, and text for infographics is an art by itself. I like a clear reading flow, a well-thought out hierarchy, and using color as an added layer of information, not decoration. No visual element in a graphic should be decorative; each needs to contribute to tell a story. Avoiding unnecessary complexity and avoiding misrepresenting or distorting data are the biggest challenges."

The visual language of infographics extends beyond its classical field of use today. Data has come to be seen as chic, and Velasco observes a current avalanche of what he refers to as data visualization.

Greater bird of paradise
Paradisaea apoda

Wilson's bird of paradise
Cicinnurus respublica

Ribbon-tailed astrapia
Astrapia mayeri

Short-tailed paradigalla
Paradigalla brevicauda

Black sicklebill
Epimachus fastosus

Magnificent riflebird
Ptiloris magnificus

Superb bird of paradise
Lophorina superba

Elevation (ft)
12,000
9,000
6,000
3,000
0

Habitat range
Species illustrated above
All other species in each genus

2 genera, 10 species

3 genera, 9 species

BIRDS OF PARADISE

They are found only from eastern Australia to New Guinea and surrounding islands. They thrive at many elevations, from swampy lowlands to cloud forests more than two miles above sea level. With abundant food, varied habitats, and few predators, the birds have been free to evolve with great diversity. The 39 species can be as small as 8 inches or as large as 49 inches, and plumage ranges from drab to dazzling.

EQUATOR

DETAILED MAP SHOWN AT RIGHT

NEW GUINEA

TROPIC OF CAPRICORN

Birds of paradise range

AUSTRALIA

0 mi   500
0 km   500
SCALE AT THE EQUATOR

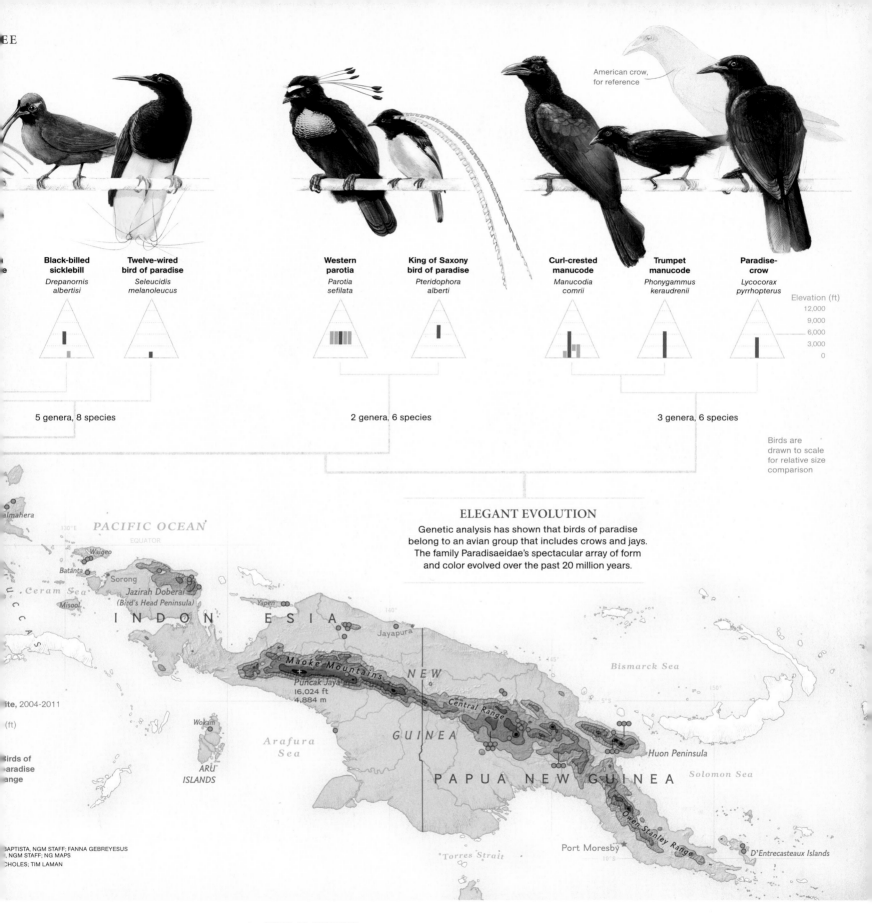

Black-billed sicklebill
Drepanornis albertisi

Twelve-wired bird of paradise
Seleucidis melanoleucus

Western parotia
Parotia sefilata

King of Saxony bird of paradise
Pteridophora alberti

Curl-crested manucode
Manucodia comrii

Trumpet manucode
Phonygammus keraudrenii

Paradise-crow
Lycocorax pyrrhopterus

American crow, for reference

Elevation (ft)
12,000
9,000
6,000
3,000
0

5 genera, 8 species

2 genera, 6 species

3 genera, 6 species

Birds are drawn to scale for relative size comparison

ELEGANT EVOLUTION

Genetic analysis has shown that birds of paradise belong to an avian group that includes crows and jays. The family Paradisaeidae's spectacular array of form and color evolved over the past 20 million years.

PACIFIC OCEAN

EQUATOR

Waigeo

Batanta

Sorong

Jazirah Doberai
(Bird's Head Peninsula)

Misool

INDONESIA

Yapen

Jayapura

NEW

GUINEA

Maoke Mountains

Puncak Jaya
16,024 ft
4,884 m

Central Range

Huon Peninsula

almahera

Ceram Sea

Arafura
Sea

Wokam

ARU
ISLANDS

PAPUA NEW GUINEA

Bismarck Sea

Solomon Sea

Torres Strait

Port Moresby

Owen Stanley Range

D'Entrecasteaux Islands

ite, 2004-2011

(ft)

Birds of
aradise
ange

BAPTISTA, NGM STAFF; FANNA GEBREYESUS
, NGM STAFF; NG MAPS
CHOLES; TIM LAMAN

BIRDS OF PARADISE
Fernando G. Baptista, National
Geographic Stock

"Much of the new data visualization seems to be more about art, design, and 'cool' visuals than about helping people understand data and the stories data can tell. It looks cool but it doesn't help. We need to keep journalistic integrity, clarity, and the benefit of the reader in mind."

New technologies have emerged to serve Velasco's purpose of conveying information effectively. "We have seen amazing new software and programming enabling smart data visualization such as Processing, Tableau, and others. We are also experiencing, very recently, a rethinking of how interactive graphics serve readers on the web; we are seeing more linear, carefully edited narratives that require little interaction from the reader, and less multiple-choice interactivity where the reader may get lost. There has been amazing progress in mapping software and techniques over the last decade: dynamic mapping linked to databases, great advances in satellite imagery and processing, and crowdsource mapping. Unfortunately, most newspapers and magazines are not taking advantage of good GIS and advanced mapping."

At *National Geographic*, they use a wide range of tools. Velasco enumerates: Illustrator, Photoshop, InDesign, Excel, Arc GIS, Nature Scene Designer, After Effects, Edge, 3D software such as Lightwave or Cinema 4D, and also pencils, brushes, clay, cardboard. The core part of the team is six Senior Graphics Editors. "Three of them specialize in cartography and three in information graphics, either data visualization or illustrated graphics. The Senior Graphics Editors are responsible for conceptualizing graphics for stories and doing the editorial and artistic development. They come up with ideas to cover them, and research them, sketch them out, and often illustrate them or produce maps. They have freedom to hire freelance researchers and artists from across the globe for their projects, depending on their needs, workload, and interests." Some work in-house if they are local, or are brought in or visited for important

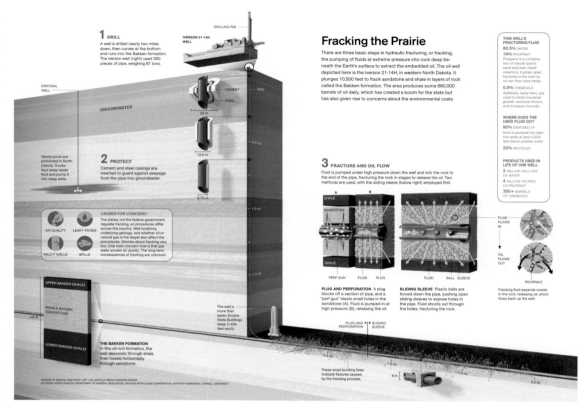

FRACKING THE PRAIRIE
Bryan Christie, National Geographic

assignments, but most freelance assignments are handled over phone and email communications. "There is a special team responsible for iPad and iPhone content—they also have their own video and layout team. We also have a research editor, two graphics editors (one doing graphics and the other one doing maps), a map text editor, a text editor, two production assistants, and we always have a few interns that make great contributions, including artwork for publication."

The people doing maps have geography degrees, as sophisticated maps are technically difficult and they require a very special eye to combine multiple layers. The rest have a combination of graphic design, journalism, fine arts, and miscellaneous degrees.

Velasco likes being very close to his team, but values the privacy of individual offices. "People think that open space layouts foster collaboration, but that's just a psychological trick. Our work requires intense research, interviewing people, and creative focus. That's hard to do in a room full of people. The important thing is to stay connected and talk to your colleagues often, and in person." *National Geographic*'s elaborate infographics call for the team to talk things through and collaborate intensely. Velasco and his team are lucky that time allows them to do so.

"Our deadlines are not tight; in fact they are really long. We may work on the same graphic for 6 months or even a year, including research and production. We don't depend on breaking news but we have to be relevant and cover the important topics of our day. Unlike newspapers, where you finish a project and then move on to the next one, we are working with multiple stories for multiple issues at the same time. You have to be a good project and time manager."

As editors and journalists responsible for their own projects, Velasco and his colleagues don't receive assignments, but generate content themselves. More than 50% of their time goes into finding relevant stories, the best experts and consultants, and often times they need to study topics in depth to be able to propose a concept or find good datasets in the first place. The actual execution of the drawings, charts, and maps takes a small portion of time. "A good idea is everything, and once we have good research we spend a good amount of time sketching and refining visual ideas. As a graphic evolves, we stay in touch with experts, sending revisions back and forth to make sure everything is accurate."

When a story is approved, photo, text, and graphics editors are responsible for independently coming up with a plan to cover that story. "Obviously, we communicate a lot with the text editor and the photo editor to make sure we are on the

same wavelength, using the same reliable sources and sharing travel and planning logistics. In most cases, we need to start before the text is written and the photos finished, so we need a degree of journalistic independence from them."

"As the art director of a large magazine you spend a lot of time in meetings, and it's a collective effort where many different people give valuable ideas. But also, you have to satisfy requests and concerns of many editors, designers, etc. In general my days are full of meetings with my team, with text and photo editors, and with experts on different topics who are providing us with information. Many of the meetings are just talking, but I also

spend a good deal of time doing hands-on work with my team, sketching out ideas or looking at the maps, art, and graphics as they evolve."

Given his various responsibilities at *National Geographic*, finding time for 5W (the company still exists, the day-to-day operations are run by his brothers from New York and Madrid) has become hard, but is also a welcome change to Velasco's daily routine. "Working independently is very rewarding, as generally you do what you want and you can be a lot more efficient about how your time is used." Over the years, 5W's offerings have turned into a good mix of editorial and corporate work, as well as consulting. Velasco's activity within the

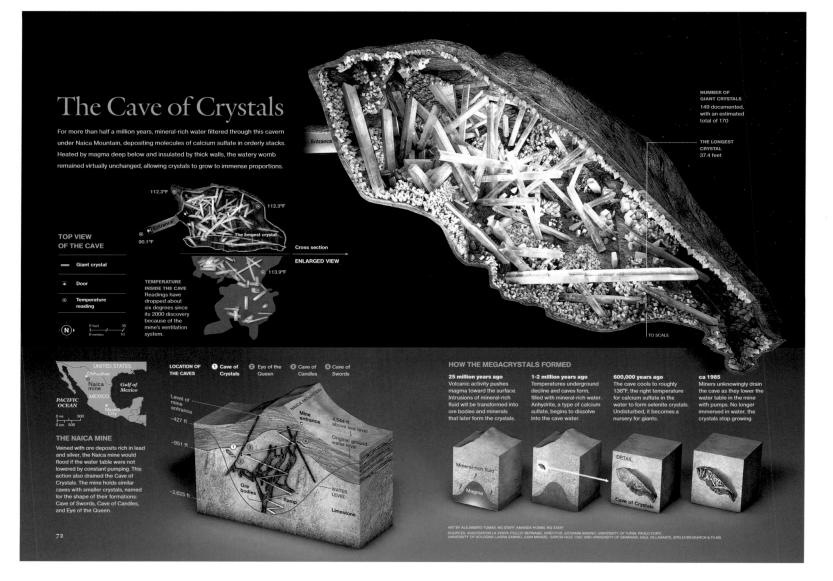

The Cave of Crystals

For more than half a million years, mineral-rich water filtered through this cavern under Naica Mountain, depositing molecules of calcium sulfate in orderly stacks. Heated by magma deep below and insulated by thick walls, the watery womb remained virtually unchanged, allowing crystals to grow to immense proportions.

NUMBER OF GIANT CRYSTALS
149 documented, with an estimated total of 170

THE LONGEST CRYSTAL
37.4 feet

TOP VIEW OF THE CAVE

— Giant crystal
↗ Door
⊙ Temperature reading

112.3°F
112.3°F
90.1°F
113.9°F

Entrance
The longest crystal
Cross section
ENLARGED VIEW

TEMPERATURE INSIDE THE CAVE
Readings have dropped about six degrees since its 2000 discovery because of the mine's ventilation system.

0 feet 35
0 meters 10

TO SCALE

THE NAICA MINE
Veined with ore deposits rich in lead and silver, the Naica mine would flood if the water table were not lowered by constant pumping. This action also drained the Cave of Crystals. The mine holds similar caves with smaller crystals, named for the shape of their formations: Cave of Swords, Cave of Candles, and Eye of the Queen.

UNITED STATES
Chihuahua
Naica mine
PACIFIC OCEAN
MEXICO
Gulf of Mexico
Mexico City
0 mi 500
0 km 500

LOCATION OF THE CAVES
❶ Cave of Crystals
❷ Eye of the Queen
❸ Cave of Candles
❹ Cave of Swords

NAICA MOUNTAIN
Level of mine entrance
−427 ft
Mine entrance
4,544 ft above sea level
Original ground-water level
−951 ft
Ore bodies
Ramp
WATER LEVEL
−2,625 ft
Limestone

HOW THE MEGACRYSTALS FORMED

25 million years ago
Volcanic activity pushes magma toward the surface. Intrusions of mineral-rich fluid will be transformed into ore bodies and minerals that later form the crystals.

1-2 million years ago
Temperatures underground decline and caves form, filled with mineral-rich water. Anhydrite, a type of calcium sulfate, begins to dissolve into the cave water.

600,000 years ago
The cave cools to roughly 136°F, the right temperature for calcium sulfate in the water to form selenite crystals. Undisturbed, it becomes a nursery for giants.

ca 1985
Miners unknowingly drain the cave as they lower the water table in the mine with pumps. No longer immersed in water, the crystals stop growing.

Mineral-rich fluid
Magma
DETAIL
Cave of Crystals

ART BY ALEJANDRO TUMAS, NG STAFF; AMANDA HOBBS, NG STAFF
SOURCES: ASSOCIATION LA VENTA (TULLIO BERNABEI, DIRECTOR), GIOVANNI BADINO, UNIVERSITY OF TURIN; PAOLO FORTI, UNIVERSITY OF BOLOGNA; LAURA SANNA; JUAN MANUEL GARCÍA-RUIZ, CSIC AND UNIVERSITY OF GRANADA; SAUL VILLASANTE, SPELEORESEARCH & FILMS

72

Panthera leo
AFRICAN LION

Alertly she watches her prey, body tense, tip of tail twitching as she advances a step at a time. Then she crouches motionless, hugging the ground. Only the quivering of her flanks reveals her tension as she waits for the unsuspecting victim to drift closer.

—FIELD BIOLOGIST
GEORGE B. SCHALLER
IN THE SERENGETI

LIFE-SIZE FRONT
PAW PRINT

ADULT FEMALE LION
Head and body length,
4'7" to 5'9"
265-400 pounds
ADULT MALE LION
Head and body length,
5'7" to 8'2"
330-550 pounds

CAT
FAMILY
TREE

10 MILLION
YEARS AGO

5 MILLION
YEARS AGO

TODAY

FELID ANCESTOR 10.8 MILLION YEARS AGO

PANTHERA ANCESTOR 6.4

BAY CAT ANCESTOR 5.4

CARACAL ANCESTOR 5.6

9.4 M.Y.A.

OCELOT ANCESTOR 2.9

8.5 M.Y.A.

8 M.Y

LYNX ANCESTOR

| *Panthera* 5 SPECIES | *Neofelis* 2 SPECIES | *Pardofelis* 3 SPECIES | *Caracal* 3 SPECIES | *Leopardus* 7 SPECIES | *Lynx* 4 SPECIES |
| LION, TIGER, LEOPARD, JAGUAR, SNOW LEOPARD | CLOUDED LEOPARD | BAY CAT | CARACAL | OCELOT | IBERIAN LYNX |

company now mainly consists of consulting trips for newspapers and magazines.

"Consultants are supposed to bring new knowledge to organizations, but you can learn a huge deal by seeing how different teams are organized, how they respond to different assignments, how they foster creativity and try to maintain high standards of journalism. I always learn something new and directly applicable to my job." Most of Velasco's work for 5W is done on the go, traveling. "I love the change of scenery, knowing new places and meeting new people."

Sometimes he combines these business trips with a short, private vacation.

"Personal balance is essential; you must have personal and family time regardless of anything that may be going on. At *National Geographic*, I am in the office from 9 am to 6:30 or 7 pm. After that it's family time, no matter how busy. If you are not disciplined about that, work eats you alive. In any case, if I have too much to do I work early in the morning, from 6 to 7:30 am, or late at night after 11 pm."

Despite his tight schedule, Velasco came up with the idea to document his projects extensively on a blog. Passionate about his trade, he assumes responsibility for his work. "In conferences and presentations you see a lot of people showing a

portfolio of their work without much explanation on how it's done and its process, which is what most people want to know. I try to offer that. Also, with the avalanche of data visualization in the last few years, I was starting to notice that illustrated infographics were starting to be perceived as less serious, rigorous, or accurate than the pure display of data in charts. I wanted to convey that every single detail you see in our illustrations has been researched extremely carefully and revised by experts."

The blog, to Velasco, is an opportunity to pass on valuable insight to aspiring creatives. "I've always appreciated receiving insights and learning from others, and I

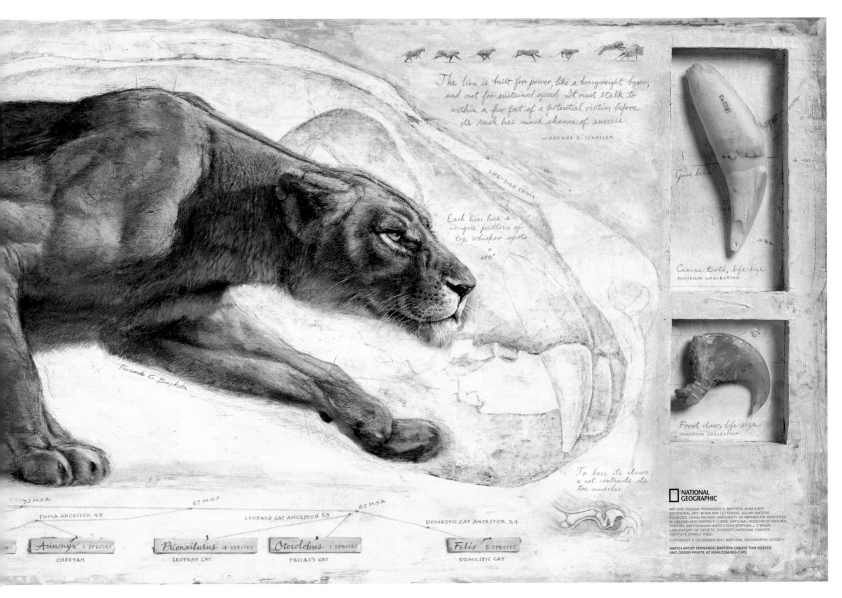

The lion is built for power, like a heavyweight boxer, and not for sustained speed. It must stalk to within a few feet of a potential victim before its rush has much chance of success.

— GEORGE B. SCHALLER

Each lion has a unique pattern of top whisker spots

LIFE-SIZE SKULL

Gum line

Canine tooth, life-size
MUSEUM COLLECTION

Front claw, life-size
MUSEUM COLLECTION

To bare its claws, a cat contracts its toe muscles.

NATIONAL GEOGRAPHIC

ART AND DESIGN: FERNANDO G. BAPTISTA, NGM STAFF
ADDITIONAL ART: BONA KIM. LETTERING: JULIAN WATERS
SOURCES: CRAIG PACKER, UNIVERSITY OF MINNESOTA; KRISTOFER
M. HELGEN AND DARRIN P. LUNDE, NATIONAL MUSEUM OF NATURAL
HISTORY, SMITHSONIAN INSTITUTION; STEPHEN J. O'BRIEN,
LABORATORY OF GENETIC DIVERSITY, NATIONAL CANCER
INSTITUTE (FAMILY TREE)
COPYRIGHT © DECEMBER 2011 NATIONAL GEOGRAPHIC SOCIETY

WATCH ARTIST FERNANDO BAPTISTA CREATE THIS POSTER,
AND ORDER PRINTS, AT NGM.COM/BIG-CATS.

7.2 M.Y.A.

PUMA ANCESTOR 4.9   6.7 M.Y.A.

LEOPARD CAT ANCESTOR 5.9   6.2 M.Y.A.

DOMESTIC CAT ANCESTOR 3.4

Acinonyx 1 SPECIES   Prionailurus 4 SPECIES   Otocolobus 1 SPECIES   Felis 5 SPECIES

CHEETAH   LEOPARD CAT   PALLAS'S CAT   DOMESTIC CAT

LIONS
Fernando G. Baptista, National Geographic Stock

appreciated people that were open to helping me. I wish I could do two blog entries a week, but the way the blog is conceived (rather long, very explanatory articles about how we do graphics with multiple examples), it's not easy." Certainly not, as he is also busy holding seminars and workshops, that, again, feed into his work at *National Geographic*. "You get to learn a lot about how other people work and what they do. Most of my workshops are overseas and I get to see the different ways of approaching graphics by professionals and students, how they deal with different issues from a creative and organizational standpoint, etc. Organizing teaching material and giving it

structure is also a great help in my day-to-day job to not lose focus on the important concepts, and also as teaching tools for junior staff or interns."

What are the milestones of a career like Velasco's, packed with state-of-the-art graphics and prestigious awards? Not so much the graphics and awards themselves, as he reckons. "I have had the immense luck of working at three places that were pivotal in the modern history of information graphics: *El Mundo*, the *New York Times*, and *National Geographic*. I have been lucky to work with many people that have contributed to shaping the field of information

graphics and to learn from them, and I also achieved my dream of creating my own independent business. At every step I was afraid to fail because everyone was so good, but somehow I'm still around. So far, graphics have given me an adventurous and interesting life full of world travel, creativity, and intellectual rewards. I love to bring visual clarity to the world and it's especially enjoyable when you get good direct feedback from readers. I always aim for that moment when I'm sketching and I find an idea that I know will 'turn on the light' for readers to quickly understand something that seemed complex and obscure."

Fashion Illustration

The tradition of fashion illustration is no less rich and longstanding than that of fashion design. Once called on to portray stiff figures draped in elaborate upper-class costumes, the field has since experienced innumerable trends and adapted looks as diverse as fashion itself. Not only has the changeable style of garments impacted the way illustrators choose to represent them, but new technologies and overall cultural developments have also expanded the toolkit of fashion designers and illustrators alike. While classic drawings with the greatest possible detailing still depict cumbersome draperies, fashion illustration now also encompasses abstract representations and high-tech garment renderings. Although fewer fashion houses employ illustrators today, much of fashion illustration still overlaps with fashion design, serving designers in putting their ideas down on paper. And although illustration as a means of fashion dissemination has forfeited a good portion of its autonomy since the rise of photography in the first half of the twentieth century, leading publications still frequently return to it as a form of visual luxury with unequalled emotional power. This chapter looks into the communication of fashion. Leaving illustration as drafting aside, it concentrates on works commissioned for reproduction in fashion magazines as part of editorial features, advertising, and promotion, and as produced by artists like Liselotte Watkins, and Tina Berning. In addition, there is a selection of fabric pattern illustrations from artists like Catalina Estrada. Connected to the fashion industry, such examples are usually produced on the basis of licensing contracts with brands to be applied to their collections. Grasping fashion not only as a field of application, but also as a distinct visual language characterized by sleek and slender couture style and its exaggerated proportions, we factor in work that is not strictly produced for fashion, but rather inspired by it.

PLACE AND DATE OF BIRTH
Braunschweig, Germany; 1969

COUNTRY OF RESIDENCE
Germany

FAMILY STATUS
Married, 1 daughter

EDUCATION / DEGREE
Diploma in Graphic Design

ACTIVE IN THE FIELD OF ILLUSTRATION SINCE
1999

BREAKTHROUGH PROJECT
28 pages fashion spread for Allegra (2002),
100 Girls On Cheap Paper (2006)

KEY CLIENTS
The New York Times, Die Zeit, Stern, Vogue,
Cosmopolitan, Brigitte, Tiffany & Co., Breuninger,
Deutsches Theater, Volkswagen, Mercedes Benz
among others

MOST RENOWNED PROJECTS
100 Girls On Cheap Paper, The Pope for the Cover
of the New York Times Magazine, 110 portraits
of contributors for the New York Times,
face/Project with Michelangelo di Battista

COMMISSIONS PER YEAR
200–300

AVERAGE TURNAROUND TIME PER COMMISSION
Something between 30 minutes and 2 months

WORKSPACE
Shared studio with her husband, a painter,
and a friend, an illustrator

EMPLOYEES
6-months interns

AGENTS
U.S.: CWC International, Inc.
Asia: Cross World Connections
Benelux: ArtBox
U.K.: Synergy Art-Partner

HOW MUCH COMMISSION DO YOUR AGENTS TAKE
25–30%

TEACHING POSITIONS
Since 2007: Drawing classes at
Kunsthochschule Weissensee

AWARDS
Every now and then

MEMBER ASSOCIATIONS
None

GALLERIES
Gallery Hanahou, New York
Galerie Andreas Binder, Munich

Tina Berning

"WHETHER YOU APPROACH A PROJECT AS FREE OR COMMERCIAL IS OFTEN ONLY A MATTER OF INTENTION."

Photo: Joachim Baldauf

Tina Berning is hard to reach on the phone, and her clients know that. "Emails are more convenient, you look at them once you have the time. I can't just jump up when the inks are still wet, then they dry up and you don't get that beautiful flow of strokes that naturally runs into each other. There is not much to be discussed anyway. I am the one who does the drawings, they are the ones who want their content illustrated. So give me content and I'll draw things up." Her forthright manner has the same sincere immediacy as her drawings. Normally, there are no corrections, few check-backs. Indeed, her phone won't ring once in the coming two and a half hours. "I got to the point where I simply didn't answer. You have to find your own way of doing things," Berning says, and she certainly has.

Successfully fusing the flow of the hand with the newfangled technological possibilities that came about in the 90s, Berning's vector drawings attracted attention early in her career. Most of her recent work is mixed media, with a good deal of human touch. "I really like that, when you don't recognize how it all came about." Some of the structures in her illustrations are painted in watercolor, others photoshopped. Some lines are penciled, others drawn with the path tool in FreeHand. However seamlessly the digital and the analog flow together in Berning's illustrations, working processes are strictly separated. There is an analog and a digital corner in her 100-square-meter studio with 6.5 meter ceilings, which is located on the upper floor of a one-story brick building in one of Berlin Mitte's placid backyards. "Some people think a studio space should be as cheap as possible. I am convinced that it must be as beautiful as possible. Investments in your workplace pay back a thousand times," Berning says. Her husband, the painter Julio Rondo, works downstairs. Purring around the house is the studio cat whose flying hair keeps the illustrator busily retouching. The two extra workspaces in the studio are those of Claudia Kefer and Gunter Rubin, both friends from Berning's student days.

BREASTFEEDING
(PAGE 148)
Cover for Midwives
Client: Royal College of Midwives, UK

**DEUTSCHES THEATER
(GERMAN THEATER)**
Drawings for 25 plays of one theater season used for all printed matters
Client: Deutsches Theater, Berlin, 2011

Berning studied graphic design in Nuremberg. "It was not an exceptionally good course, but I could focus on illustration from the beginning, and in the end, it's what you make of it." Berning started classes in 1992, the early days of desktop publishing, so the years of her studies were marked by upheaval. "We were not allowed to touch the computers during the first semester, because the professors didn't quite know what to do with them. It was in that short anarchic phase

that we were able to teach ourselves way better than they were." The disarray spurred interdisciplinary experimentation. Berning did some typography and

layout, but her core projects have always been illustrative.

She traces her fascination with illustration back to her childhood. "The only full-color magazine we had at home when I was a kid was the supplement of

my father's daily paper, the *Frankfurter Allgemeine Zeitung*. My two older sisters and I would fight about it, and in the end they would get to cut out the photos and leave the illustrations for me. So I started to love them. There were extensive picture spreads by artists like Heinz Edelmann, Paola Paglia, and Brad Holland. I wanted to do that, too." As it turned out, shortly after graduating Berning got a job as a graphic designer for the supplement of another major German newspaper, the

DEUTSCHES THEATER (GERMAN THEATER)
Drawings for 25 plays of one theater season used for all printed matters
Client: Deutsches Theater, Berlin, 2011

Süddeutsche Zeitung Magazin, titled Jetzt at that time. But she felt uncomfortable in the team environment, and soon got tired of pushing other people's imagery around. So after a year, she decided to draw on her own.

"I really blundered into advertising first, when an agency won a pitch with my drawings for Smart around 2001. Not knowing anything about pitch presentations at the time, I just did vector drawings right away—very precise, but atmospheric. They got back to me immediately, saying they'd never seen such a

well-designed presentation. Apparently, that type of illustration was all new to them." Right after the Smart pitch, the agency that had lost it booked Berning to draw for another one, this time for Volkswagen. "I was just the woman to do the layout drawings for all the car campaigns then. It went so far that other illustrators called me up to learn about my technique, for they had been commissioned by other car companies to do the same. It had developed into that strange

hype. For a while, I worked for all kinds of car manufacturers, always the same type of vector drawings, designing Christmas cards for three companies at a time." While most illustrators eke out a living through editorial jobs in the beginning, and get advertising clients later, she instead had to free herself from advertising to be able to do editorial work that she had always found more exciting. "I still do some advertising jobs, but on a very limited basis. People always think they are incredibly well paid, but they also cost much time and nerves."

Moneywise, one big advertising commission may equal ten quick editorial jobs, but Berning prefers the latter. She likes to work as independently as possible. Some clients approach her with image ideas, but she often draws something else in the end, something she finds more suitable herself. And she prefers not to work with sketches. "A sketch, by its very nature, leaves room for interpretation, it merely hints at the final drawing. In practice that means everyone sees something else. That gives rise to misunderstandings, and potential disappointment." So Berning draws finals right away. If these don't persuade her clients she starts from scratch, believing that refitments make drawings cumbersome and odd. The strategy works for editorial jobs. Berning draws quickly, and her work thrives on jotted contours and cursory touches of color. Advertising clients usually want sketches, their perceptions too rigid to allow for trial and error. Berning was asked to draw a man in a cafe for an ad recently. "There should be space for type, so I put a table in the lower front for it to be placed, which made a really nice composition. But the table hid the men's Todd's shoes, and thus had to be removed. Weird vanities, but the composition falls apart. As it's too complex to start from scratch, you start mucking around and get a result that no one is really happy with. But sometimes you have to let go and just bring things to an end. It really happened only once that I cancelled a job because the corrections were just too absurd." With that client she had agreed upon a cancellation fee of 40%. "There are usually no contracts that bind you to a project in Germany. So if the collaboration does not work out, blame is shared by both sides."

Trivial dispute and uncertainty are rare in the editorial field according to Berning, even when it comes to advertorials, which are particularly common in U.S. fashion magazines. "Advertorials involve several advertising clients who pay to have products featured on the spreads, and it's sometimes tricky to satisfy everyone. But

VOGUE
(BOTH PAGES)
In collaboration with
Michelangelo di Battista
Client: Vogue Italia, 2007

I get very clear guidelines of what needs to be in the pictures, usually catwalk pictures, from which I can either choose or combine, or use a selection of products. It is then up to me to adapt the surroundings accordingly, which is usually a very exciting and challenging task." Berning illustrates for fashion magazines a lot. It suggested itself, as the female figure has always intrigued her as a motif. Her first fashion editorial was in 2003, for the German women's magazine *Allegra*, a fully illustrated 24-page supplement. Related inquiries followed. "That's how it goes—what you throw into the world is what it reacts to. That had been the case with the cars, then with fashion. And now that I portray columnists for the *New York Times Book Review*, I get frequent inquiries for portraits. As an illustrator you find yourself in the bizarre situation of being asked to reproduce yourself over and over again." Berning soon learned to break the cycle and steer her career herself.

"If you work a lot, which I did from the beginning, there is hardly time to step aside and reconsider what you really want to do. Commercial projects can grant you financial leeway to experiment and find out." Avidly refining and propagating her creative output, Berning started the Bilderklub with some friends in 2004. "It was essentially a pre-web 2.0 blog to which we uploaded daily drawings that we had created alongside work. The idea is that of a diary or sketchbook. Every day before leaving the studio, I have to do one drawing and publish it online." Instead of just having unfinished scribbles flying around in their studios, the Bilderklub's founding members—Berning, graphic designer Sascha Bierl, and illustrators Nadine Schemmann aka LULU, Julia Pfaller, and Gisela Goppel—accumulated an extensive digital image archive that caught the attention of image editors across the globe. Two exhibitions followed, one in Berlin, one in New York. "I had started the project to liberate myself from commercial commissions, and all of a sudden clients booked me to do drawings like these," Berning remembers. "It confirmed for me that it was my responsibility to perform experiments and that these would eventually feed back into my commercial work."

It is both in her free and commercial illustrations that Berning has always worked intensively with the human figure, with fashion as its packaging. "I couldn't solely work for fashion, that would be too superficial. I love the variety of content that my job offers. But the more I engage with fashion as a subject matter, the more I see and enjoy its substance." She mentions the play with form, lines, and volumes, and how she got more versed in reinforcing her drawings with references, expression, and depth. "Especially when working for women's magazines, you are contributing to how the image of women is shaped by the media." Berning's examination into the issue "100 Girls on Cheap Paper" challenges the concept of beauty. The project begun with a bunch of discarded drawings, and extended into web-based images hosted by *Vorn* magazine, the publication of Berning's good friend, fashion photographer Joachim Baldauf. "*100 Girls on Cheap Paper* is about the discovery of imperfection," Berning explains. "All portraits in the series have some oddity to them. Then again, it is exactly these little oddities and flaws that make them beautiful." The project marks an important step in her

process. "Again, the benefits of experimentation flowed back into my commercial work. Suddenly I dared to include women that aren't perfect in commissioned illustrations, and accepted flaws in the drawings instead of smoothing them all out."

100 Girls on Cheap Paper was eventually published in book form, then toured from Amsterdam to Tokyo to New York as a traveling exhibition. Sparing no expense,

Berning took this as an investment in her career. "I strongly believe that it's worthwhile to take risks, to occasionally reject lucrative commissions and put time and money into self-directed projects." *100 Girls on Cheap Paper* brought in a harvest indeed. The day after she had submitted the book to the American Illustration award, Berning received an email from the art director of the *New York Times Magazine,* who had been on the panel of judges. "He asked me to draw the pope in the style that I had drawn the girls." Her result landed on the cover, and initiated her weekly portrait series in the *Book Review,* a project she highlights for its inspiring content.

Balancing art and illustration, Berning is clear to not give preference to one over the other. "I love the impulses I get as an illustrator, and particularly enjoy commissions that involve me in day-to-day affairs. I could not only do commercial work, for I need headspace to develop." Then again, she would not like to solely rely on the art market and its arbitrary conditions. "It's like gambling, with good contacts as jokers. Compared to fine art, illustration is a down-to-earth business, where success depends on the combination of passion and skills." Certainly knowing the right people is a plus in illustration, too, but Berning considers all the business socializing to be overrated. "I have never been part of the clubby culture of trade associations, never initiated a commission after 6 pm. I always kept a low profile and still never ran short on jobs."

Not at all. She sets lead times of about three weeks for more extensive editorial projects, as generally there are quite a few other projects in the pipeline. Extensive means something around three full pages, or three half pages, plus a few insets. Berning's illustrations rarely relate to late-breaking news, and the monthlies and weeklies she primarily works for are usually able to plan in advance. "For a single-to half-page piece I usually get about a week from the client's request. In the end the implementation rarely takes longer than half a day, but I need to have enough time to carry the text around with me for a few days, to develop the idea." Ideas usually come to Berning as products of in-

tuition and association. She likes to work with photos—not as blueprints, but from which to construe moods and themes. "Good illustration adds a twist to a given story. In my case, that is less about irony and pictorial humor than about emotionally charged connotations. I believe that illustration really works if it goes beyond the verbal content. Why should I show something that is written in the text next to it? Only so that those too lazy to read get it too? That's not my mission."

PERNILLE, LIYA & CONSTANCE
In collaboration with Michelangelo di Battista
Personal Work, 2010

Images cannot be forced, and creativity does not flow on command. "Sometimes it helps to Google keywords. First, you get heaps of clichés that tell you what you don't want—anti-research so to speak. But then, due to these weird algorithms that search engines are based on, the most absurd things pop up in between and inspire lateral thinking. Other times, it is best to develop ideas logically, in a straightforward process. But what really works best for me is time. I have to sleep on things, and then, as trite as it may sound, it is often under the shower that I have the solution. Then I go to the studio and draw it up." If the idea does not work as expected, she goes back to it later. "I don't panic anymore, I haven't for a long time. Once I get stuck I leave it for a while and continue with something else instead. I am aware of my strengths and weaknesses, have learned to accept them and canalize my

time accordingly. Sometimes I draw like a tenth grader, other times I feel like I could draw everything with ease. The latter moments I seize, the others I use to do other stuff, like my taxes. It's a matter of assessing one's own creativity, as well as the projects you take on."

In Germany, Berning did not work with an agent for a long time. She never felt the need to, but joined 2agenten in 2006. "They had just opened their office in Berlin when they called me. The fine selection of local illustrators they were already working with convinced me, it just felt right to be a part of that." Since the early days of her career both in the U.S. and Asia, she has been represented by Cross World Connections, a Japanese agency with offices in Tokyo and New York. Agents in Holland and the U.K. followed over time. She never looked for agents in other countries, thus rarely works in other markets. "If a client from Italy approaches me, for example, which happens occasionally, especially in the fashion context, I usually let my

German agents handle the project. To really establish yourself in a foreign market, you definitely need an agent." Berning's decision to establish herself early on in the U.S. market was well-considered, and Asia was serendipitous. "I had traveled to New York where I had

made appointments with six different agencies. Five of these six were typically American: 'Oh this is lovely, amazing, great, we'll certainly give you a call.'" At the sixth appointment she was received with Japanese restraint: "'We like it very much, but we don't take new artists.'" Disappointed at first, because she had liked them the most, Berning received a call the next day, asking her to come in again. "When it comes to jobs they are exactly like that—reserved, never promising too much. And they are on the dot and to the point, filtering all empty twaddle out

rights fully disbursed. Many rather work like craftsmen—daily rates, and that's it." Agreements that imply multiple reproductions in unspecified sub-publications or syndications, which allow publishers to resell illustrations, have become common practice, but Berning rejects them. "You usually get 50% if they resell a piece, but they can give it to whatever publication they like, for whatever amount they consider appropriate. Meaning that an illustration I created for them for 500 euros may be resold for 200, leaving 100 for me. That may sound okay, but I prefer to have

control and decide where my illustrations appear. So I take my ruler and the agreement to cross all that stuff out." Clients usually accept her edits.

In America, rights are regulated more precisely in the first place. Fees are substantially higher than those paid by European clients, too. "In the editorial field, you usually get about 50% more, even now, despite the crisis," Berning explains. "This is because print runs are a lot higher, but also because illustration has a higher reputation by tradition. In Germany, it's often considered a stopgap. It

of American-client conversations, reducing it to clear and concise information. I love that."

A large part of Berning's clients are from the U.S., while the bulk are from German-speaking countries. Accordingly, Cross World Connections and 2agenten are the agents she works with the most. Both truly foster their artists, she says, and represent her interests well. "Rights of use is a tricky issue, for instance, and one that I'm rigorous about. When I began to work as an illustrator conditions were ideal. Nowadays ever more illustrators don't seem to care much about getting their

FACE/PROJECT DRAWINGS #31, #33, #38
(TOP)
In collaboration with
Michelangelo di Battista
Personal Work, 2010

PERNILLE (DETAIL)
(RIGHT)
In collaboration with
Michelangelo di Battista
Personal Work, 2010

has gotten much better, and many clients now deliberately use illustrations because of their fictional and subjective qualities. However, quite a few still approach illustrators simply because their photos didn't work." And how does this translate to the fashion industry, which has traditionally worked with illustrations both in design and dissemination? "Early fashion magazines used illustration because drawing was easier than taking photos back then. Although photography slowly broke through in the 50s and 60s, fashion illustration has always enjoyed a relatively high level of recognition across the globe.

Although leading fashion houses rarely employ illustrators anymore, most designers are still schooled in drawing." Berning teaches drawing for fashion designers at the art college Berlin Weißensee—not traditional fashion illustration, but rather compositional and figurative approaches. "Every second week before the course I ask myself why the hell I am doing this, for there is hardly time to prepare something. But then I leave each class with a very positive feeling."

Passing skills and experience on to young talent has enriched Berning's practice throughout her career. She has worked with interns and assistants since 2002. They help her with organizational matters, research, scanning and preparing images, and, occasionally, work with her on illustration commissions. "Sometimes image elements can be divided up, so that I draw the figures, and an intern the insects, for example. In other cases, ink drawings and color textures can be worked on separately and overlayed in Photoshop later. It is not easy to hand over tasks—drawing is a very subjective process. But once the chemistry in the cooperation is right, it feels natural." Tasks and materials need to be prepared and Berning often lacks the time to do so, though there is not always work that can be shared in the first place. "A basic prerequisite for both my interns and assistants," says Berning, "is that they bring in their own projects to work on, so that I don't feel bad if I can't give them anything for a few days." The work climate in the studio is unbureaucratic and, most importantly, amicable. Almost all of Berning's interns stay longer than planned, and collaborations turn into friendships. "Gisi (Gisela Goppel) stayed in the studio for over four years. She had started as an intern, then became my assistant. Now working on her own, she remains one of my closest friends. It was a similar situation with Signe (Kjær Pedersen). I can only work with people that I really like on a personal level. After all, this is a very intimate thing here, like a family circle." At the moment there is no intern in the studio. Berning says she

misses it somehow, but just cannot wrap her head around finding someone right now. "I receive applications, but you simply have to get to know each other first—it takes time."

Time is precious, especially since Berning's daughter was born two and a

FACE/PROJECT DRAWINGS
#05
In collaboration with
Michelangelo di Battista
Personal Work, 2010

half years ago. Having to structure her days more clearly now, she has set working hours from 9 to 4. "It's long enough—I just need to work more compactly, which works well for commissions. With free projects, it sometimes happens that I get into the flow when it's almost 4 and wish I could continue forever." Self-directed projects account for about a third of her work at the moment. Berning would like to do more again but notes that the transition is fluid. "Certain projects are free, yet commissioned—art and illustration coincide." She refers to a project she did for the Deutsches Theater in 2011. Over the course of one

season, she illustrated every play in the program for the theater's visual communications. "They had given me all the scripts, and I read them all and just drew whatever came to mind." She created a blog where she uploaded everything that the theater's designers could then take—the daily tried and true Bilderklub strategy. "Whether you approach a project as free or commercial is often only a matter of intention."

Afloat on the fluid line between art and illustration is Berning's collaboration with the fashion photographer Michelangelo di Battista. It started with a commission for Italian *Vogue*. Di Battista was looking for visual disrupters, quirky remarks to contrast the perfection of his photos. Berning's job was to create drawings and bricolages onsite at a shooting, which were then held into the image setup to be photographed with the models, resulting in analog, surreal collages. She flew to Paris, where, much like in surrealist collage, elements of opposite worlds met. "Everything was so over the top, around 40 people on set, from the hand model to the security guy guarding the jewelry. There was Michelangelo [di Battista] in perfectly coordinated cooperation with multiple assistants. And me, tinkering around in an improvised and rather chaotic manner, spurred by the great opportunity to bring the little flaws I had experimented with in drawing my *Girls on Cheap Paper* into one of my favorite magazines." Allowing for keen experimentation is key to the strategy of Italian *Vogue*, as Berning explains. Contributors are free to do whatever they like, but usually get nothing but the production costs reimbursed. But nothing ventured, nothing gained. "The project enjoyed great popularity, and there were follow-up jobs for both Michelangelo and me."

From the *Vogue* project emerged another collaboration between Berning and di Battista: a series of large-scale portrait photos, which she reworked with brush, paint, and cutter. "We had the opportunity to exhibit the 'FACE/project' at the photo gallery Camera Work in Berlin, and

worked toward that show. It was supposed to start in early September—Angelo had sent me the last photos in June—and in July my daughter was born." She did half of the work before giving birth, half after—40 large-scale images. It seems as if the time pressure helped to ignite the project, as it thrived on blazing spontaneity. "The show was quite a sensation and sold out on the day of the opening. In retrospect, it was all a bit crazy too. I had done the largest piece of the show the night before the opening." Her husband Julio, who teaches a university course in painting, had semester break so he was able to take care of their newborn baby. Berning did not take maternity leave after that show, but has learned to say no more often.

"Once you reach a certain level in your career, saying 'no' becomes an essential part of business. I am not really good at

WEIHNACHTSGESCHICHTE (CHRISTMAS STORY)
(LEFT PAGE)
Story by Elke Naters
Client: Cosmopolitan, Germany

PORTRAITS
(LEFT, 4 IMAGES)
Selection of 110 weekly portraits of contributors for the New York Times UpFront section
Client: the New York Times

INTERNE KLOK
(RIGHT)
Client: Quest Magazine, Netherlands

it, but now, being a mom, things are a bit different. I had my child relatively late, so I found myself in the happy position of already being established in the industry. That was a precondition, as I would not want my child to be raised by a nanny." So she says no and works until 4 pm, knowing that, living two houses away from the studio, she can always come back in the evening. "All in all, I really treasure the time I finish work now. I never had that before, we would often leave the studio after midnight. I have always savored freelancing for the ability to structure my days as I wish, but felt tied up in working like a puppet on the strings of commissions sometimes. I think what saved me from burnout is my habit of taking two months off every year to go on vacation." Now that she has taken more time off every day for two and a half years, she is slowly beginning to miss her nights at the studio. "We'll find a way to organize things so that I have one or two days a week to work open-ended, with more depth, and on free projects too. Work, for me, is just a state of genuine happiness. It's such a fine feeling to be productive.

Liselotte Watkins

PLACE AND DATE OF BIRTH
Nyköping, Sweden; 1971

COUNTRY OF RESIDENCE
Milan, Italy

FAMILY STATUS
Married, 2 children

EDUCATION / DEGREE
Art Institute of Dallas

ACTIVE IN THE FIELD OF ILLUSTRATION SINCE
1993

BREAKTHROUGH PROJECT
Barneys New York makeup ads in the
New York Times for 2 years

KEY CLIENTS
Absolut, H&M, and Elle

MOST RENOWNED PROJECTS
Absolut Watkins

COMMISSIONS PER YEAR
Anywhere from 12–100

AVERAGE TURNAROUND TIME PER COMMISSION
N/A

WORKSPACE
Home studio

EMPLOYEES
None

AGENTS
Paris: Agents & Artists, New York:
Art Department, Stockholm: LundLund,
Milan: Atomo Managment

HOW MUCH COMMISSION DO YOUR AGENTS TAKE
20–25%

TEACHING POSITIONS
None

AWARDS
None

MEMBER ASSOCIATIONS
None

GALLERIES
None

"IT TAKES SOME EXPERIENCE IN THE FIELD FOR COMMISSIONERS TO BRING YOU INTO THE PROCESS AT AN EARLY STAGE, SO THAT YOU CAN ACTUALLY CONTRIBUTE TO THE IDEA AND THE BRIEF. IT IS GREAT TO SEE HOW PEOPLE ARE STARTING TO TRUST YOU AND YOUR VISION."

Fashion is fickle, and so is Swedish illustrator Liselotte Watkins. The editors of Vogue have described her visual language as "unmatchable," for it constantly evolves. Watkins proclaims that she loves the idea of fashion as transformation, and cannot resist the ever-present urge to reinvent herself and her work. To that effect, her portfolio is manifold. In recent years, she has expanded her work to include styling and set design, which she considers extensions of her illustrations. "It's like a little universe where everything kind of connects. Finding new ways to work, and never stand still and be content—that, I think, is the most important thing for me."

However inquisitive, playful, and agile her approach, Watkins's illustrations always remain marked by her signature style: highly distinctive line drawings of peculiar, lascivious figures; mostly girls, with long legs, bright faces, and round dolly eyes, somewhat exaggerated features. If there are colors, they are usually flat and full-bodied, with a flavor of the 60s: blackish mulberries, blueberries, rusts and plums, lilac, purple, and earthy shades. Some of her images could have been beamed into our time from the windows of Biba. The British boutique had, about half a century ago, begun to mix Art Deco, Nouveau, Victoriana, and the exuberance of Hollywood's golden age— a fusion of styles that reverberates in Watkins's illustrations.

Born and raised in Nyköping in Sweden, Watkins moved to the U.S. on her own at age 17. She studied at The Art Institute of Dallas in the late 1990s and moved to New York to start her career after graduation, taking things as they came along. "I didn't really concentrate purely on fashion back then, but happened to get commissioned by a lot of fashion brands and department stores." Her first big commission was a series of makeup ads for the luxury chain Barneys New York that appeared in the *New York Times* every Sunday over a two year period. "That was huge. Finally, I

could rent an apartment and didn't have to stay at the YMCA anymore."

It wasn't until after 10 years in the U.S., when Watkins moved back to Sweden, that she focused in on the fashion industry more consciously. "There wasn't really much of fashion illustration back then in Sweden. Of course Mats Gustavsson (my hero!), but he worked from New York. I worked a lot with a magazine called *Bibel* and there were a lot of new fashion brands starting up in Sweden at that time. So it was all very exciting."

COVER SWEDISH ELLE
(LEFT)
Client: Elle
With model Frida Gustavsson, who styled herself

FASHION OBSERVATIONS
(PAGE 160 & RIGHT)
Client: Muse magazine

Enjoying her field of work and fashion as a theme, Watkins became evermore immersed in it. "I believe you really have to know what you are doing in order to be good. So I read an awful lot about fashion, not just about shows but everything. A lot of biographies about people in the industry, books and magazines about the business of fashion. Also, I began to attend as many shows as I could."

Combining her untiring zest for exploring fresh creative approaches with a keen interest and growing expertise

in the field, Watkins now successfully collaborates with some of the industry's major players. Her projects for clients like MAC Cosmetics, Barneys, Victoria's Secret, Sephora, Max Mara, and Anna Sui have received broad acclaim. The Prada brand Miu Miu's 2008 spring collection featured Watkins's illustrations on 10 different outfits. In 2011, the deluxe leather accessory brand Valextra commissioned her for a range of visuals to be featured in their Milan store during the Salone del Mobile. That same year,

Absolut Watkins came out, her special-edition bottle that was received with great delight by fashion and vodka lovers alike.

Trends come and go, but Watkins's reputation remains strong among the international fashion industry. She particularly values the freedom that goes along with it. "It takes some experience in the field for commissioners to bring you into the process at an early stage, so that you can actually contribute to the idea and the brief. It is great to see how people are starting to trust you and your vision." She has arrived at a point in her career where she hardly ever feels the need to compromise. "I always put myself into the work. It's very rare that I just get a brief and have to stick with it."

For Watkins, illustration is all about storytelling. The key challenge for her is to create scenes as vivid and multifaceted as life itself. As she told Vogue in an interview, the characters in her drawings are all people to her. "I work out their whole story—where they live, if they have a boyfriend, their bank balances, and their style. That's why one girl might have only the jacket of a Victor & Rolf suit—she lost her job the week before so she can't afford the rest of it."

She wants the world to look at her drawings and see more than just a pretty picture. "I need the girls to be real. To feel real. I hate flatness and just beauty. So boring. That is also why I prefer to do my own styling or involve stylists that I trust in working with illustrations. I guess I work more as a photographer in picking my models, thinking about hair and makeup and clothes and then inventing a situation for them to play a part in. If I work with a model I envision the story before and have her act it out like a shoot."

The early stage of a new project, the phase of research and idea development, which tends to take as long as the drawing itself—these are the best moments for Watkins. "I take a lot of pictures for reference. It is so important for me to be prepared. To think and think and think and look for inspiration. I spend a lot of

PINK RIBBON
(TOP)
Campaign Against Breast Cancer

FASHION OBSERVATIONS
(RIGHT)
Client: Muse magazine

time looking at the photos I took, pairing them with clothes and fabrics and images that I find to add to the image. So in a way, the illustration is already finished when I start putting my pen to the paper. Then comes the frustrating part of drawing a picture that comes close to the one in my head. 99.9% of the time I am not completely satisfied."

Watkins draws on vellum with ArtLine0.5. "It's the only pen I can work with," she says. "Then, if I want to use color, I scan the drawings and color them

in Photoshop. My photographer friends taught me how to use the computer. So I work like them." While the technique remains more or less constant, the overall process varies greatly, according to Watkins's broad range of projects.

The Miu Miu collection, back in 2008, emerged from existing illustrations that the Miu Miu team had spotted in a book. Watkins did not even see the clothes until the opening, and without any concerns, as she commented on a Swedish website after the show. "When a company like Miu

Miu calls and says that Miuccia (Prada) likes your stuff, you go 'thank you, thank you, thank you for noticing me.' You don't demand to see anything in advance." Later, she reported how the Miu Miu team had "turned it all into magic!"

The commissions she takes particular pleasure in are those for print publications. "I love the work atmosphere at magazines," she says. She works with the big ones in fashion, like *Vogue, Elle, Bon, Tush,* and *D la Repubblica*. In 2003 her first book, *Watkins's Heroine*, was published as the result of a collaboration with graphic designer Stefania Malmsten, art director at *Bibel* magazine. *Watkins's Box of Pin Ups* followed, an exclusive box with 36 printed portraits by Watkins, including "Watkins's No 1", an album of photographs and sources of inspiration.

FASHION OBSERVATIONS
(ALL)
Client: Muse magazine

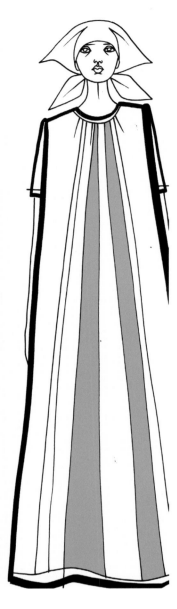

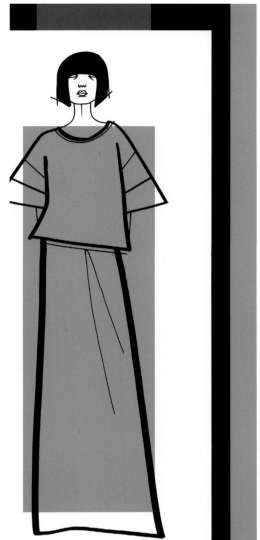

"I'm an illustrator and the most important thing is that my drawings are visible," Watkins says. Indeed, they are right there at the fashion forefront. Last year, her illustrations adorned two silk scarves by the fashion label Rodebjer, one of the most promising Swedish labels that has gained international acclaim over the past few years.

Watkins herself claims to have no interest in trends. Her work may constantly evolve but not in a chameleon-like way, to fit in, or to be "in." She worries about a lot of things, she says, but never about her style being in vogue or not. "I am so busy trying to find new ways of working that I do not have time to think about that. I also have two small children and that kind of changes your worries and priorities." She is aware of trends and takes note of the latest developments in fashion, but rejects their authority in favor of tradition. "The whole trend business gets a bit boring. I like the fact that fashion is now totally democratic, but some of the magic is lost."

Watkins moved to Milan in 2009, intrigued by the special atmosphere of the city and how it has preserved the sense of fashion as a traditional trade. "Milan is

discussing, work, pricing work. I am so bad at all that and trust them completely." Her agencies assist her in choosing among the requests she gets. "I tend to say yes to a little too much and they know my schedule better than I do, so they can stop me when I already have a lot of things going on."

local brands and believes in the benefits of personal contact. "I really like to meet people and I always have. My friends have been so important for me in my work. We work a lot together and some of my best friends I have met through working with them. I have a hard time

a fashion capital but also a small village in many ways. I love that it is not so cool here. To work in fashion is a job like being a plumber. Most people I meet work in fashion, simply because most people here do. It is a job and the tradition of fashion runs deep. The craftsmanship of it. I love the understanding of fashion that people have here. The knowledge. Then it is of course very handy to be close to a lot of fashion houses. To see the clothes upfront."

About 20% of Watkins's clients are based in Italy, and 40% in Sweden. The rest are spread across the globe, and she works with several agents, LundLund in Stockholm, Agent & Artists in Paris, Illustration Division in New York, and Atomo Management in Milan. "The agencies are so important and I have been so lucky finding really wonderful people. They mean everything! They are so much better at everything! Networking,

RODEBJER CHRISTMAS
(TOP)
2 scarves for Christmas 2012
Client: Rodebjer

ABSOLUT WATKINS
(RIGHT)
Client: Absolut Vodka

PATTERN
(RIGHT PAGE)
Client: Miu Miu

However much she trusts her agents, she also tries to get in touch with her clients personally whenever she can. "I always like to talk about a project a lot. It's good and prevents misunderstandings." She enjoys collaborating with

differentiating between work and play. It's all a bubble."

Her husband works in fashion, too. The two share a large studio/apartment near Porta Venezia, in a busy area full of shops and restaurants, together with their two children. She recently invited the Italian design platform Discipline to feature it for their "Living With" project, a series that portrays creative individuals and their homes. "I'm fortunate in that I've always thrived in working in a busy, loud environment. I'm not one of these people who needs peace and quiet," she said in the accompanying interview. The buzz of having two kids around is one thing, a bustling work atmosphere quite another. Watkins appreciates both. "I love doing set design and styling because you are part of a creative group of people. Illustration can be a bit lonely sometimes. That's why I try to involve other people in my drawings, taking pictures of models and friends and involving stylists."

Considering herself too restless to be working for just one client, Watkins has freelanced throughout her career. However, she does her best to maintain some daily routines. She has to, being the mother of two small children. She works intensely every day from 11am to 4pm, when she then picks up her son and goes to the park. "Then, I work whenever else I can," she adds, "usually at nights. My job is something that surrounds me almost constantly." What may sound daunting to many does not to her. She does not feel the need to escape. Her job is her passion, she declares, and that makes everyday feel like the weekend.

"The main problem for me is to try and take it easy with all the self-exploring. My agent in Sweden just told me to slow down with the exhibitions. I had two last year. So then I decided to establish my own little company." It is a clothing line for children for which she draws cheerful patterns, inspired by the life with her kids. "I spend so much time around them so I decided it's time for that to feed into my work." She is hoping to launch the brand sometime this year. "We will see how that goes." Her words reverberate with expectation and curiosity, proof that her thirst for new challenges has not yet been quenched.

Kustaa Saksi

PLACE AND DATE OF BIRTH
Kouvola, Finland; 1975
COUNTRY OF RESIDENCE
Netherlands
FAMILY STATUS
In a relationship
EDUCATION / DEGREE
BA in Graphic Design, Lahti Institute of Design, Finland
ACTIVE IN THE FIELD OF ILLUSTRATION SINCE
2001
BREAKTHROUGH PROJECT
Illustrations for Bon Magazine, Sweden
KEY CLIENTS
Nike, Levi's, Vespa, Swarovski, Playstation,
Issey Miyake, the New York Times, Nissan, Artek
MOST RENOWNED PROJECTS
Pavilion for Stockholm Furniture & Light Fair,
Installation for Nike 1948 showroom London,
Designs on trains for Finnish Railways
COMMISSIONS PER YEAR
20
AVERAGE TURNAROUND TIME PER COMMISSION
4 weeks
WORKSPACE
Own studio with a photographer
EMPLOYEES
None
AGENTS
NYC: Hugo & Marie, London: Dutch Uncle
HOW MUCH COMMISSION DO YOUR AGENTS TAKE
30%
TEACHING POSITIONS
None
AWARDS (SELECTION)
Communication Arts Award of Excellence
Clio Award, Gold; The One Show
Award, Gold; The Obies Award, Gold
MEMBER ASSOCIATIONS
None
GALLERIES
None

"I'VE NEVER SEEN MYSELF AS A CLASSIC ILLUSTRATOR, BUT MORE LIKE A HYBRID BETWEEN ARTIST AND DESIGNER."

Photo: Jussi Puikkonen

"To me, a grand artist is a mysterious character whose images have a certain magic in them," declares Kustaa Saksi. That magic, he believes, stems from experience, an outstanding eye for detail and, most importantly, a joyful and vivid imagination. Proving that he has plenty of each, the Finnish-born illustrator sweeps us away in a steady but energetic flow of psychedelic pop imagery. "I just like to envision concepts, ideas, and worlds," he says.

His worlds are kaleidoscopic and made up of wizard-hatted, water-spouting, twisting and turning enchanted valleys full of fantasy, where steep slopes meet thick woods with trees growing downward, and crowds of odd creatures merge into abstract patterns of organic shape. Arabesque lines recall meandering rivers, and water pools in varied aggregate states. Roundish formations resemble clouds or the Moominvalley rendered in surprisingly flashy colors. Saksi's work is a pop version of Scandinavian nature mysticism mixed with references evocative of the sixties.

When Saksi says he is inspired by nature, he certainly refers to the Nordic landscape. The illustrator's deep attachment to his homeland is chronicled in his 2008 *Offpiste: In the Land of Kustaa Saksi*. Not a classic monograph, this visual journey through Saksi's earlier career is interspersed with a selection of landscapes shot by a longtime friend of his, the Finnish photographer Matti Pyykköö. "In a way, I have always been interested in mixing illustration and graphic design with photography," Saksi explains. "In the case of this book, I felt that it provided room to breathe, and a balance to all the colorful illustration work that would have otherwise been too heavy." A real world backdrop to Saksi's otherworldly creations, Pyykköö's photos also provide a sense of biographical context and a perfect bridge to the beginning of his friend's career.

Born in Kouvola, southeastern Finland in 1975, Saksi studied graphic design at the Lahti Institute of Design. He wanted to become an architect first, but didn't pursue that idea because he considered himself bad at math. His interest in the arts and creative production emerged when his parents sent him to a local children's art school at the age of seven. "It was only in the afternoons, like twice a week, and mainly playing around, but they taught us various techniques in print-making, painting, and so on. Sometimes I was really super bored, and would have rather been outside playing football with my friends, but in retrospect I am very

PERFUME
(PAGE 168)
Client: the New York Times, 2006

REGULAR SHOW
(RIGHT)
Client: Cartoon Network, 2012

**AT THE SWAMP
AIRBORNE**
(BOTTOM)
Client: Lacoste, 2006

glad that my parents made me go, because these early experiences really pushed me in this direction." Soon he began to create covers and cartoons for the local kid's magazine run by his sisters. "I was always drawing pretty intensively—my school-book pages were full of doodling, mostly logos of bands. However, I didn't really think of my future as a professional artist before I got into the design institute in Lahti. I didn't really know what illustration was when I began to study. I didn't really know what graphic design was. I really learned all that there."

There were occasional classes in illustration, and Saksi created his own imagery whenever university breaks allowed, but on the whole he studied the full palette of general communication design and considers it a good foundation. "In fact, I've never seen myself as a classic illustrator, but more like a hybrid between artist and designer," Saksi says. Most importantly, he defines his practice by the freedom to implement his own artistic visions. And as with so many things in life, it would take a little detour to find out what these visions were.

After graduating in 2000, Saksi went to Helsinki and took a year-long job at a local design studio that specialized in classic corporate design. He then went on to work as an art director at a magazine for another year. "I was dealing with a lot of photographers and illustrators, and in a way it was nice because I was meeting loads of people. But it was mainly about managing things, organizing photo shoots, and stuff like that. Realizing that I'd really rather do the artwork myself was an important step though."

In his pursuit to become an independent artist, he began to experiment as a freelancer in Helsinki, sounding out his own visual language. It was then that he illustrated a few pages for the Swedish lifestyle magazine *Bon*, a project he would later refer to as his breakthrough. "Like many magazines they were very open

LUNARGLIDE
Client: Nike, 2009

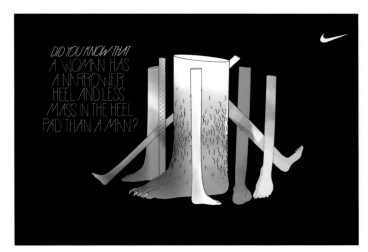

and eager to find new illustrators to work with, so the job really offered the opportunity to apply the style I had developed and show it to a broader audience." He began to work with his first agent from Amsterdam and for more and more international clients, mainly magazines.

In 2004 he moved to Paris. "I didn't speak French and didn't know many people there, but I kind of liked the sense of adventure. It sounds cliché to say that Paris is the city of artists, but I thought it was exciting to just go there, and the idea was to stay for a year or so." One year

turned into four, during which time he primarily worked in editorial illustration before leaving for Amsterdam, where he still currently lives. His studio is located in the center of the city on the top floor of an ancient cigar factory. He loves the beautiful light-filled environment, with the sun coming in from the multiple windows and skylights. He shares the place with photographer Jussi Puikkonen, a fellow Finnish acquaintance who he occasionally collaborates with. "The move to Amsterdam has been easy for me. I had always loved the vibe of the city, plus there were many people I knew, in part because my old agent had been located there."

Around 2006 he began working with his agents at Dutch Uncle in London, who are now in charge of the bulk of his European client commissions. Hugo & Marie in New York have covered the U.S. market for about 3 years. "I think London and New York are really the most important cities when it comes to commercial illustration, so you really need to have someone on the spot." About half of Saksi's

ART OF 99
(RIGHT)
Client: Nissan, 2011

BUTTERFLY
(LEFT)
Client: Vespa, 2006

IT'S GRIM UP NORTH
(BOTTOM)
Personal Work, 2008

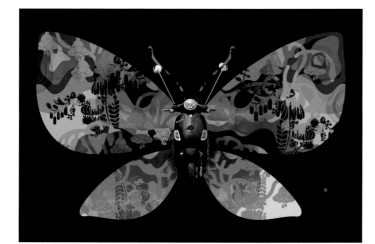

there's a problem to be solving through visual storytelling, in his words. Accordingly, he illustrates for advertising, books, tableware, fashion brands, music labels, designs window displays, sculptures, and installations. His patterns have adorned buildings, bodies, and iPad screens alike. He never consciously pushed a certain area of work, but preferred to actively cater to the greatest possible variety of clients. "I think it's nice and challenging to collaborate with people from very different backgrounds. You really learn a lot." Recently he teamed up with Swedish architect Gert Wingårdh to design a pavilion for the Stockholm Furniture and Light Fair. "I like to create spaces. I've been working on installations and large-scale artworks, but I think there is something extra special in working with a shape that gathers people inside, and really feel the space around you. I was very excited about that project."

clients are from Europe, the other half from the U.S. The only notable difference is that of time zones. "It can especially be a pain to work on West Coast time."

Saksi keeps in close touch with his clients throughout the creative process via email. Although an agent is indispensable in most cases, he likes to hand-pick a few projects that he can handle on his own. "It is crucial to find someone who fits your style and is ready to invest time in representing your art. Otherwise an agent is a waste of time." And certainly money. But both Dutch Uncle and Hugo & Marie are worth the 30% commission they take. Over the years Saksi's portfolio has grown to include key clients like Nike, Levi's, Vespa, Swarovski, PlayStation, Issey Miyake, the *New York Times*, Nissan, and the Finnish furniture company Artek.

Having started with editorial work like many young illustrators do, Saksi now feels at home in various fields—wherever

The organizers of the Fair had a rough idea about mixing architecture and illustration and approached Saksi and Wingårdh, considering them to be the perfect match for the job. They asked the two

upon in the end was a dome-like walk-in paper sculpture comprising thousands upon thousands of paper sheets, suspended from the ceiling in a vertical blind-like construction. Wingårdh came up with

of the lowest sheet in each stack, creating a 3D visual effect when viewed from underneath. From the outside, there were white sheets extending up to the ceiling to create translucent walls.

"Combining minimalist architecture and art, we managed well to create a surprise effect," Saksi says. "The artwork gave the pavilion another dimension and thought-provoking atmosphere. It was simple and complex at the same time." Preparations for construction took

months and the actual raising of the dome was a tricky task. But all in all, Saksi considers the whole experience very rewarding. He notes the carte blanche circumstances, the problem solving employed, the delicate technical procedures, the success of the final piece, and, with much emphasis, the spirit of collaboration. "It was great to work with such a talented team of people. We all shared the same level of ambition and wanted to create something extraordinary."

if they would be interested in collaborating on an installation piece to become part of the event. "They gave us largely free reign in the design and realization. There was no brief, and the furniture fair team encouraged us to let our imaginations run wild." Saksi had met with the event's producer, Sanna Gebeyehu, earlier in Stockholm, and then they all got together on Wingårdhs Architects' rooftop terrace to discuss the options and brainstorm.

"We had envisioned all kinds of crazy ideas at first. For example, we wanted to have real parrots in the installation, but that couldn't happen because the location's building regulations prohibited the use of live animals. But despite a few obstacles during the process, and budget limits of course, the project still offered countless options." The one they agreed

LUNARGLIDE RUNNING HISTORY
Client: Nike, 2009

ideas for the structure and material. Saksi drew a kaleidoscopic painting of mysterious sea creatures as a ceiling mosaic to be divided and printed on the downside

Continually approached as an artist collaborator, rather than an executive illustrator or designer, Saksi recently created patterns for the Italian fashion label Montecore's Spring/Summer 2013 collection. The design is inspired by the dazzle camouflage used on First World War battleships to avoid making classes of vessels recognizable to the enemy. "Working with fashion brands, I usually do a collection series. Some brands pay a one-off fee, others prefer contracts that depend on sales such as Levi's, for whom he did a series of fanciful prints in the past. T-Shirts, sweatshirts, dresses, scarves, and even shoes carry Saksi's designs.

Depending on the scope and complexity of his projects, Saksi still finds it important to meet collaborators for precise discussion. "Projects vary a lot, obviously. Sometimes I have a clean table to fill in my ideas, sometimes the client wants my view on things, sometimes they come up with a clear-cut brief that I just need to visualize. Despite, or perhaps precisely because of, the changing circumstances, it is crucial to always bear in mind who you're working for, what you're doing, and why you're doing it."

In 2011 Saksi collaborated with fabulous Studio Output from the U.K. on Sony PlayStation's PS3 theme "The Outer Woods." Taking on the challenge of moving his creations into a new dimension, he created "The Organic Underground" set for Granimator, a unique app for iPad that allows the user to create their own designs by selecting the images, color scheme, and backgrounds, adding the dimension of choice. Saksi took great pleasure in seeing his creations come to life, an experience he had already enjoyed when witnessing the computer renderings for his 2008 "Heroes" collection turning into 3D sculptures with the help of a Xerox printer and a 3D-artist from Helsinki. Using the Z Corp technology and corresponding

Saksi is in fashion but does not consciously try to be. "I can only do what comes naturally for me. I think many times artists' shapes resemble themselves—you can't run away from yourself." His style comes more from overglossy digitalism, futuristic features, and cut and paste than from nature. "I like to mix powerful art movements from the past in a contemporary manner, and to use the computer in a way it doesn't look like it was done with the computer." He masterfully moves between analog and digital mediums, between pencil, paint, and software.

"When the internet really started to work efficiently in the early 2000s, it completely changed the way images were created, used, and distributed," Saksi reminds us. "The same illustration trends are showcased, distributed, and made available everywhere in the world in seconds. That brought forth shrunken deadlines, cheap imitations, and sometimes a general lack of imagination, but it also promoted a bunch of excellent talents in illustration." All in all, Saksi welcomes the democratic rise of the internet, and the

STOCKHOLM PAVILION
Client: Stockholm Furniture &
Light Fair, 2013

many ways in which it has changed his professional environment. "Suddenly, you didn't have to post bulky CDs and DVDs anymore—all the data was running freely by emails and fast servers. It meant illustrators could be hired anywhere in the world and that their physical presence wasn't needed anymore."

materials, each figure was put together by building up 2,500 printed layers.

Always on the lookout for new processes, materials, and ideas to feed into his practice, Saksi is, in a way, always working. He tries to squeeze holidays into his tight schedule and has developed a preference of regular office hours and free evenings to spend time with his girlfriend. All in all, his ambition to test and explore different mediums keeps him on his toes, within or in between commissions. "Experimenting keeps the working process fresh and interesting, which is why I like to work on commercial and art projects side by side." Realizing about 20 commissions each year with an average turnaround time of four weeks, he spends around 80% of his time on illustration and design projects, and the rest on experimentation and self-initiated art. He wishes that this ratio was more balanced. "I am aiming towards something like fifty-fifty—more art, and more exhibitions."

Saksi's 3D sculptures have been put on show in the popup gallery Maxalot in Amsterdam, and later were sold in his

SWEETHEART
(LEFT PAGE)
Client: Nico, 2011

ON TOP OF THE WORLD
(TOP, 2 IMAGES)
Client: Montevideo, 2007

DEAD CALM
(BOTTOM)
Client: Falter, 2008

webshop for €1,200.00, signed and numbered, in extremely limited editions of three. They are sold out, and he has not worked on art like this since. He would like to at some point, but the idea is on hold as he has turned his attention to something new. "Lately, I've been working with wool fabrics at a weavery. It's sort of a modern version of traditional tapestry."

Creating his wool designs while keeping the final product in view can be quite challenging. While his "Heroes" could be digitally visualized during the process, the renderings here are done in his mind. "It's intriguing to finally start actual weaving and see it all come together from millions of threads. The best things often happen intuitively, or by accident." The downside of wool is its comparatively high material costs, which Saksi hopes to be able to cover through his commercial work. "I fell in love with the technique, and would love to take that all forward."

He is currently putting together an exhibition for a gallery in Helsinki in August 2013 consisting of about eight to ten wool pieces plus a few prints to support the overall theme. There are plans for it to travel to New York later in the year. He hopes to put some of the works on sale in his web shop, as he notes that the site is outdated. "I haven't had the time to update it for quite a while. But distributing my work is definitely one thing that I want to expand upon in the future." The how and when is still up in the air as are his upcoming ventures. "I would like to work more in architecture, or expand into theater or moving image. There's just too many exciting ways to go."

Catalina Estrada

PLACE AND DATE OF BIRTH
Medellin, Colombia; 1974

COUNTRY OF RESIDENCE
Spain

FAMILY STATUS
Married

EDUCATION / DEGREE
Degree in Graphic Design

ACTIVE IN THE FIELD OF ILLUSTRATION SINCE
2006

BREAKTHROUGH PROJECT
Coca-Cola Easter Campaign

KEY CLIENTS
Paul Smith, Coca-Cola, Microsoft, Paulo Coelho, Camper, Nike, Levis, Smart/Mercedes Benz, Unicef, Anunciaçao, the municipalities of Barcelona and London, and the Government of India among others

MOST RENOWNED PROJECTS
Collaboration for Paul Smith W/2007 collection, Paulo Coelho's diaries, Wallpaper collection, Anunciaçao's collections

COMMISSIONS PER YEAR
About 15

AVERAGE TURNAROUND TIME PER COMMISSION
10 days for first approach

WORKSPACE
Home studio

EMPLOYEES
1

AGENTS
1

HOW MUCH COMMISSION DO YOUR AGENTS TAKE
30%

TEACHING POSITIONS
None

AWARDS
Not submitting work for contests

MEMBER ASSOCIATIONS
None

GALLERIES
None

"MY IDEAL WORKING ENVIRONMENT IS EVERYWHERE, WHERE I FIND A GOOD INTERNET CONNECTION, NICE LANDSCAPE, AND NICE WEATHER."

Imagine a wonderland brimming with fabulous creatures and mutating florals; surreal landscapes and detached narratives poised between Latin American Folklore and Japanese Animé. Imagine it all in psychedelically saturated colors, and on gradient backdrops interspersed with ornaments and occasional polka dots, scattered through a kaleidoscopic prism. What your inner eye gazes at now, in astonishment and in a light and revitalizing state of intoxication, may come close to Catalina Estrada's illustrations.

Flaunting textures and shapes in the most exuberant digital multiplications, Estrada's work perfectly encapsulates the collision between the artificial and the natural. Her hallucinogenic patterns recall psychedelic art, though with cheerful, bright, and suspiciously optimistic tones, as opposed to melancholic and destructive undertones. Estrada's vivid imagination is powered by nature and an innate, unconditional love for it.

The Colombian-born artist grew up in the countryside, surrounded by nature and in a house she describes as full of beautiful and particular things. "My mother is an artist and she loves decorating her home and collecting all kinds of objects. She has an amazing and very personal sense of beauty and a feel for combining colors like no one else I know. Each wall of her house has its own specific color that matches perfectly with the beams and walls. It is as if every room has its own atmosphere by the colors that she uses."

Estrada soon knew that she wanted to be an artist like her mother, a fine artist in fact, but somehow she ended up enrolling in graphic design at Universidad Pontificia Bolivariana in her hometown

BOXES AND STATIONERY
COLLECTION
(TOP)
Client: Maku
Photo: Pancho Tolchinsky

CLOTHING COLLECTION
F/W 2012
(PAGE 178)
Client: Anunciaçao
Fashion design: Maria Elvira Crosara
Photo: Pancho Tolchinsky

of Medellin. After graduation, she began to work freelance as a designer. "But as much as I enjoyed things like typography and layout, I was always more in love with the image itself." She describes the early days of her career back in Columbia as an interim stage of juvenile curiosity, realizing she wanted to learn more about art history, longing for the bigger picture. "When I traveled to Barcelona, I found this public art academy, Escola de Artes Llotja, and absolutely fell in love with it. I thought: This is my last chance to study fine art. So I went for it." Estrada moved to Spain in 1999—she was 26 then—and attended the academy, specializing in lithography.

She graduated three years later, finding that the art world was neither like, nor open to the colorful and flowery images that she painted. "I tried really hard to make a living out of my art, without much success. Barcelona's art scene was totally abstract at that time and my work was way too figurative, so no gallery would take me. I even tried to be minimalist,

and I tried to be abstract, but it was not in me." Disappointed and slightly frustrated, Estrada reverted to graphic design to pay her rent. Art became something she did for herself, happy to finally work free of financial pressure. "I just produced what I felt I needed to produce, for myself, without worrying so much, and that felt perfectly healthy. When it came to making a living, I said: Ok, let's grab the computer again and do some flyers."

Estrada's transition from graphic design to illustration was a smooth one, proceeding naturally and somewhat unconsciously. Imbued by the surreal, painterly vividness of her fine art projects, her graphic language came to distinguish itself through its floral contours, organic shapes, ornaments, and a highly saturated, wide color spectrum. "As a logical consequence, I was commissioned for more projects that were not strictly graphic design, but rather decorative. At the same time, I felt more drawn to projects that, without me noticing it, were in fact more illustration than

graphic design." The first time Estrada recalls having been consciously commissioned as an illustrator was in 2005, for Gestalten's book *1001 Nights,* where her exotic images reinterpret the story of Aladdin and his lamp. She now usually presents herself as an illustrator, though she admits that she still sometimes feels more like a graphic decorator.

It was due to constant self-promotion that big-time illustration commissions would soon roll in. "I was writing to lots of magazines, blogs, etc., trying to get my work published and exposed. As a result, I started getting commissions by clients I would have never imagined, who were asking me to work on their projects using my own style." Coca-Cola Australia called her to ask for a limited-edition bottle to be included in their 2007 Easter campaign, and she received email requests from Paul Smith and Smart, while also doing ads for Motorola, Schweppes, and Bombay Sapphire.

Having more or less stumbled into big business, she had to learn quickly how to manage herself, write contracts, and handle the negotiations. Simultaneously, she began working with different illustration agents who provided her with better insight into the illustration world and a continuous stream of commissions. These were, at that stage of Estrada's career, mainly advertising campaigns. She refers to them as short-term projects to distinguish them from the extensive product lines that would soon become the mainstay of her work.

"The turning point was when I became initiated into the licensing industry." She recalls her first licensing project for the Dutch company Stationary Team, who commissioned her to design a back-to-school collection about four years ago. "Being unfamiliar with this new world, I was not very sure this was the path I wanted to take." However, as more clients began to contact her to decorate their products, she began pushing her work in that direction.

The way licensing works is that an artist or designer leases a certain image to a manufacturer or retailer. This can be something produced for them, in response to a brief, or it can be an existing piece that they chose to work with. Estrada holds a readily available portfolio of patterns and images from which her licensing partners choose. "Clients are very different. However, few licensors like to start from scratch. Most prefer to be served a series of images that you have to offer for licensing. That means that I usually work on patterns without knowing where they

TRAVEL BAGS
Client: Joumma Bags
Photo: Pancho Tolchinsky

will end up being used. I create a sort of catalog to propose potential illustrations. Or I can even propose a series of images for a collection of products."

A licensing agreement regulates how the designs can be applied to a certain product, or a product range, and allows the licensor to use Estrada's name as a brand marketing tool. In return, she receives financial remuneration, usually in the form of a minimum guaranteed

BAGS
(LEFT)
Client: Maku
Photo: Pancho Tolchinsky

CLOTHING
(RIGHT)
Client: Massana
Photo: Pancho Tolchinsky

fee, paid in advance, and as royalty on a percentage of sales. "It is great if the products sell well, but even if they don't, it's more the licensor's risk than mine. I don't have to invest in anything financially, I only invest my work. It is up to them to take care of the production, the sales, and distribution—all the things that I don't enjoy so much."

Stepping back from the operational responsibility that ownership entails,

Estrada accepts having to cut down on creative leeway. She may not always agree with her licensors' choices and art direction, but approves them with sound professionalism. "It is them taking the risk, so I have to please them. Also, they know their clients and have more experience in selling than I do. Working with a client, and with a licensing client in particular, means forfeiting full control of the design and searching for solutions

that both sides are happy with. It can be tricky, of course, but I got more confident over time."

A diverse range of licensing products has emerged over time, from stationary items and wallpaper to handbags and extensive clothing collections. Essentially, these are everyday objects, and Estrada loves the idea of turning them into something special and unique with her artwork. "Seeing the pieces produced is something that never stops entertaining me." Sometimes there is disappointment, too, when things don't come out as expected, but Estrada trusts that one can learn from mistakes, provided that they are properly understood.

Since working in the licensing industry, issues like material and quality have become more and more important to her. "The first thing I ask my clients when they present the brief is the printing technique and material they intend to use. For me, this is almost as important as the brief itself. Working with so many colors, I really have to be aware of the limitations of each printing technique. I work with so many colors, gradients, details and so on, that this brings a lot of trouble when printing, for instance with screen printing. It is very important to know what suits your style and how to achieve good results. So if a client says they use screen printing, I know that I have to work flat, with clean lines, avoiding delicate details and too many colors. I try to make the client understand that, but obviously that is not always easy. Some clients are quite stubborn—they have to make their mistakes themselves."

Estrada loves to work with clients who encourage close collaboration. Some include her in material choices that define the quality of a product. "It is great to work as a team, and around people who push and inspire you." She highlights the Brazilian fashion brand Anunciaçao in this context. "We have worked on 15 collections together and I always fall in love with the clothes that Maria Elvira designs with my illustrations. She doesn't stop to surprise me. Also, she gives me so much freedom. This is the kind of project where

SKIN COLLECTION
(LEFT PAGE)
Catalina Estrada Collection of skins for multiple devices
Client: Decal Girl

HELMET COVER
(THIS PAGE)
Client: Helmetdress

I can see my visual language evolve."

Estrada works intuitively, and loves to see the new-fangled energies set free in her fine art flow into her commercial projects. Regrettably, most of her clients stick to her tried and trusted style. "Some are afraid that my work will not be recognizable any longer if I evolve it too much. They tend to reject a new pattern the first time I show it to them. However, once they see it published by someone else, then they want it." This is the way things go in the lifestyle industry. And this is why Estrada keeps working on personal projects, where she can surely experiment and refine her visual language.

Estrada paints, mostly in acrylics. Occasionally she exhibits her work in galleries like La Luz de Jesus in Los Angeles,

Roa La Rue in Seattle, and, until they closed their doors about two years ago, at Iguapop in Barcelona. Estrada's art, as well as the sketches and notebooks that feed into it, provide a counterbalance to her otherwise entirely digital process.

Estrada's commercial projects take form in the software Illustrator. Most of the time, she draws directly onto a Wacom graphic tablet that is connected to her computer. "The fact that I studied graphic design made me feel comfortable working with vectors. Also, I have always loved working with very vivid colors, gradients, symmetries, and so on." Her technique allows her to work swiftly and flexibly. "I like to travel and have learned to be very practical and work with very few things. I just need the laptop, the

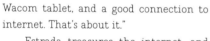

WALLPAPER
(LEFT)
Silver Stars and Deers Border
Client: Coordonné
Photo: Jordi Canosa

WALLPAPER
(BOTTOM)
Owls Forest
Client: Coordonné
Photo: Jordi Canosa

WALLPAPER
(RIGHT PAGE)
Life Tree
Client: Coordonné
Photo: Jordi Canosa

travels a lot, she rarely gets together with her clients in person. The exception is Maria Elvira from Anunciaçao, but mostly because her husband Pancho, a photographer, takes the pictures of the designer's collections. "We both travel together since I love meeting her and being part of the photo shoot." But most often, the bulk of client communication is via email, or via agents.

"I have been working with my licensing agents from Barcelona for about four years now. They take care of the negotiations, contracts, payment, and other management issues. They are very present throughout the process. What I particularly appreciate about the agents that I am working with is that the entire interaction with the clients remains fully transparent." Estrada considers her agents collaborators, rather than service providers, and attaches great value to what she calls the human aspect. "Confidence and a friendly relationship are extremely important to me." She maintains friendly and extremely fruitful relationships with Folio, from the UK, with Unit, from the Netherlands, and with Magnet Reps in the U.S. In light of Estrada's recent focus on licensing, her agents at the Spanish Grupo Edebé have gained importance as frequent and trusted collaborators.

Having worked freelance since the early days of her career, Estrada has never contemplated working in-house for a design studio or a brand; giving up her independence has not even crossed her mind. That she has never struggled for commissions may be due to well-chosen agents, or to her own knack for self-promotion and the presence that she gained through mailing lists and social networks. "To my never-ending surprise, it has always been the clients approaching me because they want to work with me on a specific project."

The only trouble with working freelance, for Estrada, is finding time for herself. The fact that she works from home does not make it easier. "During the first couple of years I was almost always working. I had to learn to work on my own schedule, to find time to rest, to exercise, to travel, to meet friends, and to enjoy life as much as possible. When I'm home I usually wake up at about 8:30 am, then it's 20 minutes of meditation, 20 minutes of yoga, a shower, and then work until 2 pm. Then I have lunch, and start working again from 4 pm to 8 pm more or less."

Wacom tablet, and a good connection to internet. That's about it."

Estrada treasures the internet, and how it has influenced her field of work over the past two decades or so. "Today, we have access to a huge amount of information, not only for graphical references but also for DIY tutorials and forums that solve most of our questions in very little time. I really believe it's an amazing age to be an illustrator. Also, it has become much easier to showcase our work, to meet and build a community with other illustrators. The internet allows us to directly connect with people who appreciate our work and with people we admire." And, this has made it possible to work for clients across the globe.

Most of Estrada's clients are located abroad, and recently there has been an influx of Spanish clients. Although she

Of course, I don't strictly stick to that schedule, and especially when I'm traveling it is almost impossible to maintain it. However, one thing is for sure: I never do nightshifts. I don't think that's healthy and I value sleep a lot. Even worse, I'm not a nice person to be around when I don't sleep enough. I have learned that resting is a very good investment. Also, I think it's important to free up some time to be able to do things that enrich your life as well as your career." She occasionally turns down a few commissions for that matter, and has just begun working with a part time assistant. "We are in trial period, finding out what her tasks are, but taking care of the graphic design for newsletters, catalogs, etc is my basic need in order for me to have more time to focus on the illustration part."

Besides commissions and free art projects, Estrada has recently started to give talks at design events and conferences.

CLOTHING COLLECTION F/W 2012
(BOTH PAGES)
Client: Anunciação
Clothes design: Maria Elvira Crosara
Photos: Pancho Tolchinsky

Most recently, she has introduced her work and projects at OFFF Barcelona and the FID design festival in Costa Rica. "It's great for me to meet other designers or illustrators that I admire a lot. Also, hearing their talks is really great because you get to really see the human being behind the projects, and then you feel connected in many ways. You learn a lot and you get very inspired."

Obviously, international events go well with Estrada's passion for traveling. "When I get invited to talk about my work at conferences in other countries, I make the best profit from it, taking my husband with me, and staying longer."

Her voice sounds as cheerful as her images look. "If we travel for pleasure," and they do so a lot, "we are usually away for a month or even more. In order to be able to do that I have learned to work on specific projects while I'm traveling. This means I might be in the middle of the jungle, but if a project has to be delivered, I will be working there and I'm fine with that. Otherwise I wouldn't be able to travel so much. My ideal working environment is everywhere, where I find a good internet connection, nice landscape, and nice weather." We see all that reflected in Catalina Estrada's work.

Narrative Illustration

While the term visual narrative is often used as an all-encompassing idiom and a generic sub-genre of visual studies itself, the label narrative illustration is most often associated with illustrated books, comics, and stereotypical superheroes. This chapter goes beyond such classic examples and beyond the general assumption that stories have to unfold in space and time. Focusing on the narrative notion, rather than its traditional forms, it portrays illustrations of various kinds and formats. Tied together by the visual sense of story, they present themselves loosely grouped and visually diverse. Unlike comics, which have over the years developed a distinct style of their own, narrative illustration in a broader sense is indeterminable in terms of genre, look, and technique. Just as different cultures have forged various ways to discern narratives from pictures in the course of history, different illustrators have put forth idiosyncratic modes of rendering them. Oliver Jeffer's children's picture books and Henning Wagenbreth's book covers represent two particularly longstanding outlets for illustration, and stand side by side with visuals produced in the context of graphic novels, animated movies, and promotional posters, like Tomer Hanuka's. Illustrators who represent and interpret the meaning of existing stories are featured alongside those who are authors themselves, and works that are produced single-handedly are featured next to collaborations with other artists, writers, ad agencies, or larger production teams. Excerpts of sequential illustrations are juxtaposed with examples that encapsulate narratives in one single image. More often than not, imagination sets the only limits for fantasy and fiction.

Tomer Hanuka

PLACE AND DATE OF BIRTH
Tel Aviv, Israel; 1974

COUNTRY OF RESIDENCE
Israel

FAMILY STATUS
Married

EDUCATION/DEGREE
Degree in Visual Arts

ACTIVE IN THE FIELD OF ILLUSTRATION SINCE
2000

BREAKTHROUGH PROJECT
Bipolar comics covers

KEY CLIENTS
The New Yorker

MOST RENOWNED PROJECTS
Marquis De Sade book cover

COMMISSIONS PER YEAR
20–50

AVERAGE TURNAROUND TIME PER COMMISSION
1 week

WORKSPACE
Studio

EMPLOYEES
None

AGENTS
None

TEACHING POSITIONS
2010–2012: School of Visual Arts, New York

AWARDS (SELECTION)
Society of Illustrators, Silver medal (2010);
Society of Publication Designers, Silver medal
(2010); British Design Museum Award (2008);
Society of Illustrators, Gold and Silver medal
(2000/2004/2006); The Harvey Award, Nomination:
Best Cover Artist (2004); The Society of Publication
Designers, Silver medal (2004) ; The Eisner Award,
Nomination: Best Short Story (2003); Ignatz Award,
Nomination: Promising New Talent (2002)

MEMBER ASSOCIATIONS
Society of Illustrators

GALLERIES
None

"THE ACTUAL PLOT POINTS EXIST IN THE TEXT. I HAVE THE FREEDOM TO SHOW SOMETHING THAT HAS A MYSTERY, THAT ISN'T RESOLVED IN A NARRATIVE SENSE."

Photo: Oscar Estrada

Each and every image by Israeli illustrator Tomer Hanuka is a story in its own right. Be it a scene, an object, or a portrait, his aim is to create a sense of narrative, a larger world, a context in which the image exists. Drawing, to Hanuka, is much like staging or directing a movie. "Any artist naturally gravitates toward a specific sensibility and would be wise to recognize that. I am a visual story teller," he declares.

Hanuka's work has an immersive quality to it, and the sense of narrative is ever-present. Stylistically, too, his illustrations recall good old adventure stories. There is a spark of nostalgia that resonates, the influence of his childhood heroes like Akira and the famous protagonists from the Marvel and DC classics. "My work is probably most closely related to whatever you think about when you hear the word 'comics,'" Hanuka says. Indeed, he was an avid comics reader as a kid, which led him to illustration in the first place.

"My earliest memory plants me on a Persian carpet, drawing, with my brother," he recalls in an interview with *Computer Arts Magazine* in 2010. "We're surrounded by American comic books, this is the late 70s, the windows are open, and a warm wind blows in. It's summer—it's always summer in the Middle East—yellow, dusty. The comics are just so mysterious and majestic; an unreachable light in a faraway land. It's more beautiful and exciting than anything else around. Years later I pack a suitcase and move to New York, looking for that hypnotic land of full-color magic. Eventually I had to concede that I'll never find it, the light remains out of reach. And that was the point—getting lost."

Hanuka attended the School of Visual Arts in New York in the late 1990s. Many of his early projects appear inspired by the comic books of his childhood: the experimental comic book series entitled *Bi-Polar* that he created with his twin brother Asaf, the self-authored and illustrated *Placebo Man*, a compilation of short comic stories, and the comic anthology *Meathaus* that he co-published with

THE FURIES
(PAGE 190)
For a short story by Paul Therdoux
Client: the New Yorker
Art Direction: Jordan Awan

mostly fiction of various genres. "There is usually a narrative that needs to be condensed and presented visually. It includes a form of editing, dramatizing, directing, pacing, etc. It's more about hiding than showing, in a sense—creating a sense of a bigger world by showing the very edge of something interesting."

Many of Hanuka's "visual stories" are told in a single image, a moment that "acts

a setting that seems meaningful to him while reading the text. "Stories naturally have that metaphoric core in them, a moment where the thing the story is about suddenly becomes very stark, or is presented in a way that echoes beyond the plot, sometimes a touch surreal or lyrical, or just very specific in some sense. It can be as subtle as a woman standing at the dock of a train station. Having read the story, you

some fellow students at SVA. But while his brother Asaf pursued a career as a cartoonist, Tomer Hanuka has come to see comics as "fun side projects," very different from the illustration work that makes up the majority of his diverse portfolio.

His portfolio includes advertising and film posters, editorial pieces for magazines like *Playboy, Rolling Stone, Business Week, Time,* and the *New York Times,* and book covers for publishers like Penguin or Random House. The latter two are Hanuka's specialty. He enjoys working with stories,

HARD APPLE:
FAN TAN
(THIS PAGE)
PING PONG SHOW DOWN
(RIGHT PAGE TOP)
CANDY STORE
(RIGHT PAGE BOTTOM)
Concept art for an animated
TV series based on the books of
Jerome Charyn. Created with
Asaf Hanuka
Client: Canal +

as a metaphor for the entire thing." When working with more literal subjects, like in advertising, the narrative is usually a message to be communicated clearly and precisely. "When illustrating fiction, the purpose is to open up a window, or expose an edge of something that will remain hidden for the most part until you read the story, making a visual that will spark someone's imagination, urging a viewer to write his/her own story in their mind."

To find the metaphorical moment in a story, Hanuka scribbles down actions or

can infuse a static scene with emotion and hindsight. The angle in which the image is drawn, the scale of the woman, her posture, the colors, how the space around her reacts to her figure—all these are choices and interpretations that can be effective in exploring her state of mind, and through it a suggestion of the larger world of the story."

Aside from twenty to fifty commercial commissions a year, each that he realizes in an average turnaround time of one week, Hanuka is currently working on his first graphic novel, a book called

The Divine, with his brother Asaf and the writer Boaz Lavie. He calls it a passion project, knowing that the amount of time and effort bears no reasonable relation to the expected financial gain. "Asaf and I were cooking this one for a while. I've created a bunch of concept art for it, and we've written a few treatments for the story. Eventually we asked Boaz, who is a great writer, to join the team and write it. He took it and made it his, and we loved the result. Then Asaf and Boaz developed layouts and now we are properly drawing it." Hanuka declares that his brother's layouts are much stronger than his. His specialty is the ink and color.

To Hanuka, color is most importantly a way of bringing images to life. "Color evokes emotion and mood specifically when tied to a narrative. I find it the most affective and effective weapon in the arsenal of an image-maker," he once told the magazine *LDN* in an interview. "Color is weakest when predictable," he went on to say. No surprise then, that most of his color schemes feel unlikely and surreal. Using color to express an internal quality of things, and to establish an emotional space where the image exists, his core aim is to make the image feel real. And real, to Hanuka, means imbued by authentic

emotion, rather than life-like and naturalistic qualities. "While the drawing is therefore the concrete, believable world, the colors are more emotional and expressive." As an illustrator, Hanuka considers it his responsibility to foresee the audience's expectations and work along/against them—along, so there is a rapport with the viewer, establishing trust; against, so the image is surprising and exciting, a new experience. That may be achieved through color schemes, or the manipulation of details, "such as a woman's feet turned into hooves," he says.

Hanuka's illustrations are surprising indeed, telling of an abundance of thoughts and fantasies. Instead of following content or clients' briefs strictly and in a servile way, they transcend alleged limitations with ease. "The actual plot points exist in the text. I have the freedom to show something that has a mystery, that isn't resolved in a narrative sense." The visual work on Hanuka's end complements content by picking up on its metaphorical core, and rendering it in a way that can be either "super dramatic or static and quiet." He particularly appreciates the opportunity to experiment with color, and his recent penchant for simplicity. "I'm drawing less scenes that involve huge crowds now, and trying to express what I need to say with only one or two figures. I think my work becomes more minimal."

Hanuka finds himself thinking a lot about the essence of ideas, and what makes a good illustration. Knowing that there is no formula, he has been trying to grab at the "fog called quality," teaching a portfolio class for seniors at the School of Visual Arts in New York. Researching references and figuring out the right approach to a new subject takes up a good deal of time in his own practice, too. After all, the approach "affects every aspect of the image—the way symbols are presented or manipulated, the color palette, the level of interpretations, etc."

Once the direction is set, Hanuka starts drawing thumbnails, up to 20 stamp-size images. Then he chooses the best

WALTZ WITH BASHIR
(LEFT PAGE)
Key frame and concept art for the animated documentary
Client: Bridgit Folman Film Gang
Art direction: David Polonsky
Director: Ari Folman

MELANCHOLIA
(TOP)
Limited edition screen print for Lars Von Trier's film
Client: Magnolia Pictures/Mondo

OVERKILL
(RIGHT)
Tomer Hanuka's monograph showcasing selected works from the first decade of the 21st century. Designed and edited by Anton Ioukhnovets
Gingko Press

three to enlarge and elaborate on. These sketches, essentially still rough line-works, are emailed to the client for approval. "Hopefully the one I liked best is chosen, but the rule is that you always get the one you hate," he reports to his students on his website. For the actual illustration, Hanuka then works with pencils, ink, and brush. Usually he transfers the sketch onto a Bristol paper at about 200 percent of the final size. Then he inks with a brush, scans the line art, and colors it in Photoshop.

The successful fusion of hand and computer work has been hailed a characteristic feature of Hanuka's work. The proportion of the digital work is growing since he has started using Manga Studio, a software application designed to facilitate

the digital creation of comics. It has tools for creating panel layouts, perspective rulers, sketching, inking, textures, and coloring. "The benefit is that you never need to leave the computer. It all happens there, from start to finish. I am using it here and there for inking, and the way things go, I'd probably use it more."

Client communication has long become completely digitized. Hanuka discusses all briefs and sketches by email, finding that it works very well. Email inquiries flow naturally, too. "My only marketing moves in the last decade were profiles in *American Illustration* and the *Society of Illustrators Annuals*. I don't have an agent. I get work from other work being out there. That is my guess at least." Regular contributions to many internationally read magazines like *Time*, the *New Yorker*, the *New York Times*, and *Rolling Stone* grant Hanuka good exposure. Numerous endorsements add to it. In 2008, a book cover he illustrated for Penguin's Classics Deluxe Editions won

the British Design Museum award. In 2009, the Israeli animated documentary *Waltz with Bashir* was nominated for an Oscar, with Hanuka as part of the art team. In 2012, Hanuka's first monograph, *Overkill,* came out, showcasing over a decade of his illustration work.

Success, of course, did not arrive overnight. There were challenges and compromises too along the way. He spent the first six months after graduation drawing cartoon dogs for a start-up company that produced reading exercise books for children. "I was glad to get a paycheck but was constantly promoting (mail-outs, portfolio drop-offs) to get the freelance thing happening." The office was downtown, right by Wall Street, and Hanuka had to dress formally, which he loathed doing. "When I got fired, I went downstairs and walked around the river and felt extremely lucky. Sometimes life just hands you a shortcut. It'll be dreary for a while, and my girlfriend at the time was pissed, but there was a long-term thing I was pursuing and getting fired got me closer to it."

Rigorous in the pursuit to establish himself as an independent commercial artist, Hanuka took on incredible amounts of commissions. For a while, he took two to four projects a week, which led to numerous discoveries and notable improvements, but also to a point where he felt burnt-out, creatively. The experience taught him to be more selective. Time for personal work that isn't client-generated is still hard to find, but Hanuka has developed an effective solution. "The secret for longevity is, for me at least, finding something for you to explore in a certain project, your own formal research, almost independent from the assignment. Some jobs offer that sense of journey and that leads to good results most of the time."

The sense of journey—into the unknown, even—is clearly exemplified in the Bashir documentary, a project that led Hanuka to explore interdisciplinary collaboration. He recalls the experience as a tough test in letting go: "You don't have much control over the final product, so it's about trusting that it will fall into place. The Bashir team was extremely committed and talented, so it worked out well." Borne out of past experience and the success of the project, Hanuka has recently wrapped a development package for an

300 FILM POSTER
(LEFT PAGE)
Part of the Zack Snyder Director's Series. Screen print edition of 300
Client: Mondo

MEANS OF SUPPRESSING DEMONSTRATIONS
(THIS PAGE)
Short story by Shani Boianjiu
Client: the New Yorker
Art Direction: Jordan Awan

animated crime TV show called *Hard Apple*, with his brother. "The story is based on a book by Jerom Charyn. Asaf and myself did all the design, layouts, and illustration. There is a team of writers and animators involved. Canal Plus, the TV studio in France has picked up the

package, so it's now in the hands of producers to take it to the next stage."

Though he has arrived at a point where he can pick and choose the assignments that are satisfying and creatively challenging, it took Hanuka a while to allow himself to experiment beyond

HARD APPLE: SHOWER
(THIS PAGE)
Concept art for an animated TV
series based on the books of Jerome
Charyn. Created with Asaf Hanuka
Client: Canal +

THE KNOWN UNIVERSE
(RIGHT PAGE)
Limited edition print for
Valentine's Day
Personal Work

commercial briefs, to break out of the deadline treadmill and take time off for longer, self-initiated projects like the graphic novel he is working on now with his brother and Boaz Lavie. Doing his best to fit both free and commercial, short-term and long-term projects into a daily schedule, from 8 am to 6 or 7 pm Hanuka keeps himself flexible in terms of location. At one point he moved from New York to London for three years with his wife during her studies. Now they are based in Tel Aviv. "All I need is a quiet studio next to a private garden, similar to the one I am working in now," he says. "I can work from everywhere."

Regardless of place, the role of the illustrator in culture and commerce is shifting these days—from the service provider to the industrious producer, as Hanuka argues: "While print publishing shrinks, illustrators have broken into making things, rather than just illustrating them." While he observes others becoming "mini-CEOs, poster-makers, puppet designers, or T-shirt warriors," Hanuka has most eminently remained true to his core business of producing visual stories—printed, unprinted, or in any form whatsoever.

PLACE AND DATE OF BIRTH

Port Hedland, Australia; 1977

COUNTRY OF RESIDENCE

United States

FAMILY STATUS

Married

EDUCATION / DEGREE

Certificate in Foundation Studies in Art and Design
University of Ulster, Belfast, Northern Ireland
BA (hons) Visual Communication University of Ulster,
Belfast, Northern Ireland

ACTIVE IN THE FIELD OF ILLUSTRATION SINCE

1999

BREAKTHROUGH PROJECT

How to Catch a Star published by
HarperCollins UK and Penguin US

KEY CLIENTS

TED, Orange UK, Lavazza, United Airlines, Newsweek,
Wired, Irish Times, the Guardian, Creative Review, the
New York Times, Kinder Chocolate, and the Telegraph

MOST RENOWNED PROJECTS

Books including How to Catch a Star (2004),
Lost and Found (2005), The Incredible Book Eating Boy
(2006), The Great Paper Caper (2008), The Heart and
the Bottle (2010), The Hueys in The New Jumper (2012),
This Moose Belongs to Me (2012), The Hueys in It
Wasn't Me (2013), Lost and Found
Animation with Studio AKA

COMMISSIONS PER YEAR

Depends on schedule

AVERAGE TURNAROUND TIME PER COMMISSION

Depends on the project

WORKSPACE

Private studio

EMPLOYEES

2 plus an intern

AGENTS

The Bell Lomax Moreton Agency

HOW MUCH COMMISSION DO YOUR AGENTS TAKE

N/A

TEACHING POSITIONS

None

AWARDS (SELECTION)

CBI Bisto–Book of the Year, winner (2012/2013),
merit (2005/2007/2008/2009); Orbil Prize Best Illustrated Book, winner (2013); the New York Times Book
Review, winner (2012); British Book Design and Production Awards, winner (2010); Irish Book Awards, winner
(2007/2012); New York Emmy Awards, winner (2010);
British Academy Children's Awards, winner (2009)

MEMBER ASSOCIATIONS

Patron of the AOI

GALLERIES

Lazarides, London, U.K.
Gestalten Space, Berlin, Germany

Oliver Jeffers

"I HAD SET MYSELF AN OBJECTIVE AND WAS QUITE METHODICAL AND LOGICAL IN MY EFFORTS TO GET THERE. LIKE MOST BUSINESSES, I HAD AN IDEA, I DEVELOPED IT, THEN INVESTED TIME, THOUGHT, AND MONEY IN SELLING IT."

Oliver Jeffers categorizes his practice into three areas: picture books, fine art, and other projects, and he does so for his own sanity. "I am constantly spinning plates in picture books and fine art. With art, the core activities are painting, meeting with collectors, liaising with galleries, researching for future projects, and of course making new work. With picture books: generating concepts, editorial meetings, proofing layouts, making the actual art, color proofing, book signings, talks and events, trade events, and interviews." The other projects category holds opportunities that arise that he cannot say no to. The bulk of Jeffers's work is visual storytelling, but he'd include "visual question asking" in there too.

Jeffers grew up in a world of stories. "Storytelling as an art form has been perfected in Irish culture, I believe. There's a lyricism, joy, curiosity, mischievousness, and duality between actual communication and entertainment that has been honed between friends, neighbors, and family in kitchens, bars, street corners, and playgrounds for generations. Humor is a huge part of it. Ireland has had a tough complicated history, so stories became a way of forgetting as well as remembering. The intricacies of telling a story are intrinsically understood, and perfected on purpose."

Born in Port Hedland, Australia in 1977, Jeffers was raised in Belfast where he went to a school he describes as "kind of rough." It was one of the first that integrated Catholics and Protestants in the city, and was new when his parents enrolled him. "To get their attendance numbers up and get funded, they took in children who were being kicked out of

other schools. Because of that, many pupils did not have an academic bent; those of us who did had to pretend we didn't like learning and that we didn't actually do our homework." Jeffers knew art was the direction he wanted to be heading in from about that time. "I caught a lucky break because I was able to talk my way out of trouble and when the other kids found out I could draw well, I was asked to draw on the bottom of skateboards and on school bags. My peers never gave me a hard time for my interest in art because of this and the teachers were supportive because I was actually interested in something." His path to art college was pretty straightforward from there.

Following a foundation course in Art and Design that covered a little bit of everything, he figured that painting was not the major subject to go for. "It seemed too nebulous at the time, and at that point I was craving structure, even though I practiced painting in my own time." He had also discovered sculpture at that time,

THE HEART AND THE BOTTLE
(TOP)
Harper Collins Publisher, 2010

STUCK
(PAGE 200)
Harper Collins Publisher, 2011

which he still dabbles in, but decided to enroll for a course in visual communication at the University of Ulster, Belfast, Northern Ireland, where he discovered his love of typography and honed his skills as a storyteller. It took him a year off in between the third and final year and six months into that last year to come up with a final project. It started as sketches that were going to become paintings, but ended up being his first picture book, *How to Catch a Star*.

Right out of art college, Jeffers practiced primarily as a commercial illustrator, receiving his first commissioned illustration for an Australian wine publication. But the fascination with picture books did not cease. He decided to get *How to Catch a Star* published, and accomplished that goal quite methodically. "I looked at what was around in the bookshops and I believed that what I had created was as good as if not better than anything else that was out there. Self-confidence is hugely important in this endeavor, as it's

more likely you'll hear lots of 'No's' before you hear a 'Yes.'" After he had read an article on self-publishing highlighting how difficult it can be—all the printing technicalities, the distribution, the economics—he deemed his attention span way too short to deal with it. So his first step was to buy the *Writers' & Artists' Yearbook* and see where to send his manuscript. "Apart from using the *Writers' & Artists' Yearbook* to research which publishers I should send my idea to, I also referred to my own collection of children's picture books. I looked to see who had published what, paying particular attention to my favorites, and which publishers popped up more often, and who I'd be a good fit with." The next step, then, was to figure out what exactly to send out.

"There are hundreds and thousands of unsolicited ideas that reach publishers every year—the slush pile—and my objective was to stand out among those, to be noticed. By asking, I found that what publishers like to see in a proposal for a new

book is the manuscript and a few samples of the illustrations, a broad idea of the feel for the book. I invested a bit of money into producing 100 copies of a small spiral bound 'sample,' with the manuscript at the start and 10 full-color illustrations after, which I put into an envelope with a letter outlining who I was and what I was trying to do, and a self-addressed envelope for them to contact me. These days an email address would probably be more efficient. I also included a small portfolio (and I mean small, 8 prints that were 14 square centimeters each) of other examples of my paintings and illustrations in the hope that if a particular publisher didn't pick up on my book idea, at least I might be able to get a few commissions while I was waiting."

The fact that he made the effort to find out who ran the children's division in each appropriate publishing house and addressed his envelopes directly to them proved worthwhile. "The point was that it would arrive at a real person's desk

LOST AND FOUND
Harper Collins Publisher, 2005

instead of some anonymous slush pile. I spent a while drawing up a big chart showing which publishers I had sent an envelope to, contact name and number, date last contacted, and room for comments. I sent an envelope to the 10 biggest publishers in the U.K., and the 10 biggest in U.S., figuring I'd start at the top and work my way down."

Expecting a healthy dose of being ignored and avoided, Jeffers was surprised to receive a phone call from HarperCollins the next afternoon expressing their desire to publish his book. It had arrived on the desk of a young editorial assistant; she opened it, liked what she saw, and immediately decided to do something about it. That offer was followed a week later by one from Philomel Books, a subdivision of Penguin in New York City, where something similar had happened. "It was as simple as that," Jeffers notes. "Simple in that they both liked what they saw and acted on it. I met with both publishers, and between the three of us we were

able to devise a cunning plan that would enable both of them to publish the book. Although I was very lucky, I had set myself an objective and was quite methodical and logical in my efforts to get there. Like most businesses, I had an idea, I developed it, then invested time, thought, and money in selling it."

Jeffers's idea, he claims, has never really been about making books for children. "I make them for me, to satisfy my own curiosity. It just so happens that what satisfies my sense of curiosity also seems to gel with a good amount of kids." Graphic novels and comics do not interests him much. He loved *Asterix* and Art Spiegelman's *Maus* when he was in high school and enjoyed looking at his brothers *Bone* comics, but it just never grabbed him. Thinking back on why, he reckons they were too visually specific. "Every little thing was spelled out and I got bored or distracted easily. I could get lost in a novel though. Perhaps because that was inside my own head."

While the Irish aren't exactly known for their cuisine, they have always enjoyed telling stories about how bad grandma's stew was, Jeffers declares with regard to himself. "I have always had a vision of the world instilled in me. That has come from all of my human experiences—the books I read when I was small, the people I have known growing up, the places I have seen, the experiences I've had, and all the stories that have swirled around me about the way the world is and the way I want it to be. Partly my books are a matter of taking this interior vision and trying to recreate it on a two-dimensional form for my own pleasure and the pleasure of others. The stories all find me in a way. Every one is based in part on reality, real encounters, actual occurrences, things I've overheard. Then I've twisted, shaped, and painted them so they satisfied how I'd like to see them exist in a picture book."

At the very foundation of each of Jeffers's books is the seed of an idea that he usually sketches in a quick drawing as an attempt to catch its essence, and then flushes out more fully to see if it's strong enough to hold a beginning, middle, and end. If it is, he starts drawing and writing the milestones. "After I get to a certain point, the story sort of tells itself. There is a fine line between predictability and satisfaction." He does not call it research, but looks at a lot of things during the process, sometimes with a semblance of organization. "It's impossible to put an amount of time on that though—I'm sort of always doing it. The big trick is recalling a certain thing I have seen or read, and then trying to remember where it is. It's like that matching memory game. Sometimes I reference the incorrect memory of something I can't find, and I'm not really sure that's a reference at all."

The most enjoyable part, to Jeffers, is in experiencing the seed of an idea taking form in the sketchbook and slowly becoming a 32-page book. Getting the flow of the story to fit within these 32 pages is what he considers the biggest challenge. There is no formula for success in the

LOST AND FOUND
(LEFT PAGE)
Harper Collins Publisher, 2005

THIS MOOSE BELONGS TO ME
(TOP)
Philomel Publisher, 2012

process of a book being made, from the idea to proposal to publication. In Jeffers's case, there's no formulated technique either. He switches between various media choices with astounding ease. While his first two picture books were entirely watercolor, he began experimenting with collage when working on the third, *The Incredible Book Eating Boy*, working digitally by making hundreds of drawings and scribbles on paper and compositing them together in Photoshop.

Now considering software like Photoshop or Illustrator tools and mediums, not unlike watercolor or oil paints, Jeffers still rarely uses them to generate imagery from scratch, but rather as platforms to composite organic drawings and textures together. For his "boy" stories he combined watercolor with a whole range of typefaces, and used printer paper to make a range of drawings, lines, and scribbles that eventually became the components of a layered Photoshop file. These days he works with pretty much anything. "I

use heavy Arches watercolor paper for my watercolor painting. I use mounting board to glue old pieces of paper to if they are to be the base of the illustration. I also make oil paintings on canvas. I've also worked with oil on canvas and acrylic over second-hand paintings and photos. Also, any sort paper (collage is wonderful), gouache paint acrylic paint, and the Dulux color matcher paint (the stuff for walls where you pick a color and they match it). I also love Letraset and old typewriters." He begins with organic materials—watercolor, collage, ink, acrylic, pencil, oil, etc.—depending on the book, and then finishes the last 5–20% in Photoshop, using it as a post-production tool.

Although happily resorting to all sorts of tools and techniques, Jeffers's choices are based on good judgment. "An important lesson I learned was when someone once brought to my attention the Mariah Carey Syndrome, where she has an 8-octave range and won't sing a song without using all 8. Just because you can do something doesn't always mean you should. Subtlety, discretion, and restraint are key in my mind to good illustration." His subtle, modest tones appear as he notes that he never really found his style. "The second I stopped trying to make my drawings and paintings look like someone else's and just listened to my hand, along it came. It's one of those things you can't force. If it's truly 'your' style, it'll be in there somewhere. Once you've realized it's there, you can turn it up."

So he did, which implied using the characteristic, jotted-down Oliver-Jeffers scrawly-handwriting, which he declares to be just the way he writes and better the faster and more he does it. "I've always labeled things, and made notes in sketchbooks, and more and more people were saying they enjoyed seeing that aspect, the more I utilized it. I'm riding a wave where lots of people enjoy my handwriting and are paying me to write things. I know it won't last forever, but it's enjoyable right now.

Even when it goes out of fashion, that'll still be the way I write."

Writing is essential to Jeffers's work, and the meaning of his words are as much a part of his style as their form. Considering the combination of pictures and words most powerful and creatively rewarding, he generates the content of his picture books himself, and states that it would be rather frustrating not to have the opportunity to come up with the words himself, as informed by his pictures. A recent foray into illustrating someone else's picture book didn't give way to this problem, as it was entirely made up

of protest letters written in crayon. "There was no opportunity to have the letters be anything other than what they were, and this provided a great structure to work from." The book, *The Day the Crayons Quit*, written by Drew Daywalt, was a chapter book, and a "different beast entirely," as unlike in a picture book, the story was told primarily through prose.

To Jeffers, writing satisfies a compulsion that drawing cannot, though in

WITHOUT A DOUBT
Personal Work, 2012

a very different way. "In the way that a hamburger won't quench your thirst, I love the relationship between words and pictures, I always have." The magic comes in finding the right balance. "I don't really know how it happens, save to say stuff just comes out of my brain, via my pencil and onto the page." He just knows when it's not right, he says, and has found it wholesome to show rather than say, to leave things as vague as possible for people to apply their personal histories to the story and thus establish a stronger hold to it. "I'm hesitant to try and dissect it any further than that for fear I may not know how to put it back together again after I've taken it apart to see how it works. All I know is that it works."

Jeffers talks and works with his editor to refine his stories. Before locking himself in the studio for 6–8 weeks to make the final art, he usually spends a few months in close contact with his editor mulling over the plot points, distilling the story so that it flows fluidly over 32 pages. With his editor located in Paris, his publishers in London, and he himself in New York, face-to-face communication is rarely possible. "Our contact is mostly via weekly emails, monthly phone calls (both of which become more frequent in the middle of a project), and then we make a point of face-to-face at least twice a year for a few days. Personal contact definitely leads to better results. You get a much better sense of what someone is saying."

The fruitful work relationships Jeffers has established with HarperCollins and Penguin began with the bizarre agreement that he fumbled into after both responded to those first blind submissions. "I happened to be in New York City the next week, even though HarperCollins approached me first, so I ended up meeting Penguin U.S. first. The editor there, Michael Green, with a small imprint at the time, said I'd be foolish to not give a giant like HarperCollins real consideration, and I knew immediately that I liked and trusted him. I asked HarperCollins if they'd give Penguin first refusal on

American rights if I signed with them. They said they would, and it's been like that ever since."

Jeffers has been working with the same literary agent, the London-based Bell Lomax Moreton Agency, since about a year after the 2004 publication of his first book. Having ventured into freelancing right after his studies, he has always considered the organizational matters that surround his business the most daunting challenge in establishing and running it, especially those related to finance. Figuring out taxes, invoices, and things alike have always been a struggle for him. "I am happy to now have someone to do that stuff for me. I hate it." Running a business with momentum and discipline entails many challenges besides, but Jeffers confronts most in his wonderfully calm manner. "It's very important to not live in a bubble, but sometimes networking for networking's sake comes across as insincere. Like all things, it should be a balance," he proclaims.

"My first job was booked based on my art college's final show. My second job was booked because of the first job, and so on. Somewhere along the line I got a website. Having been working very hard independently for over a decade, and making some tough choices along the way, I've managed to maneuver myself into a scenario where I only do what I want to do." Jeffers recently accepted a commission to illustrate a print and TV ad campaign for Ferrero Kinder Chocolate. Asked how his picture books feed into his occasional commercial illustration work, and vice versa, he notes that it is strictly one way. "Kinder came to me because they had enjoyed my books. The books are sacred though, and commerciality will never have a place in them."

Although working on occasional commissions that pique his interest, Jeffers does not see himself as a commercial artist. His main focus these days is on picture books and fine art, endeavors he considers equally self-generated. "The boundary between fine art and illustration is very blurry these days. Where I see the difference is that with fine art you are giving form to your own concept, and worrying about money further down the line, whereas with illustration, you are giving form to someone else's concept and figuring out money upfront."

For both picture books and art projects, Jeffers works backwards from a deadline—a given or self-imposed one—and breaks down every step of what needs to happen in order for a task to be accomplished. He writes everything in his calendar and schedules time quite far in advance, trying not to have any more than one or two "other projects" at any time. Among these other projects that he would not say no to are the titles and film he was commissioned to make for TED, a non-profit conference devoted to creative ideas in technology, entertainment, and design, or a project he is working on with the ONE campaign, a grassroots undertaking committed to the fight against extreme poverty and preventable diseases. Various collaborations like illustrating other authors' publications also fall into this category.

With the London-based animation studio Studio AKA, Jeffers has turned his second book *Lost and Found* into a much-awarded animated short film, which he notes as a very enjoyable experience. "I worked pretty closely with Philip (Hunt), the director, and Studio AKA the whole way through. We had a conversation very early in the process where we agreed that a moving repetition of the book would be boring, and Philip realized I love true collaboration and that I was not precious about things, and this, coupled with my trust in his vision, laid the foundation for a very fruitful project." Moving his creation into the next dimension spurred Jeffers's interest in exploring alternative ways of storytelling such as interactive ones. "I have played with this platform a little, but feel that content needs to be created bespoke for interactivity, rather than forced into it from an existing book. I'm curious to see how this whole industry will play itself

REPLACING ADRIANNA IN THREE PARTS (2)
Personal Work, 2009

out over the next few years, but content to let it happen naturally."

Since Jeffers moved to New York ("because it's New York") six years ago, his team has grown to include not only his wife Suzanne, whom he praises for managing his time and practically everything else in his life that "doesn't involve a paintbrush or pen," but also an old friend from college. "I took on Connie in 2010 just before I started work on my 8th

picture book *Stuck*. We studied together in Belfast, and she had worked with my wife first. As it turned out that we all worked well as a team, it made sense to continue that relationship. We have a similar eye so it's good to have a creative close to hand who I can bounce ideas off." There are also interns now and again at the studio, depending on what projects are coming through at the time. At lease once a week they all sit down and discuss what needs to be done, which Jeffers much appreciates for forcing him to take a look at where he is going in a practical way. Then they divide and conquer.

In Jeffers's studio there is a painting area and drawing desk, a computer desk, and a large island in the center when daily project meetings are held. "My studio is on the first floor of an old factory building in Brooklyn. It's a good size although I always wish it was bigger. I have been collecting antique flat files to store my paper and art, so I have a tower of them as you enter the studio. Most of the bits and pieces in the studio I have found on the street in Brooklyn over the years. It's amazing what people throw away. I have great natural light which is really necessary when painting."

Jeffers does not really work nine to five, as his schedule is defined by the projects he is tackling at the time and by the lighting conditions in his studio. "Currently I'm preparing for an exhibition in London, so I'm spending most of my days painting with oils in the studio while it's bright out, then dealing with other stuff that's not so light sensitive after the sun goes down. Constants in his daily routine are walking his dog to the studio and then having coffee and breakfast. "I try to get to the studio as early as I can to deal with emails, organizational things, and correspondence with my publishers in London. Then I try to do creative work in the afternoon. If there's a big project going on, I'll just stay in and work. If there's not, I like to get out on the street and experience life."

Jeffers may balance work on several different types of art pieces, picture bookmaking, self-initiated projects, and painting all at once, and other times he may be working on only one project for months. Last year he began to work on three paintings that will be part of a greater series of dipped paintings. It was all a bit of an experiment at first, but now he has been working on new concepts and a new process for the dipping and is really excited about sinking his teeth into it. "I'm also

UP AND DOWN
Harper Collins Publisher, 2010

about a third of the way through my biggest picture book yet—a collection of short stories, one for each letter of the alphabet. I'll spend the majority of the rest of this year working on it, and it will come out in 2014. It's a mammoth project, but I've wanted to make this book for a long time."

Quite frequently, Jeffers will be out meeting people, working on-site, or traveling for events and signings, which entails a lot of time on airplanes and in

hotels. "Exhibitions are hugely important, but also time-consuming. That is when the team in the studio is a great help. They come in and sort out all the logistics so I can concentrate on making the work." Recently, the *Guardian* invited him to write an article on Maurice Sendak, but that was a one-off foray into journalistic work, he notes. He accepted the offer because he was interested in writing about Sendak.

sketch books. I'm hopefully going to get working on a selection over the coming months." Jeffers does not accept the invitations to teach workshops very often, but is currently preparing for one he will be giving in Valladolid in Spain, which he finds very exciting. "Such activities that force you to look at where you are and where you're going can be both important and enjoyable when I am able to dedicate time to them. It all comes down to balance."

He has learned to spot projects that have the potential to mess with his head quite far off now, he says. He has also learned to stop working and relax. "It can be very easy to be sucked down into a vortex of your own making. Learning to say no was a huge step for me—removing 'good enough' from my vocabulary, too." When asked about other essential steps worth sharing with aspiring creatives he adds: "learning to be disciplined in my use of time; talking to people whose work I enjoy and being open about my work; being okay with the fact that I thought I was a fraud, and subsequently realizing that I wasn't; learning not to factor money into important creative decisions; figuring out a way to plan years into the future; learning that some days you're just no good and not to force it; and probably more things I can't think of."

In Jeffers's case, such steps were richly interspersed with milestones. Getting his first book published was a huge one, he says. Then, one of his paintings was hung in The National Portrait Gallery in London, and then used as the invitation image for their portrait awards. He then saw his second book turned into a short film. He won the *New York Times* Best Illustrated Books Award, had his first monograph of his art published by Gestalten, and then had a show at the Brooklyn Museum and a solo exhibition in Lazarides Gallery. He was truly honored to win the picture book awards. The list could go on, and Jeffers is likely to actively be expanding it as you read. "I am very happy," he asserts, "but not content."

It is especially when things get overwhelming that Jeffers finds it easy to prioritize. He has ceased to engage in larger side projects like "You and Me The Royal We," a miscellaneous product line he conceived and operated together with the animator and collage artist Mac Premo and Aaron Ruff of the jewelry line Digby & Iona; and the art collective OAR, which he founded along with his brother Rory Jeffers, Mac Premo, and Duke Riley. "Both

were great collaborative projects when they were around, but due to increased workloads for all parties involved we decided to let them rest."

With picture books and art being the core of his practice now, Jeffers easily feels at home with other activities that come his way. "For the past few years I've been invited to make more and more maps and from that I've worked up a long list of cartography ideas written in my

ife and four chil-
& Services Ltd.
merce and after
grace of God you

ears. Within this
ads of state have
pounds sterling,
se consignments
gold, diamonds,
bacha of Nigeria
Siera Leone, Rtd.
ory Coast (dead),
eposited with us.
lot of them are
ay ever come for
anybody except

you are able to
ased to you upon
g to Mobutu Sese
am soliciting for
s deposited with
ince he died, the
ion, some ran into
ment No. 002101
ll the information
and easy:
curity for the re-
d for documents
ry detailed infor-
will invite you for
n the deal except

for you and 10%
sure you that this
e cannot fail.

PLACE AND DATE OF BIRTH
Eberswalde, Germany; 1962
COUNTRY OF RESIDENCE
Germany
FAMILY STATUS
N/A
EDUCATION / DEGREE
Diploma (Graphic Arts),
Kunsthochschule Berlin Weissensee
ACTIVE IN THE FIELD OF ILLUSTRATION SINCE
1987
BREAKTHROUGH PROJECT
N/A
KEY CLIENTS
Büchergilde Gutenberg, Frankfurt; Berliner Festspiele,
Berlin; Die Zeit, Hamburg; dtv, Munich; Editions Attila,
Paris; Gingko Press; Berkeley, California; Insel Verlag,
Berlin; L'Association, Paris; Liberation, Paris; Theater
Lucerne; Maro Verlag, Augsburg; McSweeney's, San
Francisco; National Post, Canada; Peter Hammer
Verlag, Wuppertal; Public Bikes, San Francisco; Rhode
Island Monthly; Theater Bonn; the New York Times;
Wagenbach Verlag, Berlin
MOST RENOWNED PROJECTS
Plastic Dog, L'Association, Paris; Cry for Help – 36 Scam
e-mails from Africa, Gingko Press, Corte Madera (2006);
Wolfram Frommlet: Mond und Morgenstern, Peter Ham-
mer Verlag Wuppertal (1999); Der Vogelhändler (stage
design), Theater Lucerne (2008)
COMMISSIONS PER YEAR
N/A
AVERAGE TURNAROUND TIME PER COMMISSION
N/A
WORKSPACE
Home studio
EMPLOYEES
None
AGENTS
None
TEACHING POSITIONS
Since 1994: Professor for Illustration,
Visual Communication, University of the Arts, Berlin
AWARDS (SELECTION)
The Most Beautiful German Books, first prize (2000);
The Most Beautiful German Books (2002); The Most
Beautiful Books from around the World, Golden Letter,
first prize (1999); International Poster Biennale
Warsaw, second prize (2004); China International
Poster Biennale, second prize (2004); The Best Books
by Independent Publishers (2012)
MEMBER ASSOCIATIONS
Alliance Graphique International (AGI)
GALLERIES
None

Henning Wagenbreth

**"ILLUSTRATION PER SE IS UNINTERESTING.
LIKE GOOD ART IN GENERAL IT MUST
HAVE SOCIAL RELEVANCE AND CONTRIBUTE TO
THE CULTURE OF DISPUTE AND SOCIAL
DECISION-MAKING."**

Good stories thrive on actions, thrill-ing events, and unexpected inventions, once wrote Scottish novelist Robert Louis Stevenson in a letter to a friend. Contemporary illustration does too, con-firms Berlin-based illustrator Henning Wagenbreth, who recently translated and illustrated a series of tales by Stevenson, tales that he found to be largely un-known in German-speaking countries. One of them, *Der Pirat und der Apotheker* (The Pirate and the Pharmacist), toured through various German cities as a play reading that was then expanded into a full-length theater play, conceived and re-alized in collaboration with the puppeteer Günther Linder and the actor and stage director Albrecht Hirche. As announced in the program guide, Lindner and Hirche sing, dance, scream, and throw around light and shadow figures. Wagenbreth

and fellow illustrator Sophia Martineck accompany the performance on the man-dolin and autoharp.

To think of Wagenbreth as a jack of all trades would belie the fact that he is indeed a master of many. Comprising editorial illustrations, theater posters, book covers, illustrated books, and digi-tal formats, his portfolio is as varied as his field of interest. Having grown up in the GDR in the sixties and seventies, Wagenbreth has always felt attracted to culture and the arts, a domain that prom-ised the greatest possible independence. He aspired to study stage design first, but when he went to the State Opera for an interview he was told he didn't read enough. Fine art fascinated him, but he preferred the idea of learning the crafts of letter setting, drawing, and printing. He thus decided to apply for commercial

letterpress workshop then. Wagenbreth enjoyed the crafty process, and the ability to build on his previous knowledge of printing techniques. There was half a year of time between his college entrance exams and military service, which used to be compulsory in order to attend university, and Wagenbreth seized that time to help out with printing parliamentary papers and law gazettes at the GDR's State Printing Office. After the army, he did an internship at the print workshop of Walter Graetz. "Graetz focused on art prints. All the big names of East Berlin's art scene had their posters produced there, in very limited print runs," Wagenbreth remembers. "They printed offset, did color separations with a big reproduction camera or directly by hand, mixed inks manually—processes that would bring my awareness to the value of technical constraint and hands-on experimentation, and impact my own creative approach in the long term."

manner. He has learned to think and design in practical terms, as back when he studied in East Germany, scanners were so rare that it would take weeks to get an image scanned, and prints required governmental authorization. "There was no censorship, officially, but above a certain print run the design had to be presented to the magistrate. A rejected layout would usually be explained by the fact that there was no paper to spare. The Verband Bildender Künstler Deutschlands (VKBD), the artists association of the GDR, fought for certificates of exemption, so that art prints could be made with a print run of up to 100 without prior permission."

Wagenbreth's first commissioned book was printed in 1988, right after his graduation. The father of a friend of his, a commercial artist, had been asked to illustrate a 5th grade school book for the Sorbs, a Slavic minority in East Germany, but he didn't have time to do it. So he

arts instead, first in Leipzig, at the College of Printed Graphic and Book Art. They rejected him, "with vehemence," he recalls. "I was very young, only 18 then. In Leipzig, they favored older, more experienced applicants, preferably ones who had already completed an apprenticeship in bookbinding or a related field. So I applied in Weissensee, at Kunsthochschule of East Berlin, where I was accepted right away."

The course provided a solid foundation in painting, drawing, lithography, and modeling. "Sadly, graphic designers don't get to learn enough about these things anymore these days," Wagenbreth remarks. "In the beginning, I did a bit of everything, some poster design, some book arts, illustration too, of course. Later, I specialized in illustration and typography." Typography was still taught in the

CRY FOR HELP
(PAGE 210 & THIS PAGE)
Illustrated collection of 36 scam e-mails from Africa.
Gingko Press, 2006

In Wagenbreth's work one can typically see few, but blatant colors and lines that are tight and of unbending precision. He has come to use pen and mouse alike, with no particular preference. "Well, whatever circumstances require," Wagenbreth says, in his remarkably modest and practical

recommended Wagenbreth, who did the job well enough to be commissioned for the 8th grade book a year later. It was at about that time that he began to work in the stop motion studio of Germany's most popular children's bedtime television program *Das Sandmännchen* (Little

Sandman). "I was amazed by the procedures one would most appropriately refer to as from the stone age today," he recalls. "The job was no big money, but you did not need big money back then in Berlin, before the reunification. I would get 200 Ostmark a month from a grant agreement supporting university graduates, and could live fairly on that. So everything else I earned was pretty much on top of that."

Shortly after the fall of the Berlin Wall, Wagenbreth went to France, first for six weeks, and then again for a year after he got a stipend from a German-French artists' exchange program. He would later describe his Paris experience as an eye-opener. "It was more or less at that time in France that I first came into contact with serious comics and graphic novels. There were a few people in Leipzig who worked in that area, and I was fascinated by the work of Volker Pfüller from Berlin, who followed an interestingly subjective approach, and

MOND UND MORGENSTERN (MOON AND MORNING STAR)
An African Tale by Wolfram Fromlet
Peter Hammer Publishing, 1999

by Manfred Butzmann and his remarkable talent to combine artistic and political statements in his graphic work. Then there was a Czech, Jiri Šalamoun, whom I had admired since my early student days, and Hans Hillmann, from West Germany. But all in all, I had gotten to know cartoons as something trifle and principally funny." In Paris, Wagenbreth was thrown into a vivid scene of living antidotes that he had been largely unaware of throughout the

eighties. Sophisticated artistic approaches of cartoonists such as Mark Beyer, Pascal Doury, Marc Caro, or Jacques Loustal, and their legendary platform, Art Spiegelman and Françoise Mouly's *RAW* magazine, would open up new vistas and influence Wagenbreth's visual language significantly.

Back in East Berlin, the local art scene had begun to prosper, absorbing influences from various cultures and subcultures. The collapse of the GDR regime made it possible to print and distribute independent publications. Wagenbreth joined together with the artists Anke Feuchtenberger, Detlef Beck, and Holger Fickelscherer to form the group PGH Glühende Zukunft (Co-op Glowing Future). Feuchtenberger and Wagenbreth were classmates during their time at the East Berlin art school in Weissensee, and Wagenbreth had admired Feuchtenberger's approach to drawing and illustration from the beginning. Fickelscherer and Beck were friends, and friends of friends, respectively, who drew sarcastic political cartoons. The four worked mostly independently but shared a gallery space, located in what is now

the heavily gentrified area of Prenzlauer Berg. "We had emptied out, plastered, and painted one of these run-down abandoned premises you would find in abundance in the neighborhood at that time," Wagenbreth recalls. Here, they produced and showcased independent booklets, posters, and magazines, driven to discuss what they had not been able to openly discuss for so long.

It was at the gallery that Wagenbreth first met the publisher Armin Abmeier, a man dedicated to promoting the world's comic avant-garde in Germany and supporting its local representatives. Abmeier, inventor of *Die Tollen Hefte* (The Awesome Booklets), a biannual series of elaborately crafted books and booklets, immediately found favor with Wagenbreth's art, and would later, in 2002, included him in the series with *Das Geheimnis der Insel St. Helena. Die Wahrheit über Napoleon.* (The Secret of Island St. Helena. The Truth about Napoleon.) Wagenbreth considers his acquaintance with Abmeier a significant impetus for his career. "Abmeier knew people, and would pass my work

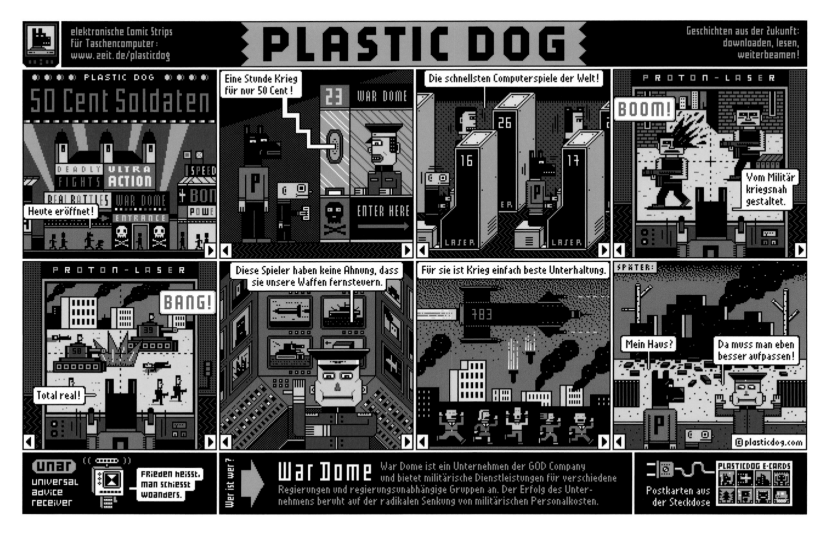

PLASTIC DOG
Electronic comic strips for Palm OS.
The 24 stories were published as
book compilation in 2012
Client: Die Zeit, 2004

around, which was extremely helpful," he recalls. "He was a great traveler, always in search of remarkable illustration projects beyond the mainstream." The *Die Tollen Hefte* (The Awesome Booklets) series was still in its infancy and the local scene very small when Wagenbreth met Abmeier in the early nineties. The few enthusiasts like Abmeier kept the scene alive, and while much has changed since then, *Die Tollen Hefte* (The Awesome Booklets) still maintains its status today as the foremost platform for the German independent illustration scene.

In 2011, Wagenbreth contributed to the series' anniversary release, *Charakter ist nur Eigensinn* (Character is Mere Obstinacy), a selection of Abmeier's favorite literary quotes illustrated by his favorite artists. Another book in the series

will be released this year. Abmeier's wife, the artist Rotraut Susanne Berner, has continued the project since her husband's death in 2012. "It may sound pathetic, but shortly before Abmeier's death, I had to promise him that I would do the number 39," Wagenbreth says. "I'm running late with this now, the deadline was supposed to be early this year. It always takes me so long to do such books, which is why I don't do that many. You have to continue with proper jobs at the same time, while with these types of projects you have all the freedom you want to work by your own rules, use special inks and all that, stuff that other clients are not usually willing to pay for." Is the freedom to experiment the main motivation for Wagenbreth? "In regard to the *Die Tollen Hefte* series, that has indeed been the

beautiful idea behind the project," he replies. "And the fact that I certainly owe Armin a lot."

Die Tollen Hefte (The Awesome Booklets) series is printed offset like is was in the early days, but the manual offset adjustment is now often superseded by digital prepress preparation. Computer simulation makes up for fiddly trial and error. "Back in the day, you had to imagine pretty much everything. Standing at the printing press, you could at most control the color intensity, that was it." Lecturing at the UDK Berlin since 1994, Wagenbreth has taught and still teaches generations of illustration students who would probably never be facing such problems if not for their love of experimenting with silkscreen and the old letter press in Wagenbreth's office.

"There has been this struggle for years at the academy about funds and investments in workshops. There are two fundamental fronts, those who think digital is everything these days, and people like me, who say it's not."

Wagenbreth finds it crucial to experiment with various tools and think across media lines. He sets examples himself. His early interest in the computer has brought about the automated illustration machine Tobot ("Half toy, half robot"), a kit of image modules that can be put together on keypress in good old and bizarre Exquisite Corpse manner. It began when Wagenbreth had Steffen Sauerteig and Sven Smital of the illustration collective Eboys in his class, who developed a modular typeface design application, and invited several people, including their professor, to contribute custom-made letters. Wagenbreth began to digitalize a hand-drawn alphabet with them, but paths diverged as he soon found it more

DER PIRAT UND DER APOTHEKER (THE PIRATE AND THE PHARMACIST)
(LEFT & NEXT DOUBLE PAGE)
A story by Robert Louis Stevenson
Peter Hammer Publishing, 2013

KOPF IST RUND (HEAD IS ROUND)
(RIGHT)
Personal Work

large-scale Tobot murals on display in a chapel during the Fumetto International Comix-Festival Lucerne. Wagenbreth is currently working on a 3D-installation of wooden building blocks for the group show "Memory Palace" at the Victoria and Albert Museum.

Since its inception in the late 1990s, the Tobot kit has grown to include several thousands of modules, and new ones are still being added. Recently, Wagenbreth has used Tobot to illustrate a series of books, a selection of stories by Edgar Hilsenrath. Gracing the covers, the characteristic Tobot elements—mostly zombie-like creatures of nineties low-tech allure—create a strong visual identity. At the same time, each book calls for very particular elements. "Generally, the idea is to choose from the existing elements, for it is exactly the severe restrictions that bring about the most absurd creations. However, when I did the cover for the book *Orgasme à Moscou* I needed

Breschnew, for example, who was impossible to compose from what the image kit offered." The fourth book in the Hilsenrath series, *Orgasme à Moscou* is the first that is illustrated throughout by solely using Tobot modules.

Pieced together to make truly bizarre compounds, Wagenbreth's image elements—he likes to call them visual terms—remain clearly identifiable, or legible as one might say. Word and image along with drawing and typography fuse in his work, amounting to a dialog full of tension, ambiguity, and substantial statements. They feel urgent and sometimes absurd—not necessarily in line with the stories they illustrate. "Illustration should seize its opportunity to comment on the content and interact with it. It can build up contradictions," Wagenbreth states. When illustrating a book, he does not aspire to direct representation. "Any kind of drawing is interpretation already and I just like to take things a bit further

interesting to load all sorts of image elements into different-shaped frames, as opposed to sticking with square modules and letters. Allowing for each drawn and digitized element to be used and reused in endless variations, the Tobot project has turned into a prolific field of experimentation. In 2008, Wagenbreth put

Ein Zitat von Francis Picabia, das schon lange zu meinen Lieblingszitaten gehört, passt gut zu dem spätdadaistischen Künstler, der sich gern zeitgeistig den verschiedensten Kunstströmungen angepasst hat

Unser Kopf ist rund, damit das Denken die Richtung wechseln kann

away. But not too much and not to superimpose my own vision, because I take the text seriously. Yet certainly so as to add a new dimension." Wagenbreth outlined his position in an interview with the journal *Jitter:* "Illustration per se is uninteresting. Like good art in general it must have social relevance and contribute to the culture of dispute and social decision-making."

Considerate of the ethics of his profession, Wagenbreth advocates a humanist

The ability to take a clear stance is reflected in many of Wagenbreth's projects. The comic strip series Plastic Dog, for example, picks up on socio-technological innovations to spin them out in the sense of ironic modern fables. One strip tells of violent computer games that the military uses to remotely fight real enemies, taking advantage of the unerring precision of unsuspecting gamers. The moral is clearly stated in the last panel, as Plastic Dog's house is hit by a misdirected missile.

Another profound piece of visual storytelling, Cry for Help, a graphic implementation of spam e-mails from Africa that Wagenbreth started to collect in 2000, was released in 2006 following a limited edition containing handmade linocuts. Wittily embedded in the satire of simple-minded criminal intents is a critical account of cultural and economic disparity. In 2010 Wagenbreth was one of a few selected artists from Berlin and Tel Aviv invited to contribute to *Tel Aviv Berlin,* a comic book

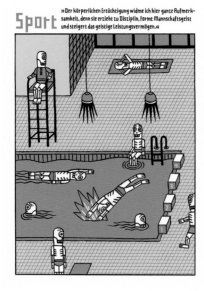

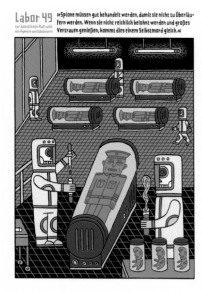

approach. He believes artists have the responsibility to critically scrutinize their ways of representation and set boundaries for themselves. Where does contempt, disrespect, pride, racism, or arrogance start? How far are you willing to go? He does not speak of political correctness here, at least not of the hypocritical kind that is spreading throughout our wary world today. "I think you can be very politically incorrect, as long as your expression contributes to an overall idea that is essentially humane and in support of core values such as the freedom of opinion, equal rights, or tolerance. Jokes at the expense of disadvantaged people are largely unacceptable. Jokes about the powerful, on the other hand, may be dangerous, but are almost always okay to make."

Initially designed to be downloaded on the Palm Pilot, Plastic Dog's print versions appeared in the German weekly *Die Zeit* in 2003. Ten years later, the Parisian publisher L'Association released a cardboard book, and a German book edition published by Walde und Graf followed shortly thereafter.

project under the patronage of the German ambassador in Tel Aviv and the Israeli ambassador in Berlin. It was conceived as a subjective travel book of intercultural metropolitan impressions. Just recently Wagenbreth finished a three-minute 2.5D opener sequence for an alternative economy program commissioned by the Franco-German broadcaster Arte.

Although Wagenbreth works internationally, he has never considered getting an agent. "I always feared that an agent would make me do stuff I do not like to do," he explains. He dislikes being told what to do, and he usually gets the last word when receiving change requests from commissioners. For the book *1989* Wagenbreth illustrated for the Italian publisher Orrecchio Acerb, he was asked to put an Uschanka,

with open eyes, it seems that projects find him, rather than the other way around. To Wagenbreth, getting commissions is less a matter of customer acquisition and more about just "going out and doing stuff." It is often at exhibitions or the theater that he meets someone who asks him for an illustration, and he maintains close contact with creatives from various fields. "Actors, musicians, many of them need illustrations to promote their work every once in a while. One works together, not

hurdles and uncertainties that increasingly burden the industry, an industry that has changed drastically and in many ways since his student days. "We were six in the course when I started to study, and only four of us graduated." At the moment there are 35 students in Wagenbreth's class. Initially, he only wanted to take on 20, but seeing the disappointment in the faces of the rejected ones, he decided to accept more. "They are all great and do amazing stuff, much better, I think, than I

the typical Russian fur hat, on the head of a soldier. "I said that I wouldn't, for I know that they only wear these in the winter, and it was not winter in that image. They were puzzled and slightly annoyed, but finally they put up with it." There are always some minor changes and discussions with the Jazz Fest posters, a project he has been working on for many years now. And there was the poster he did for Amnesty International, where he was asked to revise the final illustration. He found their changes pedantic and says that he avoids working for large advertising clients for exactly that reason.

Resolute and straightforward about what he wants, Wagenbreth communicates it in his refreshingly unassuming, open manner. Going through the world

DAS GEHEIMNIS DER INSEL ST. HELENA (THE SECRET OF THE ISLAND ST. HELENA)
(LEFT & THIS PAGE)
Büchergilde Gutenberg, 2002

to assume liabilities, but because of shared ideas and interests." That is the way it has always worked for Wagenbreth. Happy coincidences have also played a role. "When I ran out of money in Paris back in the day, I worked as an au pair for a German bookseller. It was she, through some detours, who introduced me to the people at Editions Attila, who commissioned me to do the Edgar Hilsenrath book series years later. And when I met the actor and stage director Albrecht Hirche to speak about a poster for one of his performances, he saw my illustrated book *Der Pirat und der Apotheker* and came up with the idea to do a release show, which then turned into a full-length and properly funded play."

One thing always led to another in Wagenbreth's career, sparing him from the

did when I was their age. I do worry sometimes, how all these illustrators will get by in the future. But they all really want to study illustration, and nobody can take this decision away from them. What I can do is make them aware of the fact that they need to be extremely flexible these days." Besides versatility, Wagenbreth points to the growing need for inventiveness and entrepreneurial skills. "I advise my students to join forces whenever it fits. Many do that, and it works really well. Not only can you finalize a publication a lot quicker as a group of four, but you also reach a broader audience with different styles." The trappings revolving around the product are also considerable, finds Wagenbreth, referring to conceptual and performative aspects. "A book, for

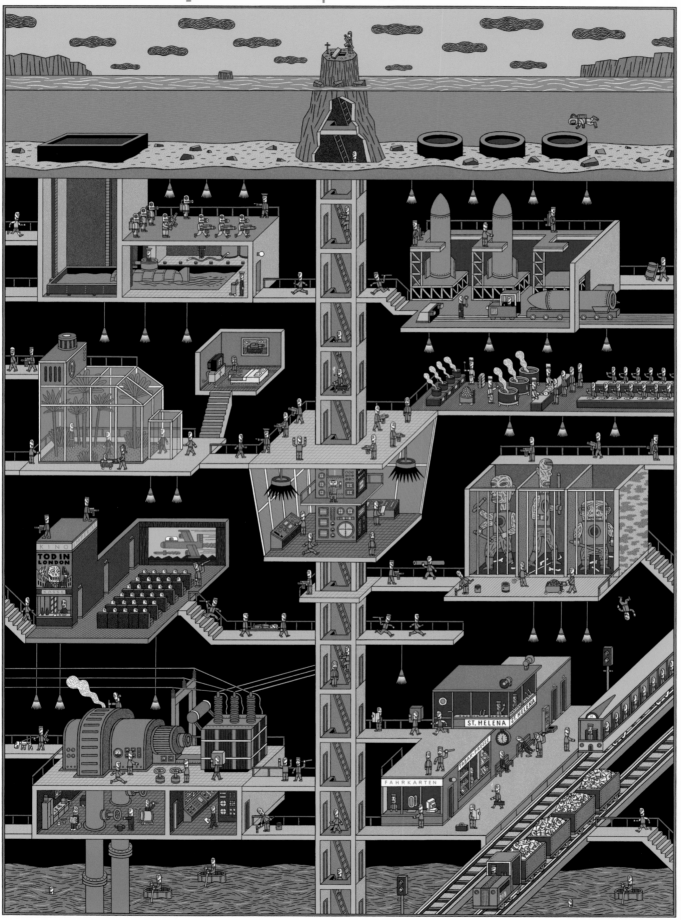

Jörg Stickan est allemand. Ancien élève de la rue Blanche, il commence par traduire du théâtre (Lenz, Wedekind, Eisler, Drach, Jahnn…) Le très remarqué *Fuck America* a été sa première traduction d'un roman. Depuis il a traduit des nouvelles, du roman et du roman graphique.
Sacha Zilberfarb traduit des livres de psychanalyse, d'esthétique, d'histoire de l'art, des biographies et du théâtre. Il écrit aussi pour la revue *Vacarme*. Accessoirement, il a appris le yiddish, langue de ses grands-parents paternels, afin de lire Sholem Aleikhem dans le texte.
Le duo a reçu le prix Gérard de Nerval (SGDL/Institut Goethe) pour ses traductions de l'œuvre d'Hilsenrath.
Guerre froide, 1970. La fille du patron de la mafia new-yorkaise, Anna Maria Pepperoni, connaît son premier orgasme lors d'un voyage de presse à Moscou. Le responsable ? Sergueï Mandelbaum, dissident juif fauché doté d'une étonnante propension à susciter des orgasmes. La mafia met tout en œuvre pour le faire venir aux États-Unis afin d'épouser Anna Maria, mais le passeur qu'elle a recruté est un dangereux dépeceur sexuel. Les obstacles, et pas seulement diplomatiques, s'accumulent…
AEROFLOT
Après le succès américain du *Nazi et le barbier*, le cinéaste Otto Preminger commande un synopsis à Hilsenrath, qui écrit en six jours *Orgasme à Moscou*. Dans cette parodie de roman d'espionnage, version déjantée d'OSS 117, l'auteur de *Fuck America* abandonne toute limite et se livre à une mémorable surenchère burlesque. Truffé de références à la situation politique de l'époque, le livre, dénué de (presque) tout sérieux, est un divertissement électrique sur fond de Guerre froide.
L'AUTEUR DE LA COUVERTURE
Henning Wagenbreth est un dessinateur, affichiste et décorateur d'opérette allemand, qui partage son temps entre Berlin et San Francisco. Professeur de communication visuelle, marqué, entre autres, par la gravure, l'imagerie des pays de l'Est et la culture pop, il a travaillé pour *Libération*, le *New York Times*. Ses dernières publications sont *Plastic Dog* et *Der Pirat und der Apotheker* de Robert Louis Stevenson.
23 euros
9782917084526
Edgar Hilsenrath
Orgasme à Moscou
Attila
Edgar Hilsenrath
Orgasme à Moscou
Attila
Attila
Né en Allemagne en 1926, Edgar Hilsenrath a connu les ghettos durant la guerre, avant de partir pour Israël, puis pour New York.
Toute son œuvre s'inspire de cette expérience, mais sur un mode burlesque et satirique. Longtemps refusé par les éditeurs allemands, qui craignent les réactions à son approche, très crue, de la Shoah, il est d'abord publié aux États-Unis, où ses livres sont des best-sellers.
Prélude totalement déjanté à *Fuck America*, où chaque héros porte le nom de son plat favori, *Orgasme à Moscou* est une étonnante pochade sur la situation géopolitique mondiale dans les années 1970, qui met en scène, à côté de toute une mafia de pacotille, Brejnev, Nixon, Moshe Dayan et le président du Conseil italien, obsédé sexuel (déjà !)
Écrit en 1979, entre *Le Nazi et le barbier* et *Fuck America*, ce livre hautement "politique" relève du divertissement loufoque et survolté.
Une nouvelle preuve du génie inclassable d'Edgar Hilsenrath.

DAS GEHEIMNIS DER INSEL ST. HELENA (THE SECRET OF THE ISLAND ST. HELENA)
(LEFT PAGE)
Büchergilde Gutenberg, 2002

ORGASME À MOSCOU (ORGASM IN MOSCOW)
(TOP)
Bookcover, one of a series of books by Edgar Hilsenrath, printed with three spot colors. Éditions Attila

example, can be launched with an event, where it's sold and put on display with a series of related posters. There could be music, too. I believe that the overall experience counts a lot these days."

Wagenbreth usually spends two days a week passing on his integrated approach to illustration to his students at the UDK. Otherwise, he works on his own projects from home. His apartment doubles as his studio, with no clear spatial allocation and no fixed working hours. Wagenbreth has little time for private life, and when asked about his top personal achievements, he once named the ability to stay awake for up to 36 hours. Asked if he has someone to assist him with office work, he refers to his tax accountant. Exhibitions are the most work-intensive he says, and call for a lot of administration and organization, but he enjoys doing them occasionally. Last year, he exhibited in a screen-print workshop in Bologna, in the context of the BilBOlBul comic festival. Up next is the show at the Victoria and Albert Museum, and one in Antwerp, which he will do in collaboration with his companion and fellow illustrator Sophia Martineck.

It almost seems as if private and working life must flow together for Wagenbreth's world to be in balance. He used to have a studio, when his son was little, so that he could work undisturbed, but he recalls it as a terrible back and forth. "Every time that I wanted to work at home in the evenings, I had to get all my working material from the studio." At the moment, he works every day, including many evenings. "There are just so many beautiful projects underway. But I travel now and then. Tomorrow, there's a reading of *Der Pirat und der Apotheker* in Bremen." Wagenbreth speaks as if that is a holiday for him. "I may also visit the academy there. I have held two workshops there in the past and haven't been back since they moved to Überseestadt, the redeveloped historical seaport area." He will meet a few old acquaintances, too. "I think it is just impossible for me to not merge private into business life, and the other way around. As soon as I visit a city on vacation, I snoop around its antiquarian bookshops, which are a great inspiration for work. I guess the only activities that really have no connection to my work are the bicycle tours I occasionally do. And I recently started making music again, but that occasionally relates to work too." As aforementioned, Wagenbreth plays the mandolin on stage, accompanying the theatrical interpretation of *Der Pirat und der Apotheker*. Rehearsals are underway.

On top of Wagenbreth's list of personal achievements, prior to staying awake for extended periods of time, is the ability to reinvent himself and his practice again and again. Recent undertakings go in the direction of self-generated content. He is writing the latest in the *Die Tollen Hefte* series, *Honky Zombie Tonk*, in versified form. "Finding the right balance between text and image is quite tricky. I am fiddling with that now. And as I have the freedom to change content myself, it all takes longer than expected. That's why I am so late this time." He still enjoys commissions, but thinks of himself more so as an "illustration author" now. "I think this is a natural development that comes with time and age. Like actors who begin directing their own plays, there comes a time when you are not satisfied with simply following the instructions of others. You have your own ideas of what you'd like to do." Wagenbreth says that he has a long list of such ideas, long enough to last another decade to come.

Illustrated Lettering

Almost half a millennium after Gutenberg's invention of mechanical movable type printing, the world seems supersaturated with prefabricated typefaces. With the abundance and availability of fonts of all kinds comes the prestige of custom drawn letter shapes. Once the sole means of written communication, they are now broadly understood as visual luxury and are a welcome recourse to less complicated, cozier times. Less generic than ready-made type, illustrated letterings not only expertly support and establish the creative direction and image of a brand, but also have emotional power and distinct features with which publications gladly avail themselves. After all, today's densely populated markets call for competitors from various industries to stand up and stick out. Besides the increased esteem of personalized details as a means to raise market recognition, the implied presence of the human hand grows in virtue with the ongoing digitization and overall visual equalization of our surroundings. Along with the current wave of small edition products, hand-printed graphics, and non-chain restaurants offering homemade bread and locally brewed beers, illustrated lettering reasserts itself as a worthwhile sphere of activity for illustrators and graphic designers alike. The artists featured here are masters in the field. Mostly hand-sketched and digitally produced, their custom logotypes, taglines, and headlines cater to the specific needs of commercial and editorial clients. Showcasing Alex Trochut's sleek creations, Jessica Hische's delicately decorated characters, and the bold sign-painterly work of House Industry's Ken Barber, this chapter presents the plentiful art of lettering in many fine words.

KEN BARBER
2012

PLACE AND DATE OF BIRTH	Reading, Pennsylvania, United States; 1972
COUNTRY OF RESIDENCE	United States
FAMILY STATUS	Married
EDUCATION / DEGREE	BA in Fine Arts, Temple University, Tyler School of Art
ACTIVE IN THE FIELD OF ILLUSTRATION SINCE	1993
BREAKTHROUGH PROJECT	N/A
KEY CLIENTS	House Industries
MOST RENOWNED PROJECTS	Logo design: Jimmy Kimmel Live!; logo design: Only Vegas; typeface design: Chalet; typeface design: Ed Benguiat Font Collection; typeface design: Studio Lettering; typeface design: Blaktur; typeface design: Smidgen; typeface direction: Neutraface; typeface direction: Eames Century Modern
COMMISSIONS PER YEAR	25
AVERAGE TURNAROUND TIME PER COMMISSION	2 weeks
WORKSPACE	House Industries studio
EMPLOYEES	11
AGENTS	N/A
TEACHING POSITIONS	Maryland Institute, College of Art, University of Delaware
AWARDS (SELECTION)	Art Directors Club ADC New York City, Award for Excellence in Type Design (2005/2008/2012); Association Typographique Internationale, Letter 2 Type Design Competition (2011); Design Museum London, Nomination: Design of the Year (2011); National Design Museum, Smithsonian Cooper-Hewitt (1996/2003)
MEMBER ASSOCIATIONS	N/A
GALLERIES	N/A

Ken Barber

"THE BEAUTY OF HAND-LETTERING IS THAT ITS UTILITY ALLOWS IT TO BE TAILORED TO VIRTUALLY ANY APPLICATION."

"While a handful of typefaces have come close, few can match the genuine warmth of hand-drawn letters. Writing and lettering speak in friendly and familiar tones—even formal, elegantly written script is personable and approachable." In reaction to our standardized visual surroundings, more and more local businesses, marmalade manufacturers, family-brewed breweries, artisan bread-makers, and handmade books are enthusiastically received. For the same reason, custom letterings such as those of Ken Barber are having a revival. His practice thrives on the tension between tradition and technology. "The past decade or so has seen a resurgence in 'craft,' which I believe is due in part to a reaction against our hyper-digital culture. Consequently, there seems to be a parallel movement focusing on craftsmanship and handmade objects. I,

for one, am really happy to see it, because I like both sides. I'm not a super tech-geek, but ultimately I do digitize much of my work. I like the combination of the two."

Ken Barber is a letterer, type designer, and type director at Delaware-based design studio and type foundry House Industries. His work is in the permanent collection of the Smithsonian Institution's Cooper-Hewitt National Design Museum and has been honored by the New York Type Directors Club. Association Typographique Internationale recently selected several of his typefaces for inclusion in its decennial design competition. Barber's success can be largely attributed to the connections he's made along the way. "I think I was really fortunate; I met the right people at the right time. School was helpful, but mainly because it was there that I met a lot of folks who would

LIBERTY AND
INDEPENDENCE
(TOP)
50 and 50 State Mottos Project
Client: Dan Cassaro, 2011

ONE
(PAGE 224)
Celebrate 65 Anniversary Book
Client: Type Directors Club, 2012

soon be in the design industry, and who I'm lucky enough to call friends today."

Barber studied graphics at Tyler School of Art, part of Temple University in Philadelphia, Pennsylvania. He was attracted to graphic design from a young age, he says, before knowing exactly what it was. "As a child, the lettering and illustration of *MAD Magazine* had a considerable influence on me. Then, from the world of skateboard art, I was introduced to the likes of Jim Phillips and Vernon Courtland Johnson, two extremely talented guys

who worked for Santa Cruz and Powell-Peralta respectively; they combined illustration with hand-drawn letterforms, something that held tremendous appeal for me. When I began playing in punk and hardcore bands as a teenager, I was hand-lettering 7-inch sleeves and fliers advertising shows." While still in high school, Barber was hired by a local grocer to make in-store signs advertising weekly specials, discounted items, and featured products. "I wasn't a skilled card writer; apparently my only qualification for the job was that

I had neat handwriting." By the time he attended college, letter-making suggested itself as a viable career option.

It was during his studies in Philadelphia that Barber became friends with Allen Mercer, one of the former partners of Brand Design Company, which would later spin off House Industries as a separate font division. In 1993 Mercer introduced him to Andy Cruz and Rich Roat, the company's founders, who gave him the opportunity to take some of his academic lettering projects and develop

THE TITLE OF Benevolent Dictator OF THE UFO FOR LIFE Is HEREBY CONFERRED UPON *Tal Leming*

ROBOTHON 2012 · ROYAL ACADEMY OF ARTS · DEN HAAG

them into fonts for the new type foundry. "The fellas at House Industries had more work than they could handle, but didn't want to give up clients, so they gave me a freelance job," Barber recalls. His first professional piece was done shortly before graduating from college: an illustrated and lettered postcard advertising a play for a local theater company. "I got paid $300, which felt like a million dollars to a poor art school student."

During the final year of his studies, Barber's cooperation with Mercer, Cruz,

BENEVOLENT DICTATOR
Client: Robothon, 2012
Ben Kiel
Photo editing: Bondé Prang

and Roat materialized. "Between the odd pieces of lettering and typeface designs for the nascent foundry, I think we shared a sense that we'd work together on a more permanent basis at some point in the future. In fact, when Andy finally called to invite me on board full-time, he said that they would have asked sooner if only they had enough cash to hire me." Instead, after Barber had graduated in 1994, he moved to New York, biding his time by working for design agencies in Manhattan. Barber had never really entertained the idea of going

it alone. It was a matter of playing the waiting game—not a question of "if," but "when" he would start working at House. When he eventually received the call in 1996 he gave up the city he had grown to love and relocated to Yorklyn, Delaware to join the company full-time.

The studio's offerings have varied from the start, ranging from design services to retail fonts and related products. "During the mid- to late-nineties, it seemed like I had my grubby little hands in practically everything," Barber recalls.

COFFEE BREAK
(TOP)
The People's Pennant
Client: The People's Pennant, 2012
Photo: Jessica Karle Heltzel

TYPOWEEK
(LEFT)
Client: Typoweek, 2013
Christian Giribets and
Marc Salinas Claret

DAILY DROP CAP "B"
(LEFT)
For Jessica Hische, 2010

GO GO
(LEFT)
Client: Penny Pimentel, GO GO
Marketing & Distribution, 2012

"In addition to typeface design and lettering, I contributed to catalog layout, illustration, commercial design work and even copywriting. Then, as we managed to add more talented folks to the crew, I was able to focus primarily on drawing letters and directing freelancers doing the same. Today, while it's not uncommon for everyone to offer their two cents when a project is brought into the studio, there's a greater degree of specialization. Andy Cruz is an amazing art director; nothing comes in or out of the studio without his eyeballs on it. He works closely with Bondé Prang and Jess Riddle, who do all the heavy lifting when it comes to graphic design, including the production of catalogs, promotional mailings, apparel, retail items, and our Photo-Lettering app. These projects almost always involve some element of custom type or lettering, which is where I come in. Adam Cruz and Chris Gardner contribute all the illustration, while Rich manages the nuts and bolts of various projects, including day-to-day studio operations."

Lacking a formal type design education, Barber initially failed to appreciate the differences between lettering and typography. "To me, they were practically the same thing." It took him some time to learn that both are comparatively unique disciplines. Today, calling himself a lettering and typeface designer, he divides his time between the two, with a recent focus on the former. "The focus on lettering is probably because I'm impatient and the payoff is practically immediate, not to mention extremely gratifying. Typefaces can take months or even years to complete, while a hand-drawn logo can be cranked out in a matter of days." Needless to say Barber still derives a great deal of pleasure from both disciplines and the ways in which the two complement one another. "After all, there are a number of similarities in the thinking that drives both practices. Even in my own lettering work I notice a certain methodology that produces somewhat predictable results. Like other artists, my creative routine is shaped by personal experience, preferences, and working habits. Such discernible patterns can be programmed in a smart and sophisticated typeface, even if I'm not the one handling all the technical hooey."

"Specializing in any one field provides the opportunity for designers to really hone their chops," finds Barber. Working with the alphabet day in and day out has enabled him to get acquainted with the subtleties and nuances of tools, techniques, and styles. "Designers don't begin with a clean slate or create within a vacuum, not that anyone would want to. As a letterer, I am not immune to what has come before me. As such, it's critical to remain aware of the conventions that I must work within, along with the freedoms that I possess. People commonly associate emotions with certain ideas, as well as how those notions are traditionally represented in letterforms. Consequently, it's nearly impossible to escape cultural or

STUDIO LETTERING
(TOP)
For House Industries, 2007
Glass gilding: Larry Polzin
Photo: Carlos Alejandro

KANAI
(LEFT)
Client: Kanai, 2008

LB MONOGRAM
(LEFT)
Client: Lynn Eva Barber, 2010

THANK YOU
(LEFT)
Client: Craig Walsh, 2009
The Society of Design

historical influences. With that in mind, research plays an important role in my personal process. While conventions can't be ignored, they can most certainly be pushed. I like to investigate various ideas and see if they can't come together in a single piece of lettering, whether it's referencing different periods of typographic history, or imaging a tool that combines qualities of different ones."

While Barber won't say that he has developed a definitive style, he does acknowledge that certain habits—especially in regard to production processes—have contributed to giving a specific look to his work. "I do a fair amount of brush lettering—both analog and digital—and translating a stroke made with a pointed brush loaded with ink presents particular challenges. The organic nature of the materials involved—the viscosity of the ink, the bristles of the tool, and the texture of the paper, to name a few—are all influencing factors that affect the silhouette of the

strokes. Taking the character of the brush and interpreting it into vector artwork can be likened to translating an idiomatic expression: you have to understand the essential meaning of the original before communicating it in a different language. The same holds true for tracing handmade marks in a digital environment. Staying close to the appearance of the actual mark made by the original tool is usually impractical and often impossible; at worst, a poor automated computer-tracing betrays the actual production method. It's necessary to find meaning in the language of points and lines so that the spirit of the letter and materials is not diminished." Technology has changed the process of letter-making drastically, but Barber feels that its essence has remained largely unaltered. Among the tools he considers to "get the job done" are Lamy pens ("great for broad-edge calligraphy") and Winsor & Newton Series 7 brushes ("unbeatable when it comes to advertising script lettering"). Regular No. 2 pencils and tracing paper are also old standbys for him. For vectorizing wordmarks, it's Adobe Illustrator. When it comes to typeface editing, however, he uses RoboFont.

As the primary letterer and typeface designer at House, Barber has shaped the company's style—and vice versa. In acknowledging that he has refined his approach while working at House, he cites the input of the studio's co-founder and art director, Andy Cruz, as one of the biggest influences on his method of working. "He's been hugely influential in shaping my thinking in regard to lettering and typeface design. While we don't always see eye-to-eye, we both want the best result. That prevailing attitude, as well as an unhealthy obsession with perfection, contributes immensely to House Industries' aesthetic." Cruz has also helped keep Barber on his toes. "He's consistently pressing me to go further with my lettering and typeface design. Of course, plenty of hard work and determination can't hurt either."

Barber certainly works with determination and drive, but does not adhere to a fixed plan or strategy to get there. However, he has observed certain preferences in his routine. "Although I use a number of different tools and techniques for sketching, whether it's a broad-edge pen or a pointed brush, I almost always refine my initial explorations with pencil. In fact, I often start with a pencil rendering, drawing on my familiarity with various writing instruments. A logo or headline will usually start its life as a thumbnail sketch, in which I focus primarily on composition and the general proportions of the mark. Then I'll tighten up any number of directions in a series of increasingly detailed tissue comps. However, it's not uncommon to hit on a fairly realized idea in the first one or two drawings. Next, the piece is carefully vectorized before finally going through some fairly rigorous testing and proofing."

To Barber, lettering and typeface design represent microcosms of other design

practices. "Similar to other disciplines within the field of visual communication, the general problem is fairly basic: positioning certain elements within a particular environment to achieve the desired result. Much of that boils down to balancing positive and negative space, which is the essence of lettering—harmonizing form and counterform whether it's within an individual character, a string of letters, or a group of words. Letter-making gets to the root of design, stripping things down to a relatively small set of variables. Of course, this is oversimplifying the matter. There are countless ways to imagine a Latin script letter, for example; the alphabet is surprisingly malleable. Yet, there is only so far one can stray from the essential nature of letterforms. At some point,

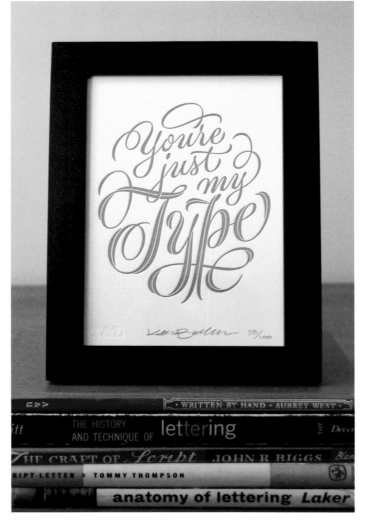

they will break. Finding a sweet spot somewhere in between—that ideal combination of freedom and restraint—is what makes drawing letters both challenging and exciting."

The search for the right form is largely defined by the individual needs of the commissioner, and Barber's approach is as broad as the client list of House Industries. He refers to the acclaimed American typeface and logo designer Donald Young, who often pointed out that certain letter styles are more appropriate than others for certain applications. "However, Young also maintained that nearly all letters can be hand-rendered under the right circumstances. For example, the delicate refinement of formal scripts is particularly well-suited to concepts of luxury, quality, and elegance. On the other hand, consumer packaging aimed at communicating notions of convenience, affordability, and ease of use commonly utilize less formal styles like bold straightforward sans serifs or casual brush letters. Of course, the beauty of hand-lettering is that its utility allows it to be tailored to virtually any application."

Despite the huge number of inquiries from various market segments, House Industries is very selective as to which projects they take on, doing less and less commissioned work these days. "If the right commercial job does come along, or the House coffers grow a little light, we'll take on the occasional commissioned logotype or piece of lettering." The bulk of time, however, is divided between designing typefaces that are almost always retail products, in-house projects, collaborations with other artists and manufacturers, and the production of self-promotional material such as catalogs and mailers. Tasks are organized flexibly but with clear priorities. "Juggling many projects at once, especially with a considerably small creative team of seven people, means that some projects have to be moved to the back burner from time to time. It can be difficult to interrupt progress in one direction, only to shift gears and move in another, but fortunately the work is engaging enough that the disruption is minor. Commissions with hard deadlines obviously get immediate attention, and often take precedence over personal projects."

Barber and his colleagues also carefully choose who they work with, doing their best to partner with clients who they believe understand their work and trust them to do the job right. Close consultation is important to them. "Talking directly with the client or art director is necessary to get a firm idea of the project's scope. After the general creative direction has been established, the crew will kick around a few ideas before putting pencil to paper. We're careful not to throw any stray dogs into the mix, which means that we may present one idea or a half dozen to the client. It all depends on what we think will be appropriate and effective. A lot of self-editing takes place before reaching that point, so the customers rarely see more than a handful of sketches."

"The smart use of handmade letters allows artists the ability to offer clients a broader range of design options and potential solutions," says Barber, pointing to the fact that there are no defaults, thus few limitations and plenty of leeway. "Unlike the impulsive scrawl of writing, or the systematic nature of typographic forms which need to work in any conceivable order, hand-lettering exists within a single fixed context. This offers considerable creative freedom in shaping the letters, allowing them to be arranged in a potentially dynamic composition. As a result, a powerful and distinctive word-image can serve not only as the medium for a message, but become the message itself. While reading a book or magazine, ideally the reader will look past the typography to appreciate the content of the text. With hand-drawn logos, on the other hand, lettering cannot only shape how the content is literally communicated, but also how it's perceived. In this sense, the appearance of a well-executed hand-lettered wordmark is inseparable

LIGADURAS
(TOP)
Client: Catalana de Tipos, 2007
Marc Salinas Claret and Carlos Cabañas

STUDIO LETTERING TYPEFACE COLLECTION
(RIGHT)
For House Industries, 2007

from its message. Examples of highly expressive lettering can even take on an illustrative quality."

While it is critical for lettering artists like Barber to be responsive to the needs of a client, it is also natural that they insert themselves into the creative process. As he puts it, it is impossible not to inject one's personality. "If design is problem-solving, then it's not surprising to see a pattern emerge throughout a designer's body of work. The problem is

when a particular form of visual expression ignores or eclipses what is necessary to satisfactorily complete the task at hand. Hopefully, the requirements of the job are met without sacrificing aesthetic integrity, and any tension resulting from potentially conflicting demands is imperceptible to the audience." To Barber, an adept lettering artist can add just the right amount of personality to a headline or logotype while still remaining true to the needs of a project. "Because it's custom, lettering isn't bound by the same limitations of typography; it can be molded to fit any application and to behave in ways impossible for conventional typography. In this sense, the use of calligraphy and hand-lettering allows for a fuller degree of design authorship."

Aside from the individual needs of a client, there are technical requirements to meet, and those vary considerably with the type of commission. "The primary difference between hand-drawn logotypes and advertising/editorial lettering is the final application," says Barber. "Each plays a different role, appearing in different settings under various conditions. These factors have an effect on the way the projects will be handled. Logotypes should be tested within a broad range of sizes and in a number of environments, such as in print and on screen. Lettering for advertisements and editorial pieces typically has very specific yet limited uses and can therefore be more forgiving. This also means that it can be more illustrative and elaborately detailed."

Generally, the more illustrative and detailed the lettering the longer it takes, but given that one never knows when creativity will strike, turnaround times can be unpredictable. "In some cases, the first idea turns out to be the best one. Other times, pages of thumbnails are drawn before reaching a good solution. That means a job can take anywhere from a few minutes to a few days." Barber gives himself a few solid hours to sketch rough initial concepts. In most cases these are ready to be tightened up with a final pencil

composition in two days. "Depending upon the scope and complexity of the lettering, and assuming it's a necessary step, it may take longer to vectorize it. If time permits, I also like to live with the piece for a while. It's helpful to be able to walk away from it before returning with a fresh perspective. Finally, there's the proofing stage; this is especially crucial for logotypes. Making sure a wordmark performs under the rigors of physical and digital environments can't be stressed enough. I look at both hard copy and on-screen versions at a range of sizes in both positive and negative to make sure the final mark will meet the demands of real world applications."

Barber and his colleagues prefer face-to-face time with their clients and collaborators, which helps to sustain long-lasting business relationships. "Networking is

LETTERING WORKSHOP
(TOP)
Personal Work, 2012
Photo: Lynn Eva Barber

ALLEN AND ANITA
(RIGHT)
Personal Work, 2013

such a sleazy word, but it is important to make friends, and there's no better way than breaking bread in person. Although we may not share the same room as a client until after a job has been completed, an effort is still made to meet face-to-face

at some point. We've become increasingly interested in doing good work for good folks, and it doesn't hurt putting a face to a name."

From its base in Yorklyn, Delaware, House Industries works for clients across the globe. When asked whether they have observed cultural differences among these clients, Barber proclaims that those biases are usually self-imposed. "In regard to lettering and typeface design, for me it's an opportunity to explore novel ways of thinking about letterforms, and more importantly how they're perceived within different societies. Alphabetic expression among cultures can vary surprisingly, which only adds to the charm of written language." One retail font project that investigates this idea is Studio Lettering, a font set that includes different scripts of sign-painterly appeal. "The challenge to create the collection's 'colloquial' character sets—which reflect nuances and preferences of native speakers—began during a trip to Sweden. It was in Stockholm that I noticed a peculiar gilded storefront window featuring what appeared to be an 'o' with a tilde above it. Naturally I was intrigued, especially considering that no such letter exists in the Swedish alphabet. After a little sleuthing (and some very helpful local friends), it became clear that the letter in question was an 'o dieresis.' It turns out that the pair of dots are commonly replaced by a squiggle-like accent. Noticing similar diacritic simplifications, structural differences in letterforms, and a slew of other curiosities in various languages, I set my mind on pursuing culture-specific character sets. The fonts' bloated glyph sets and challenging programming—wrangled expertly by Ben Kiel and Tal Leming respectively—made the project extremely demanding, but also very rewarding."

In order to expand their international scope, House Industries has been working with the Tokyo-based agency Yayoi Cannon over the past few years, who has initiated collaborations with acclaimed Japanese clients like Found, Muji, Uniqlo, Medicom Toy, Nakagawa textile company, the ceramic manufacturer Hasami, and Hermès Japan. Beyond Yayoi Cannon, Barber and his colleagues have not felt the need to work with other representatives. "Rich and Andy's smooth talking manages to pull in a fair amount of work. In the end, it's about making friends with people who you respect. If something comes from the relationship, all the better."

Collaboration is paramount at House, be it with clients or among the team. "We all work in the same room so that we can see what one another is working on—no cubicles or glass conference rooms here. Rich likes to call it 'the roll over factor,' which means that we can easily slide our chairs around the office to have a look at what folks are working on and offer on-the-spot feedback. At any given time, we're each juggling two or three projects,

but we remain open to new perspectives and differing points of view. This collaborative spirit has been integral to House Industries' approach since the beginning. Most importantly, we trust one another. We believe that each of us wants the best possible result in the end. We may not al-

ways agree on every point, but that trust allows things to run relatively smoothly."

"The studio is pretty laid back," says Barber, and although he is referring to the studio's overall atmosphere, this applies to their work hours as well. "Andy likes to refer to our schedule as a 'semi-retired' work pace." They maintain a 9 am–6 pm schedule, with summer Fridays off. Two days a week, the staff works remotely from home, but keeps in touch "thanks to the wonders of today's technological gadgetry." Every now and then, a pressing job comes along that demands overtime, but they're few and far between. And Barber makes time for vacations with his wife Lynn, a former House employee.

With a supportive wife who currently stays home with their two children, Barber also teaches an experimental type course at the Maryland Institute College of

Art and co-runs the online letter-vending service and iPhone app Photo-Lettering. And as if his plate was not full enough, he works on occasional freelance jobs, mostly for friends, as well as on self-initiated projects. A selection is featured on his personal website, www.typeandlettering.com, along with information about tools, techniques, his general design process, and an online shop offering a fine selection of prints and type-related products. Barber started the site as a resource for his students and for the participants of the many hand-lettering and typeface design workshops he conducts throughout the year. "I've come to realize that instructing others on how to letter is an essential part of my own approach. Taking someone through the creative process step by step forces me to be more observant, especially when it comes to personal work. Questions about tools and techniques, which may have never been raised, lead to more research and investigation. I'm constantly refamiliarizing myself with various aspects of my approach, fine-tuning it and hopefully perfecting it. Students also offer fresh perspectives, which sometimes opens my eyes to points that I might have otherwise missed."

Barber looks back on his career and diverse activities with a healthy mix of critical self-awareness and pride. "It's hard to look back and not see all the flaws and oversights in your previous work. However, it is encouraging to notice the things you happened to get right. Of course, it's always flattering to be recognized by folks and organizations that hold your respect. I'm pleased to have my work in the Smithsonian Institution's Cooper-Hewitt National Design Museum, and to have the online Photo-Lettering service nominated by the Design Museum London as a Design of the Year recipient. Being honored by Association Typographique Internationale and the New York Type Directors Club are highlights as well. Most of all, I feel incredibly fortunate to work with my friends—people with an enormous amount of talent and integrity to match."

PLACE AND DATE OF BIRTH
Charleston, South Carolina, United States; 1984

COUNTRY OF RESIDENCE
United States

FAMILY STATUS
Married

EDUCATION / DEGREE
BA in Fine Arts,
Tyler School of Art, Temple University

ACTIVE IN THE FIELD OF ILLUSTRATION SINCE
2006

BREAKTHROUGH PROJECT
The Daily Drop Cap

KEY CLIENTS
Penguin Books and most major U.S. publishers,
Wes Anderson, Tiffany & Co., The U.S. Postal Service,
American Express, Neiman Marcus, Papyrus, BBDO,
Leo Burnett, and other agencies

MOST RENOWNED PROJECTS
Daily Drop Cap; Should I Work for Free; Title Design
for Wes Anderson's Moonrise Kingdom; Penguin
Drop Caps, 26 classic books featuring artwork;
Buttermilk typeface

COMMISSIONS PER YEAR
50–100, depending on travel schedule

AVERAGE TURNAROUND TIME PER COMMISSION
Books: around 4 weeks from sketches to final,
advertising: anywhere between 3 days and a month,
editorial: around 1–2 weeks

WORKSPACE
Shared with Erik Marinovich, another letterer

EMPLOYEES
None

AGENTS
Frank Sturges Reps

HOW MUCH COMMISSION DO YOUR AGENTS TAKE
N/A

TEACHING POSITIONS
None at the moment, but frequent lectures and workshops

AWARDS (SELECTION)
Print Magazine's New Visual Artist, 20 under 30;
Forbes Art and Design, 20 Under 30; Art and Design,
ADC Young Guns; Graphic Design USA, People to Watch;
Society of Illustrators; Type Directors Club; AIGA 50
Books/50 Covers; American Illustration;
Graphis, Communication Arts Typography;
Communication Arts Illustration

MEMBER ASSOCIATIONS
The Type Directors Club, Board of Directors

GALLERIES
Solo show at The University of the Arts in Philadelphia
plus a few gallery exhibits

Jessica Hische

"I JUST LOVE TO SPEND HOURS AND HOURS MOVING BÉZIER CURVES AROUND AND PERFECTING THE FORM. I GET SO EXCITED AS I WATCH IT EVOLVE AND GET BETTER AND BETTER TO THE POINT THAT I OFTEN FIND MYSELF HYPING MYSELF UP OUT LOUD AT THE STUDIO."

The common phenomena of postponing urgent tasks for less urgent but more enjoyable ones may result in a severe loss of productivity and social disapproval for not meeting responsibilities. For Jessica Hische, it resulted in a remarkable career as an illustrator and lettering artist. As a student at Tyler School of Art at Temple University in Philadelphia she was tasked with many fine art briefs that she put off in favor of painting, drawing, glass, and woodworking. She found herself replacing mandatory assignments with those that arose from a design elective she had enrolled in rather arbitrarily.

"A good way to figure out your passions is to look at what you enjoy doing while procrastinating from everything else," Hische asserts, adding that she enjoyed design-directed problem solving, rules and restrictions, and the need to communicate clear-cut messages for

people to get. This stands in opposition to fine art, "where if people get it right away, you're probably doing something wrong." In 2006 she received a BFA in Graphic Design, took on a job at the Philadelphia-based studio Headcase Design, and began working as a freelance illustrator, designer, and "procasti-worker."

Her penchant for drawing letters emerged early and out of necessity. "Too broke to buy decent fonts as a student, I knew that I could either approach every design project with my limited number of typefaces, spend days digging through terrible free font websites to find anything even remotely acceptable, or draw

PENGUIN DROP CAPS
(PAGE 234 & 235)
Series of 26 collectible hardcover editions of fine works of literature, designed in collaboration with Penguin Art Director Paul Buckley
Series Editor: Elda Rotor
Client: Penguin Books, since 2013

BARNES AND NOBLE CLASSICS
(THIS PAGE)
Series covers of classic books. Leather bound and foil stamped in two foil colors, designed in collaboration with Jo Obarowski
Art Direction: Jo Obarowski
Client: Sterling Books/ Barnes & Noble, 2010–2012

more personal and more cohesive. Plus I loved to do it!"

Over time, a fair amount of hand-drawn typography accumulated in Hische's portfolio, leading to her hire by New-York based lettering specialist Louise Fili, who she acknowledges as having fanned her passion. "All day every day I drew words and phrases for her. I lettered for logotypes and book covers, magazine headlines and pretty packaging." Working for Fili allowed Hische to hone her lettering skills and she soon found herself incorporating more and more letters into her editorial commissions. First treating them as a component within illustration,

managing your time. Because most of my freelance work was illustration, it was a lot easier for me to manage freelance projects than a lot of my designer friends, who had to juggle lunchtime meetings and sneak phone calls in the middle of the day. Most of my clients were very forgiving about the fact that I had a day job and were fine to communicate via email alone. I tried to be incredibly respectful of Louise's time and never conducted business during the day when I was on her time."

After two and a half years, Hische left Fili's studio to focus on her freelance career. She remembers it as an easy move, as her freelance income already doubled her salary. "It felt like something I had to do to maintain my sanity, and because freelance was coming in consistently it didn't feel scary." By that time, her lettering work was already her greatest asset. Fascinated with the process of drawing letters, she particularly appreciated the ability to work on something that was "less illustrative." "Even when you're inventing, you're not inventing out of thin air, so it's not intimidating to start a project—letters have to be based in some way on a historical model or at least a model that exists. Otherwise they wouldn't be letters, they'd be illegible shapes." The challenge is to navigate between familiarity and experimentation. Taking great pleasure in the letter, Hische exceedingly loves drawing capital R's because they have a bowl, a stem, and an arm, and therefore a lot of elements to play with.

Over time, Hische's keen interest in the physicality of letters extended from typographic illustrations and hand-letterings to typeface design. "I'm still figuring out how to streamline my process so that I can work more efficiently, but my love for type design is growing by the day," she declares. A recent commission to design a font for the titles of Wes Anderson's *Moonrise Kingdom* reinforced her desire to do more type design work, with all its nitty-gritty details. "It requires a lot more time and discipline than lettering, but the process is very rewarding for me. The few

my own "fonts.'" She says this in quotes in discussing the misuse of the word font—a mistake she made all the time when she was younger. "I noticed that the more I drew fonts for my own projects, and the more I lettered titles and logotypes and headlines for fake magazines, the more my work started to stand out from my classmates. Everything felt

she soon offered conceptual solutions that were entirely letter-based. What followed was a constant flow of pur sang lettering commissions, requiring upwards of 16 working hours daily—9 for studio work and at least 7 for freelance illustration.

"The main challenge when you establish a consistent freelance career while working in-house somewhere else is fonts that I have released and the ones that I have in the works were made entirely by me, though I will be collaborating with Font Bureau when releasing the typeface from *Moonrise Kingdom* so that they can help me with the stress testing and making sure that it is as idiot proof as humanly possible."

Having come a long way since she believed that type and lettering were one and the same, Hische now sells her fonts and the benefits of custom solutions alike. "A well-done lettering is so perfectly suited to a project that it feels like they couldn't have existed without each other before. Many people think that because of

the thousands of typefaces that are available, custom lettering is unnecessary, but I couldn't disagree more." She refers to logotypes as an obvious place for lettering, as well as one-off items that do not need to be systematized. "For instance, if I were to design a wine label for just one wine, it would be amazing to do something crazy and lettered. If it needed to

BARNES AND NOBLE CLASSICS
Series covers of classic books. Leather bound and foil stamped in two foil colors, designed in collaboration with Jo Obarowski
Art Direction: Jo Obarowski
Client: Sterling Books/ Barnes & Noble, 2010–2012

be a series of ten wines (and the client didn't have an outrageous budget) I would suggest that they use lettering and ornaments for consistent items (like the logo or the wine variety) and pair that lettering with complimentary typefaces for the rest of the labels so that the series could be easily expanded."

Most of Hische's current work is for books and advertising. "There are plenty of instances when a typeface might suffice, but even with thousands and thousands of typefaces available, finding one that is exactly perfect in every way for your project is incredibly difficult. By commissioning custom art, you get

something amazing and unique that no one else has, and something that was inspired by the thing it's meant to communicate. You can inject so much emotion into letterforms, especially when you're not worried about them becoming an engineered system of glyphs meant to work together in endless combinations. You can experiment more, and can often arrive at a suitable solution way faster than if searching for the right type."

Speaking of letterings as custom art, Hische underscores that the "what is art and what is illustration" argument is a tired one. When it comes to the content of form, she prefers to point to the difference between designing/illustrating

and decorating. "If you don't focus on the content and communicating that content in a conceptually interesting way, you are decorating. There is a place for either, but I always try to think conceptually when making lettering work rather than just making something that is beautiful but has no ties to the content."

For advertising projects, the art director usually gives her a rough sketch to begin with, so a lot of the conceptual work has already been done. For logo work, she tries to show options of comparatively elaborate sketches early on in the process, because when working with non-creatives she says it can be difficult for them to

grasp what's happening in a sketch. For both books and editorial work, the process is fairly standardized, broken down into reading the content and presenting several sketches, and once one is approved, she takes it to final and does revisions if necessary. "Each kind of work has its own rewards. I prefer to keep a variety of each on my schedule because while I love the research and conceptualizing stage of editorial and book work, I sometimes like it when I have a project put in front of me and the art director knows exactly what they want and they just need me to do the thing I'm best at and make their concept shine."

Hische likes to work very closely with her clients and regrets that she rarely gets

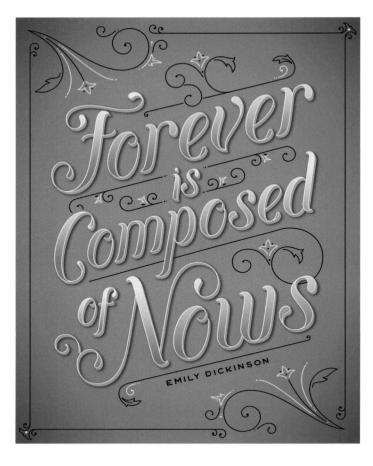

EMILY DICKINSON

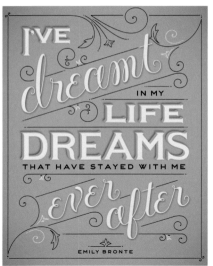

EMILY BRONTE

client is a painstaking process but a thrill to Hische. "I just love to spend hours and hours moving Bézier curves around and perfecting the form. I get so excited as I watch it evolve and get better and better to the point that I often find myself hyping myself up out loud at the studio." She creates letterings in Illustrator and designs type in RoboFont.

"For illustration and lettering work, I always start with pencil sketches—not because it is my preferred way to work, but because clients need to approve something before I can move to final. My pencils used to be quite rough but because I've been doing more and more lettering work

to meet anyone in person. "I wish it happened more, but as it's just not a common occurrence as a letterer or illustrator, I try to get on the phone as much as possible. It isn't the same, but can help a lot to make sure a project starts off on a good foot and that everyone knows the personality and tone behind the emails to come in the future," she explains. "Building trust with a client is incredibly important to make sure everyone is happy and knows that you're as invested in the project as they are. Many artists like to say that complete creative freedom is ideal, but for me that's not the case. I love constraints. Without constraints it's hard for me to complete projects or know where to begin. Communicating with the client early on, making sure that their needs are met and that they trust me completely to create something to perfectly suit their needs is my favorite way to work."

Creating type and lettering and fitting it to the particular needs of a commercial

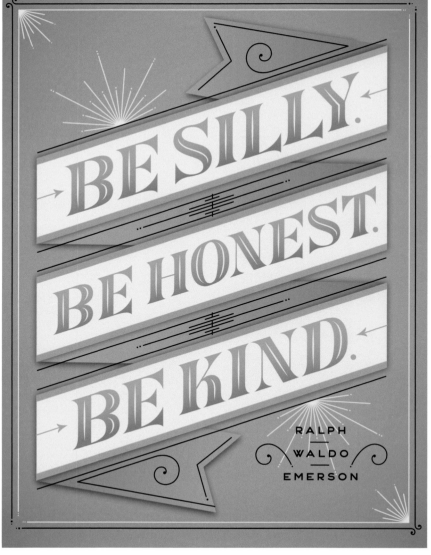

RALPH
WALDO
EMERSON

for advertising clients, they've become more refined. After a sketch is approved, I jump into Illustrator, usually not tracing my sketch for the final. I believe that the translation from sketch to final without tracing helps me correct my mistakes as I go. I idealize like how you would if you were drawing a person from memory versus from real life."

She mainly uses the basic pen tool in Illustrator, and after a few years of working intensely with the program it has become more natural for her than drawing by hand. "I don't use a Wacom tablet—I hold a pen like a child holds a crayon, in a tight fist that will only catalyze the carpal tunnel—just a mouse or the trackpad on my laptop. I usually work with the grid on at first, starting with a single weight line and then adding thickness or ornament later, depending on what I'm trying to achieve. I make general decisions at the beginning to figure out what kind of lettering I want to draw (a script? slanted or

TODAY IS THE DAY
Pocket planner
Client: Galison, 2010

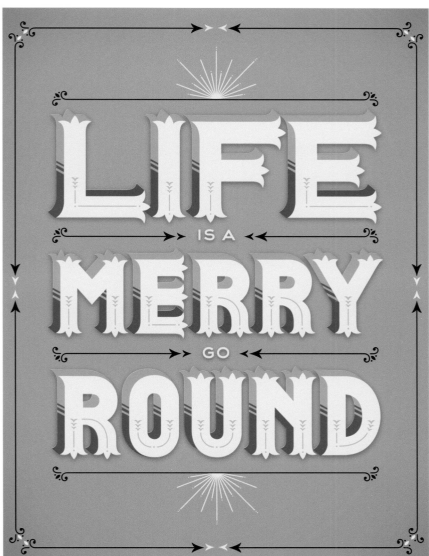

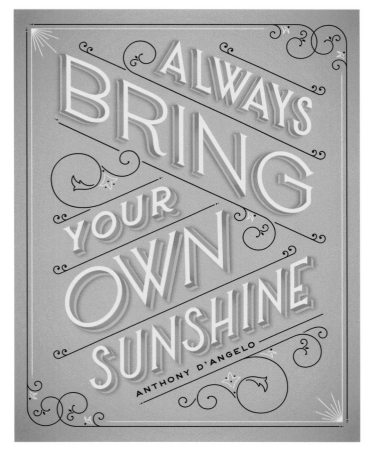

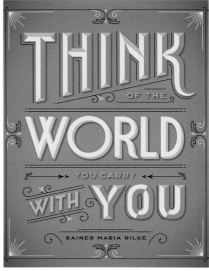

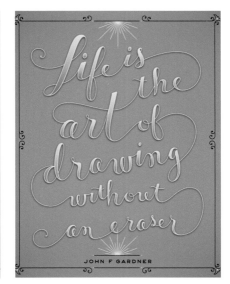

upright? thick or thin? sans serif? retro feeling or more modern feeling?) and then add decoration or ornamentation after the skeleton is drawn."

Designing type in RoboFont, Hische generally starts with the lowercase then works her way to the uppercase, punctuation, and additional characters. "When you're designing type, you constantly have to look at all of the letters in context to each other and design as much for whitespace as for the positive shape itself. I think usually with letterers, the thing that makes their work consistent is the medium they work in. Since I work almost exclusively in a digital way (aside from my pencil sketches), all of my work,

NEW YORK LOTTERY
Client: DDB / New York Lottery

composition. "I like to think of myself as a pretty warm and happy person, so my work is very optimistic. It's incredibly difficult for me to work on projects that have a dark or twisted side to them—in the end everything I make has a friendliness to it that is hard for me to hide." Asked about the vintage quality to her work, Hische agrees that it contains "small nerdy bits of history," but rarely historically accurate references. Clients that hire me don't want to make something that is tightly tied to history but instead something that feels a bit timeless or at least not hyper trendy. I don't actually do a ton of historic research before I begin a project unless the project calls specifically to a certain era."

whether I'm working on a blackletter, a script, or a sans, feels consistent."

Her signature style is a reflection of both the methods she prefers to work in and her personal preferences for color and

Genuinely dynamic, many of Hische's letterings appear to have effortlessly flown into form. Needless to says it is never that easy, and the time and effort that goes into each piece varies greatly with its degree of complexity and its context. With advertising work, the concept is often established before she is even hired, leaving her plenty of time to "grow the client's seed of an idea into something beautiful." Book covers, however, tend to call for extensive preparation. "I usually have to read at least half of the book to get a good enough sense of what I want to do, though prefer to read the whole book, which is a research stage that can take weeks depending on the book length and whether it's an easy read or not. I do word association brainstorm lists the night before I plan to sketch and then walk away from it so that I can let ideas formulate."

If possible, Hische sleeps on the reading, researching, and brainstorming for a night before she starts sketching. She thinks it helps eliminate bad ideas and allows for strange and interesting ones to pop into her head. When sketching, she likes to start loose and tighten up later, doing her best to get the basic layout in place without tracing the sketch perfectly. "This allows another round of editing and refinement to happen—it's almost as if you're drawing from real life instead of tracing. I've started to add another stage of finalizing to my work, especially when it comes to scripts, where I will retrace all of my artwork as shape after I've built it up as stroke and shape. This lets me smooth out all of the kinks that might have happened at connection points of the thicks to the thins, but adds a significant amount of work to the process, so I save it for things that will print enormously or for logos, which have to be 100% perfect." While her sketches usually take between one hour and three hours, the completion of a final piece following the revisions to the sketches and the client's approval can take anywhere from four hours to two days.

Clearly set timeframes are of great virtue for Hische, as they help her get

ideas straight and drive the process forward. The same applies to feedback and creative exchange. Even when working on personal projects she gives herself deadlines and briefs and discusses her work with friends. While she never struggled to get commissions after her shift to fulltime freelance, she does struggle sometimes with working on her own. "I miss collaborating with people in the same way that I collaborated with Louise (Fili). I try to replicate that process when working with clients but because I'm always working with new people it

can take time until you get into a good flow with a client."

Due to her preference for close creative collaboration, Hische is not opposed to the idea of joining a design studio again some day. For the time being, however, she enjoys acting out her innate people skills in benefit of her freelance career. She wouldn't speak of networking, but agrees that friendly relationships and her overall outgoing nature have contributed to her success. "I'm just a really friendly person who loves talking to people. I am the textbook definition of an extrovert: I get all of my power from interacting with other people. The more I'm out and about meeting and talking to people the more energized I feel, which gets me excited to do work."

It comes as no surprise that her ideal working environment is a shared, buzzing office. She likes to mix it up, she adds. "Sometimes I work from other people's offices just so I can be around loads of people, and I often work in coffee shops to feel like I'm out and about and not just 'at work.' I end up talking a lot to other designers just because it's fun to talk to people you know you already have a lot in common with. Most successful freelance designers get most of their work from referrals. The more you're out and about

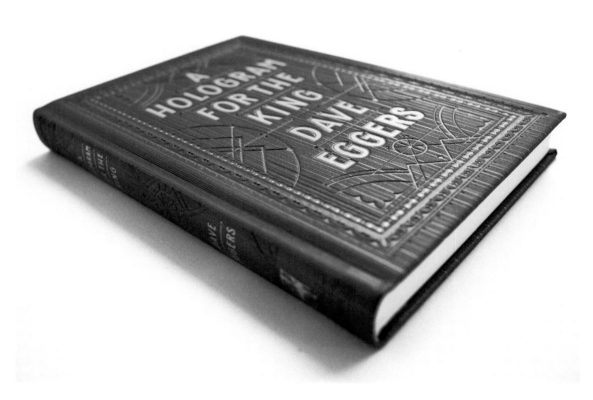

to reach a lot of people instead of mentoring only a few." She says that for her, live exchange is much more worthwhile than gallery exhibitions, adding that most of the exhibitions she participated in were done more out of obligation than her own excitement. "I do love giving workshops and find that the interactions that I have with students get me excited to make my own work, and often make me talk about my process in different ways."

Looking at her career in retrospect, Hische believes that one of the biggest jumps came when she first began public speaking, and she refers to her first major international talk at Semi-Permanent in Sydney, Australia. The "Drop Cap" project earned her wide attention and the moniker "That Drop Cap Girl." "Of course there have also been a few commissioned pieces that had an impact on the kind of work I was taking in. The first was 'Why We Love Boston in Winter,' a series of covers for the *Boston Globe*'s *G Magazine,* which was constantly referenced by incoming clients—people love that series. It also brought about a big jump in work for me making ribbon lettering, as one of the pieces included ribbon lettering and people went wild for it. For a year, many of my commissions had to do with ribbon." The most recent major step was the title design for Wes Anderson's *Moonrise Kingdom,* which provided the opportunity to take her occasional type design experiments to the next level.

Hische has always tried to have a mix of commissioned work and side projects, many of which are web-centric—she calls web design her hobby. Her sites include several educational micro-sites including "Mom This is How Twitter Works," "Should I Work for Free?" and "Don't Fear the Internet," in collaboration with her husband Russ Maschmeyer, an interaction and product designer, and Facebook employee. "It's only when I don't have a balanced workload between free and commercial work that I get really stressed out. I like to leave holes in my schedule for when really good projects come along

talking to people, the more likely you'll be on their mind next time they're asked to recommend a letterer."

Although Frank Sturges Reps handles all of Hische's incoming jobs, most come in by referrals or from people that have found her work online or through one of her side projects, which enjoy great popularity in the design community. While happy to pass on all of her organizational work to her agent, who she calls her sanity keeper, Hische enjoys handling most promotional work on her own due to her success, a lively web presence, and extremely popular side projects.

She started the very popular "Daily Drop Cap" project in 2009, creating a new illustrative letter each day, working through the alphabet a total of twelve times, with a thirteenth round featuring guest letterers. At its peak, the site had more than 100,000 visitors per month. "There wasn't much strategy involved in any of my side projects," Hische says. "I do tend to make things (and to want to make things) that I know will make people

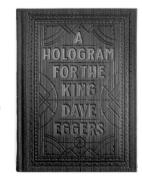

A HOLOGRAM FOR THE KING
Client: McSweeney's

happy. 'Daily Drop Cap' was easy eye candy so it was passed around a lot. My other projects are resources that I try to keep light and funny so that you can learn from them and refer others to them, but they're not dry and technical. I think as long as you make work that you delight in or find useful, there will be others out there that delight in it to. Think about the work that you pass around when you encounter it—what about that thing made you want to share it with everyone you know?"

On her website, Hische does not only present herself and her work but also shares a good deal of knowledge and experience. The valuable how-to information for aspiring creatives includes advice on pricing or finding the right agent. "I just love teaching and get a lot out of helping others. I had so many people give me advice over the years that helped me get my career off the ground and I really feel for young designers that are struggling to get going. I just want to help in whatever way I can, and writing articles and making resources is an easy way for me or in case I have a moment of inspiration on a side project and have to work on it immediately." Hische works fairly irregularly, she says, even though she is usually at the office every day from 9–7. "During that time I will often get tied up with email and all the unpleasantries that come with running a business."

Hische presents herself as an accessible person online, and correspondingly she gets a lot of email that her mom helps her organize. "I have tried this year to not be as on top of my inbox as in previous years—I found that last year I would spend up to 7 hours a day answering emails. Email just begets more email, so I've found the best way to keep the amount of emailing I do to a minimum is to not respond immediately to requests unless

FLORENCE AND THE MACHINE
(LEFT)
Client: MSN/Florence and the Machine

BECK: SONG READER
(RIGHT)
Client: McSweeney's

they are about current client work, new client work, or a deadline for something I'm already committed to. Now I probably spend 3–4 hours a day emailing, answering interviews, having phone calls, and doing administrative stuff, which is still way too much in my opinion but it's hard to keep it under that." Her most quiet and therefore most productive hours are early in the morning or after 4 pm "Once clients stop emailing I can have some peace to work. I love working at night because I can work for long stretches of time completely uninterrupted by the internet. I also love to work on the weekends on my own projects, but find that harder to do in California since so many people keep very consistent office hours and there are far fewer freelancers."

stressful to manage client work while I'm abroad. This fall I was out of my office for all but a few days each month due to work-related travel. To me, working is relaxing. I love to have time to work on my own projects—it's when I'm the most happy and most relaxed. When I'm 100% on holiday, I find that I go stir crazy after just a few days. Even on my honeymoon, we were away for a week and that was about all the relaxing I could handle."

Besides her untiring ambition, it is active creative exchange that keeps her energy level high. What she hopes to expand upon in the future is working with people that treat their time together as a collaboration rather than a transaction. "When I worked on the title design for Wes Anderson's *Moonrise Kingdom* it

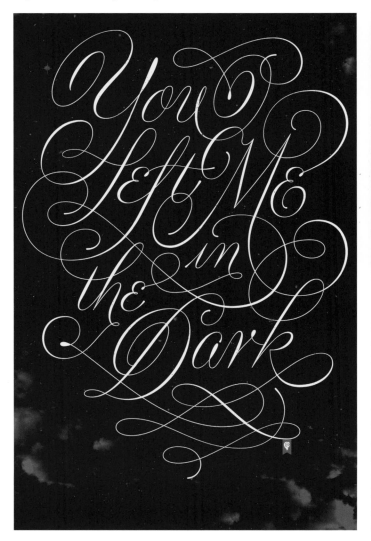

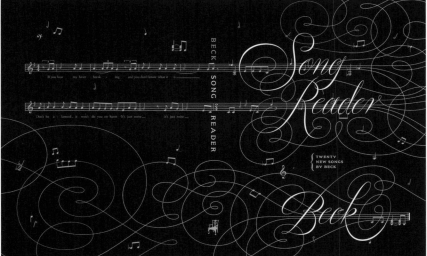

Hische recently moved to San Francisco because the city offered better career options for her husband. Most of her work is for U.S. clients, and she believes her aesthetic is most suited to the U.S. "I've worked a bit for international clients but the time difference between California and Europe makes it very difficult." She holds workshops and conferences across the globe. "Because of the conference travel that I do, I constantly feel like I'm on holiday, and while it's wonderful to be able to travel the world, see new places, and meet new people, it's incredibly

was the first time in a while where I felt like whether or not they could throw a little more money at the project I would do whatever extra work was necessary to make it awesome. I miss that feeling—the feeling that you have early in your career when you just want to go so far above and beyond on every project. It's been my goal over the past year to reclaim that feeling and so far it's working. I just try whenever I can to work with good people that are passionate about the project so that we can partner together to make it awesome."

PLACE AND DATE OF BIRTH
Barcelona, Spain; 1981
COUNTRY OF RESIDENCE
Spain and United States
FAMILY STATUS
Single
EDUCATION / DEGREE
Degree in Graphic Design
ACTIVE IN THE FIELD OF ILLUSTRATION SINCE
2001
BREAKTHROUGH PROJECT
www.binary-prints.com
KEY CLIENTS
55DSL, Absolut, ADC*E, Adidas,
Another Planet Entertainment, Arcade Fire, BBH,
Burton, British Airways, Coca-Cola, Converse, Chandelier, Chivas, Ecko Enterprises, Esquire UK, Estrella
Damm, Fallon, FTC Skateboards, ING, JWT, K2, Lane
Crawford, Mother, MTV, Muller, Nexus Productions,
Nike, Nixon, Non Format, Page, Puig Group, Red Bulletin, Saatchi&Saatchi, Sixpack, Standard Life, the
Economist, the Guardian, the Rolling Stones, TBWA,
Topshop, the New York Times, Universal Everything,
Vampire Weekend, Vicelona, Villar Rosas, Wired
Magazine, Wieden+Kennedy, Zip Design, Zune
MOST RENOWNED PROJECTS
Rolling Stones Rolled Gold Album Cover, Binary Prints
COMMISSIONS PER YEAR
Around 50
AVERAGE TURNAROUND TIME PER COMMISSION
From 1 day to 1 month
WORKSPACE
Shared studio
EMPLOYEES
1
AGENTS
7
HOW MUCH COMMISSION DO YOUR AGENTS TAKE
N/A
TEACHING POSITIONS
ELISAVA, Barcelona
AWARDS (SELECTION)
Certificate of Excellence Type
Directors Club (2005/2009); D&AD Book Award (2009);
Graphis, Nomination: Poster, Gold (2008); ADC Young
Gun (2008); Communication Arts (2008); Illustrative
Berlin, Nomination: Young Illustrators Award (2009);
Laus Or (2008); CQ Award (2009)
MEMBER ASSOCIATIONS
AGI, Col.Legi Oficial DeDisseny Grafic de Catalunya
GALLERIES
Solo Shows: Atlantis Festival, Split;
Trochut+Apparatu, Vol.1, Otrascosas Villarrosas,
Barcelona; Trochut+Apparatu, Vol.2, FTC, Barcelona;
Terrassa Escola Municipal d'Art, Barcelona;
Group Shows: Icograda 2009, Beijing;
Resist! London; Life in 2050, London; Pick Me Up,
London; Don't believe the Type, The Hague
Lubalin Now, New York; Record Time, Sydney; Ink This 3, London; Loft is in the air,
Barcelona; Noho Next, New York TDC,
Beautifully Banal, New York; Beautiful
Decay from A to Z, Los Angeles

Alex Trochut

"THERE IS NO ONE CREATIVE IDENTITY FOR ANYONE. SOMETIMES STYLE IS A PRISON THAT YOU PUT YOURSELF INTO. JUST KEEP DOING THINGS, AND IN THE END, THAT BUNCH OF THINGS IS YOU."

Mere words are not enough. The world needs lettering, and Alex Trochut has made it his mission to illustrate language and enrich it with what he calls a secondary level of communication. "Communicating on that level is always the goal when illustrating type," he notes. In following that goal, Trochut extends, rather than disrupts, the communicative value of words. "Although communicating in two different ways, the image should complement the word and say the same thing. Ideally, it brings across the idea so well that you get it without understanding the word." Illustrating the words "More is More," Trochut uses Art Deco-esque embellishment. The cover of his 2011 monograph *More is More* is lavishly embossed with ornamentation.

More is more is Trochut's motto, he says, and one can find that clearly reflected in his exuberant portfolio. "It is my way of saying yes instead of no. I like to be open to many things. That is more fun, with more possibilities to change and develop. It doesn't mean I don't like less is more, and the modernist ideas behind it. But sometimes less is less, and I prefer to have many options in the way to represent something." Trochut has been called a chameleon by many. His versatile style allows him to adapt to diverse client needs and potential audiences. A key requirement of a glutted industry? An opportunity, rather, of an industry that fosters innovation and progress, Trochut finds. "Back in the day, you needed to be forty years old to really become a master of something. Technological advancements enable you to get there much quicker these days. We have the opportunity to learn and progress so fast." For Trochut,

experimenting with different styles is one effective way to do so. "There is no one creative identity for anyone. Sometimes style is a prison that you put yourself into, thinking too much about what you want to be. I believe that you are whatever you want to be. So you should do whatever you feel like, in order to create yourself. Just keep doing things, and in the end, that bunch of things is you."

However diverse Trochut's visual language may be, there is an unmistakable essence to it. The palpable aura of organic transition fuses elements of rigid geometry with fluid forms. He aims to make both connect, and does so with ease. His work is greatly inspired by nature and

MOMENTUM
(TOP)
Map illustration
Client: Nike, 2007
Agency: VillarRosas

ABSOLUT BLANK
(RIGHT PAGE)
Lucy on the Sly with Demons
Client: Absolut Vodka, 2011
Agency: TBWA

X-FUNS
(PAGE 244)
Type and Soul are hidden in the fluid shapes
Client: Xfuns magazine, 2008

by the Mediterranean spirit that has also shaped generations of Spanish artists before him, with whom he feels closely affiliated. In his monograph, he refers to masters like Miró, Picasso, and Dalí in this context. He also speaks of the illustrator and designer Javier Mariscal, whose work he finds to reflect "voluptuousness, warmth, enlightenment, free expression, energy, optimism, and the joy of living under palm trees." If "digital revolution" can be put in place of "enlightenment," one has aptly outlined what reverberates in Trochut's own visual language.

Born in 1981 in Barcelona, Trochut studied graphic design at the local Elisava School of Design and Engineering.

"I loved to draw and already knew that I would go down the expressive path, but instead of going into illustration right away, I preferred to have the broad foundation of visual communication, so as to learn to develop ideas and communicate them. Graphic design really gives you a good base in all that. Then from there, all the tools are so accessible. I believe that anyone who wants to become an illustrator has the option to develop their skills from there."

Trochut spent a year of his studies in Berlin as part of the Erasmus exchange program, and interned at the communication and design firm Moniteurs for six months. "The stuff they do is very different from what I am doing, but they really educated my eye," Trochut recalls. "I also got the chance to work on typography projects with Alexander Branczyk, the husband of one of the partners at Moniteurs, and cofounder of the design company Xplicit." Trochut returned to Barcelona for the last year of his course, and after graduation he got a job as an in-house designer for the local design studio Toormix. Two years later he moved on to Vasava, another young design firm and a hotbed for expressive design approaches poised between illustration and typography.

Trochut's interest in drawing letters emerged over time. "It was that time of change and transition. You could sense that things were about to happen, between illustration and design. This was around 2002, or something like that." Illustrative approaches gained in standing and relevance in the design field and Vasava was one of the studios that explored the symbiotic relationship in unexpected, expressive ways. "I guess I just happened to be in the right place at the right time. The studios I had worked at before had been rather rational, more about organizing information in a very synthesized way, and then I got to Vasava, where people illustrated and experimented a lot. It was there that I found my own way of expressing myself through drawing letters." It began with letters in logos that he would treat visually, rather than conceptually. "From there, it became ever more expressive, ever more complex. Little by little, it turned into something like my formula." A formula of success, as it would soon turn out.

When Trochut branched out to freelance work after two years at Vasava, major commissions for the likes of the *New York Times,* Nike, Adidas, and Coca-Cola were not long in coming. Illustrating type and occasional liquid ornamental patterns for large business clients, the music industry, fashion, and editorial, he never gave priority to any particular business sector or field of application. "Exciting briefs can come from all fields alike. I really always

look forward to what other people propose for me to do. That is the way to evolve. The best thing that can happen to you is to have a creative counterpart on the client's side who can see beyond the projects in your portfolio, and ask for things that you would not have thought of yourself. That can be an art director, a creative director, or the client himself. Each commission is a dialog, so everything really depends on how the collaboration works. The final result is a product of ideas from both sides."

At the beginning is the brief and a good deal of intuition. "I need to feel that sense of excitement about a project. Once that is the case, there is not much to worry about. I really need that initial feeling of curiosity, the urge to explore what I can make of it. Once I get in the flow of trying things, it all works rather quickly, and I can easily do a very detailed poster in two to three days. If I don't get into that flow, I start to get lazy about things, and easily distracted by stuff like emails and phone calls, so all drags on rather slowly, sometimes for months if the timing allows it." Editorial commissions rarely come with generous timing, which is why Trochut is rather selective about taking them on. "If I take on short-term editorial projects it is usually because I already know the solution. Of course, sometimes I think I have the solution, and then realize that it does not work. Tight deadlines can be good in such cases, as they really force you to work with intensity, which can again establish the sense of flow. But that only works if there aren't loads of other projects on your back. And usually there are."

Trochut normally works on two, three, or four projects at a time, and often finds himself taking on too many. "That is because I am super bad at saying no. I have the tendency to throw myself into impossible missions. I guess that is really one of my biggest problems. Working alone, there is always a limited amount of work you can take on. And stress doesn't help you at all." These are challenges especially if one loves to research and gather references, like Trochut, who says he

VAROOM
(TOP AND NEXT PAGE)
Cover and backcover design
in collaboration with NonFormat
Varoom magazine, 2009

takes clues from many places. "Especially valuable are those that you don't find online, but randomly. I consider myself a big thief. I think much of my work is a combination of little robberies. The work is new, but emerges from various elements taken from elsewhere. Ideas are not born inside of you, I think; they emerge from all kinds of things that you pick up from the outside."

There are always plenty of ways to approach a design project, and at least as many possible solutions. Trochut's comprehensive visual vocabulary calls for close agreement with the client. "I try to communicate a lot, to avoid surprises. Sometimes clients tell me to just do my thing. But I can do my thing in so many ways. So I always try my best to make them understand what I plan to do before I start doing it. And I really try to

make people explain what they want, in advance. Some clients tend to use you, as a designer, to think and find out what they need so that they just have to say yes or no. There are some projects that are indeed pretty straightforward, but with others, it takes quite a while for both me and the client to really figure out what it needs to be." Trochut likes to work with mood boards, and to show provisional results during the process. He sometimes does many rounds, emailing them to the client. Changes are made directly in FreeHand and Photoshop, the two software applications he uses the most. "I cheat a lot," he says, meaning that he works with technical features, like filters and brushes. "The computer offers great hints, but in order to make things look nice, and interesting, you need to apply and combine them in your own way. For example, right now I am working on a ripple effect, on type. I use existing filters as a reference. The filter itself looks bad, but it gives me a lot of valuable information, visual hints of how the distortion works, for example."

Working on commissioned projects, Trochut's process is almost entirely digital. Except for occasional sketches by hand, he solely works with the Cintiq, an interactive pen display that combines an LCD monitor with Wacom's patented pen technology. The tool combines a natural flow of the hand with the digital cleanliness that is so typical of Trochut's work. "I used to be a mouse person, because I hadn't managed to work with these old generation tablets, where you draw in one place and see the result in another. But then they released that screen thing, around 2008, and I tried it and it worked really well from the beginning. It really facilitates and speeds up the process. Also, it gets you a bit closer to the manual process. Your hands are tools that never need an update, they are just always learning. I miss that a bit, miss many things about crafty techniques, and the surprises you get. In a way, analog processes are a lot richer than digital ones, which are always reduced to certain options. I would love to work more with my hands. I never trained in calligraphy, or anything like that, for example. That is something I would like to learn, if I had the time."

He does take the time to work on self-initiated projects every now and then. Many involve tactile materials like paint. "The only way to do something really exciting is to leave the routes that you take all the time. It is so crucial to escape your routine. I would love to develop the concepts of the things I am doing further, and take them beyond the commercial context, to make people think instead of just making them buy stuff." He does look for accidents and surprises to invigorate his practice, and now that he is working with paint, he photographs his experiments to process them digitally. "It is really rare that you can take the risk to experiment

VAMPIRE WEEKEND
(RIGHT)
Gig poster for band Vampire Weekend
Client: Another Planet Entertainment,
2010

with things like that when facing a deadline. So I experiment for myself, first. Once I have a better idea of how it works, I can offer it to clients. It often goes like that—you put a self-initiated project on your website, because you like it, and then some client sees it and asks you to do something along these lines."

Balancing between commercial and free projects, Trochut works to capacity. He was teaching for a few months, at his old college, Elisava, in Barcelona, but soon found that the regularity was breaking his workflow. "Also, I don't feel 100 percent ready for it. I need to get better in communicating and learn to immerse myself in other people's work processes to be able to teach them. Being good at what you are doing yourself does not make you a good teacher. I still do some lectures here and there, and might teach regularly again in the future. But now I'm busy enough doing what I do." He has been this busy ever since he started working freelance. "I think that today, once you have a likeable portfolio online, chances are good to become very busy. It's a great time. I wouldn't be working as I am if there wasn't the internet, with all the opportunities it has brought us. Ten years ago, I'd probably sit in some studio, maybe doing stuff that I don't like."

In the here and now, Trochut finds himself doing what he likes and that is what he considers a perfect working environment. In his studio in Barcelona, he works alongside a bunch of other creatives, some of whom he knows from his previous job at Vasava. Others joined later, and there are about 15 of them now. Most work in motion design, video, and 3D. Everyone works on their own projects, but they share competencies whenever needed. "It's all easy and friendly. And flexible and spontaneous, when it comes to helping each other. It broadens your toolkit to have people with other skills around. We are a bit like a family. It's a nice feeling and I feel very comfortable working there." Recently he rented a little workspace in New York, together

with a friend, and he is there as we speak. "It's rather a desk than a studio," he says, "but I decided to spend some more time here, and see how it goes. I just really love the city, it has this great energy. There are also more opportunities to work here, and even though you can basically work from everywhere these days, many clients prefer to work in the same time zone." At the

moment, about 50% of Trochut's clients are located in the U.S., but it changes constantly. "I kept traveling back and forth between Barcelona and New York, and now I got an artist visa." His agent acted as a sponsor.

Trochut works with several agents. Representing him in the U.S. and the U.K. is Debut Art's Sam Summerskill, who had approached him when he just started freelancing. "He had seen my website and asked me if I could come in for a presentation. Then we had a little trial period, and it worked really well. They really did a good job and helped me develop my career. It became a personal relationship over time, and it's nice to experience that kind of evolution with them. I think it's very good to work with an agent, because they are setting up the best conditions, both for the artist and for the client. I

better chance to really explain what they need. You can get deeper into it. It's not necessary, but certainly a plus. The only problem is time. And that I am not very good in selling ideas, in terms of talking. My agents certainly negotiate rates way better than I would. I often think of my agents as my bad cops. I handle everything organizational things like email conversation and production issues. He works alone from half past nine to six, then heads off to do some sports. "I used to often work at night, when I started, because I was having these high intensity, flowing moments. Now I hate it, because I don't see things clearly. Once it's getting

started to work with Debut Art when I was really young, and they helped me to get more and better jobs beyond the local market." Today, Trochut works globally—asides from the U.S., his clients are mainly from the U.K., France, and his home country of Spain.

"I really love when I get projects from Spain. Communication is usually closer then—there are no limitations in speech and there is always this connection, some kind of Mediterranean feeling to it." Trochut appreciates personal communication, and getting to know the people he works with. "U.S. clients really like to meet, have a personal communication, while in England and France it's all much more to the point and pretty straightforward." Now that he is in New York more often, many of his U.S. clients tend to ask him to come to meetings. "It is usually very interesting and people have a

10 WAYS TO GET A JOB
(TOP)
Client: Computer Arts Magazine, 2008

THE DECEMBERISTS
(RIGHT)
Gig poster for the band the Decemberists
Client: Red Light Management, 2009

GOTYE
(NEXT PAGE)
Gig poster for Gotye
Client: Another Planet Entertainment, 2012
Photographer: Javier Tles
CGI artist: Gerardo del Hierro
Stones: Todoazul

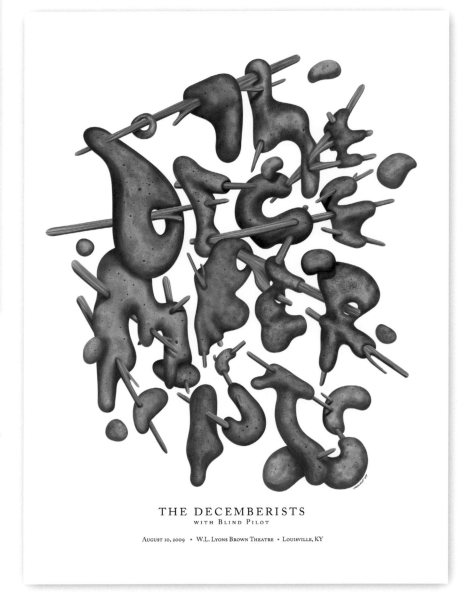

THE DECEMBERISTS
WITH BLIND PILOT

AUGUST 10, 2009 • W.L. LYONS BROWN THEATRE • LOUISVILLE, KY

creative, they do the rest. I like to design, but really don't enjoy all the organizational stuff the job entails."

For about three years now, Trochut has worked with an assistant who comes about once a week, helping him with the late, I feel my energy dropping. Then I easily get grumpy and lose the love for what I'm doing. So, even if there's a close deadline, I now prefer to leave things and start fresh and positive in the morning. Life has become very routine now

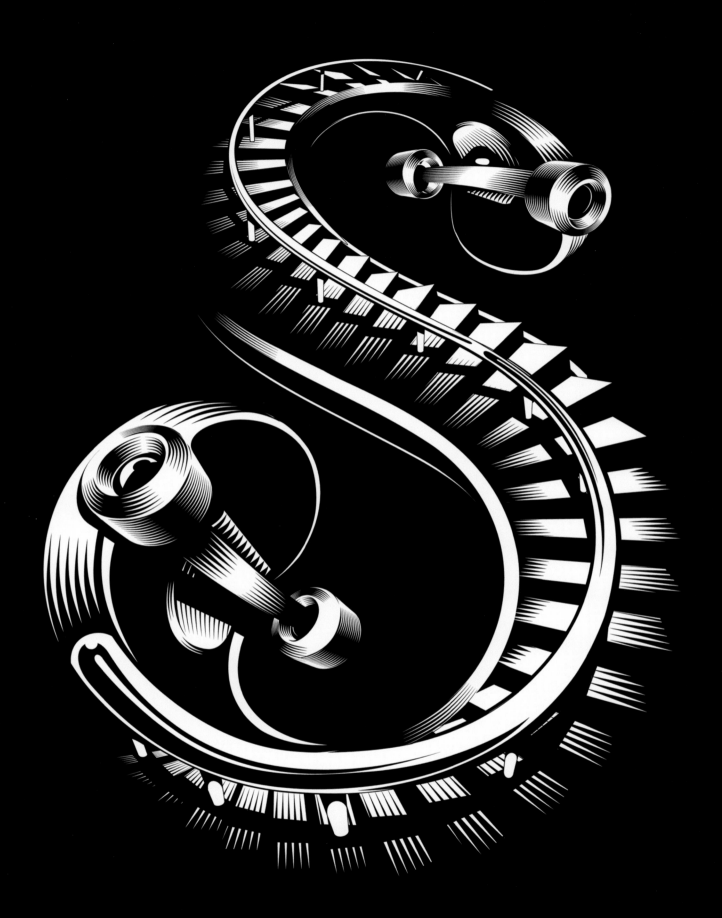

during the week. I do work on the weekends, sometimes, if there's nothing else planned. Of course some weeks are full, others more relaxed. If there's time, I allow myself to go out for lunch." More often than not, he gets delivery and eats in front of the computer.

The world needs letterings, indeed. A welcome counterbalance to an ever more equalized visual environment, custom typography continues to gain popularity. "Custom lettering is the opposite of McDonald's culture. We are fed

S - K A T E
(LEFT PAGE)
Illustrated letter "S" as the initial of *Street* and *Skateboarding*
Personal Work, 2009

P U M A
(TOP)
Client: Puma, 2012
Agency: Gregory Bonner Hale

up with seeing things that are totally homogenized. In a way, we are going back to the good old days." He refers to tailor-made approaches, like sign painters once offered. Illustrated typography has a history longer than type itself, and now it is experiencing a revival. "This is also because design has come to be socially more respected. The world's eyes are more demanding in terms of quality. The visual side of things is more appreciated now than it has been in the decades before. There are so many young

people doing amazing stuff, picking up on old times." Trochut is certain that the computer does not drown, but instead revives tradition. "The young generation is taking it all back and that is good to see. I am very optimistic. Many people are like 'oh no, everything has been done,' but I am certain that the best is yet to come."

A Life in Illustration

THE MOST FAMOUS ILLUSTRATORS
AND THEIR WORK

This book was conceived, edited, and designed by Gestalten.

Edited by Hendrik Hellige and Robert Klanten
Texts by Anna Sinofzik

Cover and layout by Hendrik Hellige
Cover illustration: Jonathan Burton
Typeface Headline: Grumpy
Typeface Text: Quister, Zimmer;
Foundry: www.gestaltenfonts.com

Chapter intro illustrations: page 4—Patrick Morgan, client: Tom Ford / page 46—Jan Van Der Veken, client: The New Yorker / page 92—Peter Grundy, client: Interoute / page 146—Tina Berning, personal work / page 188—Tomer Hanuka, personal work / page 222—Jessica Hische, client: John Bertram Architects

Copyediting and proofreading by Rachel Sampson
Printed by Livonia Print, Riga
Made in Europe

Published by Gestalten, Berlin 2013
ISBN 978-3-89955-485-4

For more information, please visit www.gestalten.com.

Bibliographic information published by the Deutsche Nationalbibliothek.
The Deutsche Nationalbibliothek lists this publication in the Deutsche Nationalbibliografie; detailed bibliographic data are available online at http://dnb.d-nb.de.

None of the content in this book was published in exchange for payment by commercial parties or designers; Gestalten selected all included work based solely on its artistic merit.

This book was printed on paper certified by the FSC®.

FSC
www.fsc.org

MIX
Paper from responsible sources
FSC® C002795

Gestalten is a climate-neutral company. We collaborate with the non-profit carbon offset provider myclimate (www.myclimate.org) to neutralize the company's carbon footprint produced through our worldwide business activities by investing in projects that reduce CO_2 emissions (www.gestalten.com/myclimate).

myclimate
Protect our planet